GEORGIA STUDIES: SELECTED WRITINGS OF ROBERT PRESTON BROOKS

Georgia Studies

Selected Writings of

Robert Preston Brooks

EDITED AND WITH AN INTRODUCTION BY

GREGOR SEBBA

PROFESSOR OF ECONOMICS

UNIVERSITY OF GEORGIA

Essay Index Reprint Series

BOOKS FOR LIBRARIES PRESS
FREEPORT, NEW YORK

STANDARD BOOK NUMBER:

8369-1025-7

LIBRARY OF CONGRESS CATALOG CARD NUMBER:

69-17565

PRINTED IN THE UNITED STATES OF AMERICA

Contents

PART TWO: GEORGIA GOVERNMENT AND FINANCES

PART THREE: IN DEFENSE OF THE SOUTH

PART FOUR: THE UNIVERSITY OF GEORGIA

PART FIVE: TRIVIA

Foreword

By Tomlinson Fort

In its origins the European university was a company of scholars. Its main purposes were the advancement of learning and the preservation of existing knowledge. The function of teaching was an adjunct to these primary objectives. The universities of Europe have remained fairly close to the original pattern with research and advanced teaching of prospective scholars their main purpose. However, in America the situation has been quite different. Here colleges which were devoted solely to undergraduate teaching took the name "university," although they were not universities in the traditional or European use of the term. However, the turning of a few Americans to Europe for study and the founding of the American graduate school in the latter part of the nineteenth century marked the beginning of a new era in scholarship for the United States. Unfortunately for us of the South most of the graduate schools were in the North.

Preston Brooks followed in the steps of the pioneers, turning to Europe for further study after graduating from the University of Georgia. He was a Rhodes Scholar at Oxford from 1904 to 1907. In 1910 he entered the graduate school at the University of Wisconsin where he was awarded the Doctor of Philosophy degree. He has taught at the University of Georgia almost continuously for forty-five years. During this period he has always advocated high scholarship, research, and the support of learning in all its branches. He is one of those who have constantly helped the State of Georgia toward the building of a greater University and helped its people to a higher level of culture. Some of his friends under the leadership of Professor Gregor Sebba are sponsoring the publication of this volume of some of Dr. Brooks' own writings to show him an appreciation of his work and to call the attention of the people of Georgia to some of the fine things that have been going on in their midst.

The following persons have been particularly helpful in bringing about the publication of this book. The thanks of all of Dr. Brooks' friends are extended to them: Mr. Robert W. Johnson of Johnson & Johnson Company, Mr. G. O. Lienhard of the Chicopee Manufacturing Corporation, Mr. M. J. Witman of Lorraine Farm near Macon; also Messrs. Harry Hodgson, Sr., Malcolm Bryan, Richard and Malon Courts, and Mills B. Lane, Jr.

Editor's Preface

THIS BOOK IS DESIGNED TO HONOR A GEORGIA SCHOLAR BY making his scattered papers of four decades once more available and useful to people of his state, and to friends and students of the South.

Four historical essays, published between 1911 and 1917, are brought together in Part One. The first two studies analyze the rise of farm tenancy from the debris of Georgia's ante-bellum plantation economy, and throw light on the economic race problem in the various sections of the state. The second of them, *The Agrarian Revolution in Georgia, 1865-1912,* is still the outstanding work on the subject. There follow an essay recalling Howell Cobb's decisive role in averting secession in 1850, and a pioneer study of Conscription in the Confederacy.

Part Two offers material on Georgia government and on problems of tax reform in the state over the past twenty years, supplementing Dr. Brooks' recently-published *Financial History of Georgia, 1732-1950.* Part Three contains three pieces published between 1913 and 1926 in which issue was taken with critics of the South. They are reprinted, not as a statement of their author's present views, which are the result of much review and revision, but as a bench mark from which to measure the remarkable changes in the Southern attitude that have taken place since then.

Part Four offers an unpublished survey of the University of Georgia which its members, alumni, and friends will read with interest, and an article written in 1947 that goes to the heart of the educational issue in this institution.

Part Five contains some *obiter dicta,* unpublished pieces

whose dry humor and mellow, personal tone make them a fitting postscript to the volume.

So much for the contents.

Except for the scholarly papers of his earlier years, Dr. R. P. Brooks wrote mostly in generous response to the demands of the day, producing a wealth of articles in magazines and newspapers, of speeches and lectures, of pamphlets and short, timely monographs, of reports and memoranda. But what is written for the day will perish with the day, unless it has significance and usefulness beyond its immediate occasion. The usefulness and significance of the writings here assembled lies in the fact that they bear upon so many of the great social, economic, and cultural issues in the state of Georgia and that they indirectly reflect the great changes in Southern thinking and attitude over the last four decades. But this significance is all but lost in the profusion of papers from which the material here reproduced has been drawn. To let the greater picture emerge from the writings themselves, without falsifying them by any act of commission or omission, has been the main editorial task.

It will be obvious that it was not an easy one. Briefly, the call was for meticulous preservation of the original tenor and flavor of the papers, while exercising great freedom in editing them for the general reader of today.

The care taken in preserving the original character of Dr. Brooks' work extends not only to the selection but to such seemingly minor matters as spelling and terminology. To quote but one outstanding example, Dr. Brooks' early writings have "blacks," "darkies," or "negroes," expressions common and accepted in scholarly work at that time, while his more recent papers use "Negroes" as is now the custom. These differences have been retained, just as opinions no longer held by the author are reprinted without change or comment. The reader will therefore do well to note the year of origin of each piece, conspicuously displayed at its head.

On the other hand I have not hesitated to abridge the studies of the agrarian revolution by omitting most of their rich illustrative and statistical material (adding the three maps and charts in the text); to drop, condense, or rewrite paragraphs in newspaper or magazine articles; and to summarize portions of pamphlets and monographs. Thanks to Dr. Brooks' sparse, incisive style, I have as a rule been able to use his own wordings in this task. The editorial treatment given each piece is briefly indicated in the note preceding it. Footnotes are given in their original style, and editorial opinion is clearly marked as such. In the interest of continuity I have refrained from interrupting the text by marks indicating where cuts have been made; this book being a survey of a lifetime's work, the scholar interested in the details is referred to the original publications.

So incisive a task of editing would have been impossible without the full cooperation of the author who graciously gave me a free hand with his papers, prepared at my request valuable new material, and did some of the rewriting himself. Moreover, Dr. Brooks has (except for my Introduction) read the whole of this book both in manuscript and in the proofs, restoring some cuts—notably in the last essay—and making occasional improvements in the original wording of the pieces. The text as presented here thus bears the stamp of approval by the author himself.

This, of course, does not relieve me of the sole responsibility for the selection made and the editorial treatment applied. Needless to say, the responsibility for the Introduction and the Bibliography is also mine.

It is a pleasant task to acknowledge information and advice received from many of my colleagues and friends in the University of Georgia, especially the members of the former

Honors Committee of the College of Arts and Sciences: Professors James A. Alexander, Calvin S. Brown, Tomlinson Fort, S. Walter Martin, and above all, Albert Saye, who suggested the idea of this volume and whose initiative got it over the financial hurdles.

I am no less indebted to Professors Rollin Chambliss, E. M. Coulter, James E. Gates, Rubin Gotesky, and R. T. Segrest, and to Mr. Harry Hodgson, class of '93. Professor Wimberley W. DeRenne, custodian of the Rare Book Collection, and the Secretary of the Georgia Alumni Society, Mr. William M. Crane, Jr., have been very helpful in tracing elusive material and in checking dates. Thanks are also due to Dean Gordon Siefkin of Emory University, and to Dr. Frank Aydelotte, American Secretary of the Rhodes Scholarship Trust, who kindly responded to a request for information about Dr. Brooks' Oxford years and who permitted me to quote from his answer.

Finally, I wish to thank Mr. Ralph Stephens, director of the University of Georgia Press, for giving this volume his special attention. Permission to use published material has been kindly granted by the *Georgia Review*, the Harvard University Press, Mentzer, Bush & Company, the *Mississippi Valley Historical Review*, the *Nation*, the *Political Science Quarterly*, and the University of Wisconsin Press.

Athens, Ga., Easter 1952.   G.S.

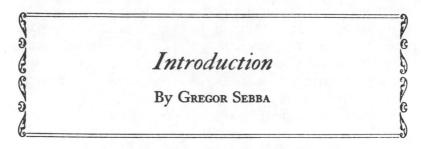

Introduction

By Gregor Sebba

Greift nur hinein ins volle Menschenleben,
Und wo ihr's packt, da ist's interessant.
                                              —Goethe

THE NEWCOMER TO THE SOUTH SOON BECOMES AWARE OF
an odd discrepancy between appearances and realities, especially when he views the scene from the placid campus of a
state university. Reaching out into its environment with its
every fiber, serving the people of the state with all it has,
the state university throbs with the life of the greater community; but of the profound issues that divide the minds,
hardly a ripple is felt. There is a stateliness, an aura of hos-
pitable friendliness about its academic life which reflects
the ways of an old ruling class that has long since gone the way
of all flesh.

Underneath is an uneasiness which seeks an outlet in heated
discussions of educational purposes and techniques, of administrative problems and reforms. It is about the only outlet
open. For though there is great freedom of thought and expression, tacit agreement exists that such freedom shall not
be used to throw "hot issues" into academic discussions. The
principle understood by all is *quieta non movere*. This is
understandable. Education is infinitely precious to the people
of the state, and the fast-rising institutions of higher learning
are not yet secure. Comparison with the old European universities, often made, is unwarranted. They, too, went through

this stage before reaching a degree of freedom that even the foremost American institutions dare not yet assert. In appearance, the state university is stagnant, tradition-bound, dedicated to immediate usefulness at the price of resignation from intellectual struggles; in reality, strong forces are at work underneath, ready to break surface.

Outside the academic halls the same discrepancies exist. Nothing seems to move, yet change is so rapid that every new set of statistics is a surprise to those that know how to read them. The state legislature operates by a system and by methods that have been denounced for decades; politics of the crudest kind are rampant; passions and stubborn insistence on small vested interests obstruct progress; yet this very same legislature will produce model law after law, keeping up with the needs of a rapidly developing state. Oddest of all is the discrepancy between the thought of people and the realities with which they grapple; between the notions of yesterday that dominate sentiment and the needs of today that govern action; between an emotional refusal to let the wounds of a long-distant past heal, and practical common sense effectively dealing with the issues of today and tomorrow.

There are many ways of coming to grips with this situation. One consists in taking the life and work of one man, a quiet, unostentatious work that spans half a century, and looking at it as it unfolds: preserving its characteristics and its flavor, and watching it for signs of change. Such is the task of the present book.

II

Robert Preston Brooks was born in Milledgeville, Georgia, on July 23, 1881, only eleven years after the occupation of Georgia by Federal troops came to an end. It is well to remember that fact.

His father, the Rev. James Henry Brooks, was a Methodist clergyman. It was perhaps a reaction to strict upbringing that made the son permanently suspicious of religious traditionalism of any kind. As soon as he graduated from the Georgia Military Academy at the age of eighteen, he struck out for independence. Working as a stenographer for two years, he earned enough money for a start in college. In the fall of 1901 he came to the University of Georgia, which was just emerging from its Centennial celebrations, including that memorable state dinner in which the second century of the University, a century of lemonade and ice water, was ushered in with flowing champagne.

It was a small institution, more like an old-style European *Gymnasium* than a contemporary university. There was a faculty of twelve men, all told. The Chancellor doubled as professor of metaphysics and ethics, teaching all the four courses in that field. The offerings consisted mainly of the classics in their original Latin and Greek, some mathematics and science, some history, English, "teutonic philology," and a few romance language courses. The student body was small.

Contact between professors and students was close. These professors were a far cry from the modern type. Their research output was negligible. Southern gentlemen born or acclimatized, they were at their best when engaging in the now all but forgotten art of civilized conversation. But their impact on young minds was powerful. They taught not so much by instruction and drill as by living example. Proud citizens of the academic world, they cast their students into the classical mold by making the great thoughts and great deeds of the past come alive.

The freshman from Milledgeville found the place congenial. He liked the leisurely academic life as much as he liked the intellectual earnestness that pervaded it. The environment was small-town, the campus a conglomeration of a dozen buildings, mostly ante-bellum. Living costs were small; a student's annual expenses were listed as ranging from

a low $125 to a "very liberal" $247, but the catalogue
hastened to add that "expenses are frequently brought under
the lowest estimate by strict economy," a claim somewhat
at variance with the philosophical statement: "The incidental
expenses of a student are just what he makes them, and the
patrons of the University are urged to take into their hands
the control of a matter which no college regulation can
reach." The matter of student conduct was disposed of in
one sentence: "The honor system prevails and formal regulations governing student conduct are few and general in
character." *Tempi passati.*

Preston Brooks worked his way through college by serving as secretary to the Chancellor, the modest beginning of a
long, successful administrative career. In his academic work
he did well. During his third and last year at the University
he won the Horace Russell prize in psychology with an
essay on "The Imagination." In the same year, 1903-04, the
highest prize open to an American undergraduate of the
day fell to him when he was awarded the first Rhodes
Scholarship to be given a Georgian.

III

Cecil Rhodes died in 1902, having established in his will
a scholarship trust as spectacular and controversial as one
would expect from this financial titan and last of the white
empire builders. Dreaming idealist and ruthless realist,
Rhodes had as a very young man conceived the idea that the
future of civilization depended upon the establishment of a
Pax Britannica, a planetary peace protected by the union of
the English-speaking peoples of the world. He understood
well enough that such a union, to be effective and lasting,
must spring from spiritual sources and from a common way
of life, not from transient political and economic interests.
Hence the singular device he designed in the grand style of
Plato's State of the Philosophers and of Hitler's *Ordensbur-*

gen: young men, vigorous of mind and body, were to be drawn from all parts of the British Empire, from the United States, and (as an after-thought) from Germany, to pass three of their formative years as Rhodes Scholars at Oxford. Did he expect this ancient seat of learning to turn these young hopefuls into budding captains of industry and builders of empire like himself? Or was he merely paying tribute to his alma mater where he had spent eight utterly undistinguished years doing what others would brilliantly do in three? Embarrassing questions.

There is no indication that these questions particularly bothered Preston Brooks as he came to Oxford in the fall of 1904, entering Brasenose College, as another young American Rhodes Scholar, Frank Aydelotte, did the year later. There was no trace of deeper significance in the work he did: reading the musty documents of old England, studying one brief phase of European history (the era of the last kings of France), and spending almost a year and a half on a minute study of a mere twenty years of English history, the years of Oliver Cromwell. He read masses of documents, absorbed a vast literature, tracked down references, wrote paper after paper only to have them pulled apart by his tutor; and when he knew all there was to know about Oliver Cromwell, he took his degree with Third Class Honors, left, and never in his life came back to the subject again. On the surface this looks like "ivory-tower" education at its worst, keeping the student away from contact with the burning issues of his time, and crushing him under a mass of useless learning. Actually, it taught him the use of the tools of his trade, and what more does an able, imaginative young man need to do a job? When he returned to his home state, he effortlessly tackled one of its burning problems and came up with a craftsmanslike analysis which has not lost its qualities in the course of time.

Still, one wonders about the impact the Rhodes Scholarship

had on him. Judging from the long lecture on Oxford he gave upon his return, the answer is none. Dr. Aydelotte, his roommate during his last year at Oxford, implicitly confirms this in a letter to this writer: "I am afraid that we were a very economical and hard working pair with few adventures which would be of interest in a biography. I think we took life at Oxford in our stride with no particular violent reaction to the different environment or the kind of life we lived. I remember Brooks as a fine Rhodes Scholar, a little on the quiet side and keenly alive to the intellectual opportunities of Oxford. I know that our life together made a firm basis for a strong friendship which has endured to the present time." And Dr. Brooks recently wrote of his friend: "My daily association with him was a blessing—so exuberant, so inspiring was he." But of the deeper impact, not a word.

Yet the same thing had happened in the case of Cecil Rhodes himself. Oxford students must choose between work for an honors or a so-called "pass" degree. Rhodes Scholar Brooks, in the lecture mentioned, pithily put the difference thus: "Students coming up to Oxford are allowed to elect whether they will be reading or non-reading men, *i.e.*, workers or loafers." The founder of the Rhodes Scholarships elected to be a loafer, spending eight full years in that occupation. Mr. Carleton Kemp Allen, until recently Warden of Rhodes House at Oxford, says of him: "The . . . remarkable feature about his Oxford days was their entire lack of distinction or even of any apparent purpose. He seems to have done nothing but ordinary things among ordinary people—and perhaps even that is an overstatement, for he did not even live the ordinary undergraduate life." Indeed not, unless commuting between Oxford's quadrangles and South Africa's diamond mines and rising from bucket-and-shovel digger to financier and colonial legislator constitutes ordinary undergraduate life. Yet Oxford's influence upon the man was such that he made her the executor of his great dream.

The truth is, of course, that education (as distinct from training) is a slow and still mysterious process, whatever the Ph.D.'s may say. It took R. P. Brooks more than twenty years to discover that Oxford had been the most important force in his life. Oxford had molded him into a future citizen of the world, capable of gradually emerging from the parochial notions and heavy prejudices with which he had started life; there he had become a hard fighter for those values that the needs of the day tend to smother. Above all, Oxford had made him the very essence of a scholar in spirit and attitude. It bespeaks the quality of the old University of Georgia that Dr. Brooks, when acknowledging Oxford's role in his life, never fails to add that the influence of his Georgia teachers equaled that of the great English university.

A sprouting bean will quickly develop stem and leaves while its root is still weak and infantile. It will shoot up fast, its progress measurable from day to day. But an acorn may lie around for many months, doing nothing. When you try to pick it up, you find that it has sunk a tough, almost unbreakable root deep into the earth. Acorns have a hard time in modern educational institutions, what with those quarterly, monthly, weekly, and daily tests for stem and leaf development. But oaks live longer than beans.

IV

Upon his return to Georgia, R. P. Brooks became Adjunct Professor of Georgia History and Sociology at his alma mater. One year later he married Miss Josephine Reid of Eatonton, Georgia. Mrs. Brooks' natural hospitality, her fine sense of humor, and her interest in community life proved to be great assets as the young professor's academic rise led to increasing social responsibilities. The Brooks home soon became a regular meeting ground for colleagues, friends, and students. More important still, Mrs. Brooks made that home a haven rather than a burden for the tempestuous scholar, enabling him to put all his energy into his work. He himself says that without her he would never have been able to maintain his research during those later years as an administrator when drab routine duties threatened to smother it.

In the fall of 1910, R. P. Brooks went to the University of Wisconsin for his doctorate, which he earned within a year and a quarter. His thesis, *The Agrarian Revolution in Georgia, 1865-1912*, received recognition as one of the two theses of the year to be published in the University of Wisconsin Bulletin. His reward at Georgia was an associate professorship, and two years later, in 1914, he became DeRenne Professor of Georgia History.

V

Schopenhauer somewhere remarks that mental energy reaches its climax well before the age of thirty-five, and that the first forty years of our lives provide the text to which the following years will furnish the commentary. Dr. Brooks is no exception to Schopenhauer's rule. All his extensive scholarly writings fall into the brief period between 1911 and 1917, his thirtieth and thirty-sixth year. From then on, it was that slow intellectual work of expanding, organizing, sifting, testing, connecting—in short, of maturing: "Only he *who grows old* will obtain a complete and adequate concept of life," to quote Schopenhauer once more.

A historian by choice and instinct, the themes of his early writings were dramatic: Howell Cobb, torn between allegiance to the Union and advocacy of states' rights and slavery, wrecking his political fortunes in his native Georgia to prevent secession and civil war; conscription in the Confederacy, adopted as a desperate measure to avert military disaster and ultimately failing because insistence on states' rights checked the Confederate government which was waging war for these very rights; the history of Georgia, dramatic in itself, and presented with a high sense of drama which made the social and economic forces stand out as prime movers. But his largest and most dramatic canvas was *The Agrarian Revolution in Georgia* to which the study of race relations in the Georgia Piedmont was a prelude.

The main theme was, of course, well known: it was "the destruction of the old order of master and slave, the fall of the plantation system, [and] the rise of the former slaves to the position of free laborers, tenants, and land owners . . . But the successive steps in this agrarian revolution have not thus far been worked out in detail for any Southern state " (Preface to *The Agrarian Revolution*.) Preston Brooks' at tention had been drawn to this theme by "Uncle Dave" Barrow, Chancellor, mathematician, and plantation owner. Not satisfied with second-hand sources, he traveled over a large area of the state, interviewing numerous planters, farmers, renters, croppers, and laborers; he gathered a great deal of fresh material which, preserved in the library of the University of Georgia, now forms a precious record of the period. The monograph resulting from this painstaking study has remained a classic in its field.

The burden of his thesis is that the character of Negro labor was the major factor in the transformation of farming and in the shifts of the rural population in Georgia after the Civil War. The old plantation system had depended on coercive supervision of slave labor; as the Negroes won freedom of movement and work, most of the large plantations had to be broken up into small units. But the qualities of the Negro as a laborer were such that white supervision remained essential if farming was not to suffer; and Dr. Brooks' main point, reiterated time and again and supported by overwhelming evidence, is that in the South (as distinct from other regions) share cropping is the better tenancy system because it leaves planning and supervision of farming in the hands of the competent white landowner, while "standing renting" or cash tenancy as a rule gets the Negro tenant into a quagmire of debt, bad farming, more debt, and finally bankruptcy, simply because he lacks the essential qualities of an independent farmer. Only when living in a predominantly white farming area, spurred by white competition and imitating the white example, does the Negro make a good farmer and a good neighbor. Thus the analysis leads back to the bitter issue that lies at the heart of most Southern problems: the Negro question.

VI

The date is 1913. We read: "On the whole slaveholders were as religious, moral, highminded a race of men as ever lived." " . . . [their] sense of large responsibility produced a race of men whose superiors in masterful qualities have never existed." "If [the slaveholder] were so ignorant and brutal as not to know his own interests, he might maltreat his slaves, thus reducing their efficiency as workers." "Negroes were lazy, inefficient and unintelligent." " . . . the Negro, like all stupid and ignorant people, was stubbornly opposed to new ideas." " . . . the slave was simply a child . . . " "In many respects [the Negroes] received more benefit from slavery than any other class. Coming to America as savages, members of a race which had never contributed anything to civilization, the enforced labor of two hundred years taught a considerable portion of them habits of industry. No primitive people ever got their upward start under such happy auspices as did the American Negroes." The date, we repeat, is 1913; the writer, a young man of high purpose, strong temperament, and decidedly liberal leanings.

The quotations are from the chapter on slavery in R. P. Brooks' *History of Georgia*, a high school text written with young readers in mind and officially used in Georgia schools for ten years. Those state leaders who today are in their late forties or early fifties learned their Georgia history from it. The slavery chapter is evidently (which need not mean consciously) apologetic. As its writer said a great many years later: "By nature a partisan, I can see few faults in my friends." But the point is that he was honestly stating the then dominant beliefs of educated Southerners, rooted in their daily experiences: "By living in long and intimate contact with the lower race," he concluded, "the white man of the South learned the black man's character; he valued the essential fidelity of the slave, and is not too greatly exasperated at the present-day Negro's shiftlessness and aversion to work. This insight into the nature of the Negro gives the Southern man a vantage ground of great importance in studying the race problems resulting from the Civil War."

Studying the race problems resulting from the Civil War from this vantage point, he did find some successful Negro farmers and renters everywhere he went, and he said of them: "They are the hope of the race because they are a standing refutation to the belief . . . that the Negro is incapable of advancement." But they were exceptions: "The mass of the race are wholly unfit for economic independence."

VII

Preston Brooks had grown up in an environment which he took for granted without realizing how different other environments were. His thinking was shaped by the fact that he was a member of a dominant race whose viewpoint quite naturally became his own. To him, as to the overwhelming majority of his social group, the disaster that had befallen their people, their society, and their culture overshadowed all else. It was impossible to forget it.

The European observer can readily find many examples of similar unforgetfulness in recent European history. He may think of the French who have forgotten their invasions of Germany under Louis XIV and Napoleon I, but who will never forget the day when the Prussians entered Paris in 1871. He may find a close parallel between the

unhappy life of the Austrian republic after 1918 and Southern life after 1865, both examples of traumatic shocks poison-
ing a community for decades, just as early childhood shocks
can leave a permanent mark on the personality.

In his brilliant note on "Facts and Valuation in Social
Sciences" (in *The American Dilemma*) Gunnar Myrdal
throws much light on the anatomy of the bias which arises out
of unquestioned beliefs, a bias of which no social scientist
is ever free, whatever he may claim. Discussing both Southern and anti-Southern bias, Myrdal writes: "The place of
the individual scientist in the scale of radicalism-conserva-
tism has . . . strong influence upon both the selection of
research problems and the conclusions drawn from research.
In a sense it is the master scale of biases in the social sciences."
And so it is. Preston Brooks was thoroughly conservative,
by nature as much as by environment. His realism precluded
any other attitude. He wanted to know what had happened,
not what should be done. It is not by accident that his first
and abiding love was history. Nor is it accidental that his
later turn to economics led him straight to *laissez-faire*, by-
passing the institutionalism so attractive to American economists of the 1920's and 1930's. For *laissez-faire* is essentially
a conservative attitude. And if he called himself a liberal,
as he was accustomed to do, he was fully within his right;
for liberalism has been conservative ever since it ceased to
be revolutionary some one hundred and sixty years ago.

VIII

In his *Kulturgeschichte Afrikas* of 1933, Leo Frobenius
said: "We shall not forget that even one generation ago educated Europeans thought of . . . the natives of Africa as half-
animal barbarians, as a slave race, a people whose coarse
depravity had produced fetishism and nothing else whatever . . . The concept of the 'barbaric Negro' is of European
make; it has . . . dominated Europe right up to the beginnings
of this century." This concept of the Negro as a savage

primitive, common to Western man around the turn of this century, fitted the popular notion of evolution as a straight-line rise from the simple to the complex, from the shapeless primordial nebula to the well-ordered cosmos, from lower to higher stages of life and civilization, from the amoeba to *homo sapiens erectus*. In this picture, the "primitive" is to modern (Western) man as the child is to the adult: savage, amoral, thriftless, shiftless, ignorant, uncontrolled, and ir-responsible, but also endowed with imitativeness and fi-delity, the saving graces. No wonder that in the Southern version of this evolution myth the Negro was "simply a child" while the slaveholder became the image of the good father.

The researches and development of the subsequent decades have smashed this simplistic conception. In 1913 it was quite possible for a conscientious writer to say that the "lower" race of tribal Africans had never contributed anything to civilization: little to the contrary was as yet on record. But Frobenius had already led his first expeditions into Africa, unexpectedly uncovering Negro civilizations under the debris left in the wake of the white man's destructive sweep; the pioneers of modern art in Paris, in Munich and elsewhere were hailing the sculpture of the African Negro as a model of that formful, disciplined, sovereign expressionism that they, in open revolution against the classical forms, were trying to establish as the modern idiom in art; modern composers found in Negro jazz the liberating stimulus that returned rhythmic freedom to music; and the spirituals of the slaves, long recognized as part of the national American heritage, were coming to be accepted as a genuine American contri-bution to music. In this period, American culture came of age, producing its own poetry, its own architecture, and a distinctive style that pervades all that Americans typically make and do. The American Negro's contribution to this culture is now recognized.

Within the wider confines of Western civilization as a whole, the beginning of this century was the time of the Great Break: modern mass civilization broke through the walls of classical form in art, music, thought, science, to find its own mode of expression, for better or worse. In 1907 Bernhard Berenson, authoritative expert on Italian renaissance painting, adviser and oracle to millionaire-collectors, could with impunity call the van Eyck brothers "miniaturists," or condescendingly write: "The trouble with Northern [mediaeval] painting was that with all its qualities, it was not founded upon any specific artistic ideas." Today not even a junior in the art department could write that and still pass. The change in thought has been nothing short of revolutionary.

IX

To the Southerner such considerations are cold comfort. Whatever he may think of the Negro, he still has to live with him, and vice versa. Neither party finds the task an easy one. A casual remark in *The Agrarian Revolution* throws sudden light on a vital aspect, easily overlooked, of this complex problem: "The economic motive that urges men of other races to labor is weak in the Negro. *Any influences which would tend to increase his wants are to be welcomed.*" It would be truer to say that this urge to labor is typical of Western man only, and of him only during the most recent centuries of his age-old history. Reaching its climax in the American way of life, this urge has unleashed productive powers of such magnitude that peoples' wants must continually surge onward to provide new outlets for these powers. Production has taken ascendancy over consumption. For the colored people of the South to "increase their wants" would by no means solve all the race problems; but it would produce a kind of economic integration between white and colored which would transform it.

But can the Negro, can non-Western peoples in general,

be influenced towards abandoning contentment (or resignation) with one's lot in favor of that insatiable desire for more and more of the good things of this world? This seems to be the issue that will ultimately determine the character of the societies and economies to rise out of the tremendous transformations taking place outside the Western world today. The limited local agrarian revolution which R. P. Brooks so carefully studied has its counterpart in that world: democratic and nationalistic ideals are shattering established social orders and structures; vast masses of uneducated people, unaccustomed to economic independence, complete strangers to modern production management, are throwing off coercion and supervision; feudal forms of landholding are under attack and appear doomed everywhere. But the differences are no less conspicuous. In the American South the transformation worked itself out through innumerable individual actions taken in the course of everyday business and within a stable and progressive society. The leadership of the dominant race was never in question. In the vast areas now seething with revolt, the very fabric of society is changing; the white man's supremacy is challenged or overthrown, and dictatorial native governments are in the process of imposing by coercion and propaganda new systems of planned output and distribution. Where the issue is still in the balance, this country is striving for ways of giving aid and leadership in order to guide the social forces at work towards the American system and the American way of life. In this effort we may yet discover that studies of the earlier American transformation are not without contemporary usefulness.

In 1930-31, Dr. Brooks made a world tour as an Albert Kahn Fellow, which took him across the Pacific to Japan, China, and India, and on to the Near East and Europe. His report to the Kahn Foundation, significantly, was on *The Independence Movement in India*. He had seen the great

Asiatic upheaval in the making. He recognized that nationalism was the greatest of the social forces of the era, and that it was about to destroy the cosmopolitan dream of a rational, just, peaceful century.

Two years later there came the sudden and unforseen outbreak of planned, purposeful beastliness in Germany, one of the most civilized countries of the world. It brought somber confirmation of the view long held by Dr. Brooks and many other liberal-minded Southerners that in acknowledging the evil facts about race relations in the South one should not forget that race relations tend to be violent everywhere and that the situation in the South was remarkably better than in other areas of the world, considering the magnitude of the Southern problem. His faith in the ability of the South to combat and eventually suppress race violence by its own efforts he also found vindicated by events. While such violence is being more and more confined to ugly isolated outbreaks, while steady though slow progress is being made in improving the Southern race situation, South Africa is abandoning the ways of Cecil Rhodes, thereby creating an enormous, and enormously dangerous, new problem; and in Russia the institution of coerced human labor has risen again. Perhaps this spectacle of mounting nationalism and race hatred has done more than anything else to convince Dr. Brooks over the last two decades that everything possible should be done to create equal economic and cultural opportunities for all, regardless of color; but his final word points up the distance between ideal and reality: "we are still far away from the brotherhood of man."

X

In 1919 Professor Brooks suddenly resigned from the University of Georgia to take an executive position with a bank in Macon, Georgia. The reason was simple enough—his salary was insufficient. A year later he was back, this time as Dean of the School of Commerce. He had quickly enough discovered that the academic halls were his proper habitat, and the University had removed the financial obstacle by elevating him from the lowly rank of professor to the lofty heights of an administrative position. In this process, both parties were losers, on balance. The University gained an able administrator and lost a proven and promising scholar, which is a net loss. Moreover, the DeRenne professorship went by default when he resigned, and there has been no chair of Georgia history since. As to Dr. Brooks, he gained security (or so he thought) for his growing family; but he had to sacrifice his love for history and his scholarly ambitions. Administrative grind and constructive research do not mix well. He himself has said all that needs saying in his amusing yet bitter little piece on deans (p. 275). His doggedness in pursuing research in the face of multiplying duties was admirable. Having started as a historian, he now mastered economics, and still later turned to state finances. His bibliography attests to his ceaseless activity as a writer. But the cold fact is that he never again achieved, or indeed attempted, anything of the order of his first great studies. His creative period was cut short when he was made a dean.

XI

He was a good dean. Under his leadership the small School of Commerce grew into a modern College of Business Administration with a remarkably liberal program and widening professional and vocational offerings. In his twenty-five years of college deanship he showed considerable administrative imagination, founding organizations which proved their worth to the University but also taxed his strength by saddling him with an ever-increasing load of executive and editorial responsibilities. In 1920 he helped organize the War Memorial Fund drive, took part in the reorganization of the Alumni Society, and founded the *Georgia Alumni Record*, which he edited for several years, an important medium for keeping alive the contact between alma mater and alumni.

In 1929 he reorganized the Institute of Public Affairs which for eleven years brought a galaxy of scholars and public leaders to the University and served as its window to the world. Under his direction the Institute also held annual round-table conferences on Georgia's constitutional problems, county administration, and public health which produced concrete proposals that gave impetus to the reform movement. In the same year he founded the Bureau of Business Research, now one of the great assets of the University in its program of service to the people. There followed in 1938 the Institute for the Study of Georgia Problems, a sounding board for the economic and financial reforms that he and his associates were advocating.

Earlier in 1917, he had been one of the organizers of the Georgia Historical Association and was its secretary and editor for three years. He was also one of the founders of that lively group, the Southern Economic Association, which made him its president in 1934. Four years later he became president of the American Association of Collegiate Schools of Business.

He relinquished his deanship in the College of Business Administration in the turbulent year 1945 and assumed the difficult position of Dean of Faculties, that is, coordinator of the multifarious activities of the institution, guardian of its rules and regulations, and top executive under the President. He held this post until 1947 when he reached the retirement age for administrators and returned to the College of Business Administration as professor of economics. In these two years he saw the University mushrooming as thousands of veterans filled the classrooms, and what he saw did not make him entirely happy. He saw a lot of concrete being poured, a host of new teachers being hired, huge appropriations being made and spent; but he also saw mass education endangering the idea of a university by making it hard for the superior student to get the tough, absorbing work he needs for intellectual growth—making it equally hard for the teacher to give his best to the superior student. And so Dr. Brooks, as soon as he was free of all administrative duties, began his last fight in the University on behalf of his most courageous and far-sighted project yet: the establishment of a system of honors work such as his friend, Dr. Aydelotte, had pioneered at Swarthmore College, whence it spread to become an integral part of modern American higher education. It proved to be an unequal fight. Within two years Dr. Brooks and his collaborators had to admit defeat. It was a bitter day when he made the motion that the program be discontinued. But the problem of serving the mass of students without hurting the elite remains. If the institution is to do its duty towards the future leaders in the state and nation as any true university must, it will have to solve it soon.

XII

In the early 1920's Dr. Brooks became deeply concerned with the fact that in far too many cultural and economic matters his native Georgia was at or near the bottom of the ladder. He maintained that the people themselves had it in their power to change this condition, provided something could be done about the "rotten system of state finances" that produced insufficient revenue, favored some services above others, and distributed the tax load most unequitably among the people of the state. But it took a major shock to make him direct his free energies towards this problem. The shock came in 1931 when, returning from his world travel, he stepped off the train at Athens to hear from the Chancellor, who met him, that faculty salaries had been cut one-third—"a financial blow from which I never recovered," he would state twenty years later. As he resumed his administrative work, he quickly found that salaries were but one victim of the economic hurricane: the financial foundations of Georgia education were giving way altogether.

His reaction was characteristic of the man. He made a painstaking study of Georgia's complex revenue system, comparing it with that of the other states in the Union and of many foreign countries. In the process he became one of the foremost experts on state finances. In January, 1933, he was ready to act. He wholeheartedly threw himself into the fight for financial reform, hammering away at public opinion with facts and figures, in speeches, articles, pamphlets, working with organizations and as an individual expert, preparing memoranda and reports for the state government, the legislature, for business and civic groups, examining in great detail every suggestion for improvement made, and proposing feasible reforms. Little did he care whether he made enemies or friends in the fight for what he considered best for the people.

In all this he remained the scholar. Unbending, he spurned the ways of the politician, trusting the power of the argument rather than harnessing emotions and self-interest. His arguments were meticulously factual, his presentation often passionately eloquent. Out of pro and con, proof and counterproof, claim and counterclaim, there would arise a cogent conclusion, to be driven home with hard-hitting strokes. In fighting for tax reform he taught the people of Georgia to understand public finance.

He found much that needed immediate remedy. The main question, however, was not how to stop abuses but how to find new sources of abundant revenue. The obvious answer to that would have been a general sales tax. No other tax could match it in productivity and simplicity.

Yet his sense of justice revolted against this remedy. He had sharply criticized the inequalities in Georgia's existing revenue system; a general sales tax would place the main burden squarely on the shoulders of the poor. In his view, ability to pay should be the main criterion for taxation. For almost fifteen years he fought the general sales tax though

he realized all the time that it offered the only practical solution. But during this period his views gradually changed.
He began to see the problem as a dynamic one: by liberally
spending money for education, welfare, and other services,
the state would help the low income classes attain a higher
standard of living and a decent cultural development. As the
Great Depression wore off and wartime and post-war pros-
perity came to Georgia, his attitude gradually hardened. He
began to wonder why those who were to benefit from
higher government spending should not contribute their part,
a part which he estimated to be a negligible burden on the
individual (about ten dollars per capita—but then he did not
consider that even at that rate the burden would be rather
heavy for low income families with many children and de-
pendents). In 1946 he unequivocally came out for a general
sales tax.

The reform of Georgia's revenue system has, by and large,
proceeded along the lines he favored. For the first time in
its history the state has ample funds at its disposal. Together
with the rapid progress of industrialization and the no less
rapid changes in agriculture, this makes for an outlook bright-
er than ever.

XIII

It must have been hard for so active a man, immersed for
four decades in all kinds of daily business, to step down and
move back to the quiet of the classroom, preparing for
the inevitable day of retirement while there was still so much
usefulness in him. One by one his friends and boon com-
panions had left the scene; new men with new ideas had
risen about him, and he was walking among them like a
stranger. The time had come to take stock and draw the
balance. What remains of a scholar's life and work?

There remains what he has said and written, though much
of it now sounds foreign; the written word is fixed while
the mind grows. There remain the students he taught: in

their blossoming and fruiting he may recognize traces of the
stuff he gave them on their way. There remain distinctions
and honors, matters of the past. There remain the people he
served; he would like to think them the better for that service, but what is a scholar's solitary effort compared to the
immense forces that forge the destinies of a people? Ultimately, there remains the university.

"It is the quality of its men that makes the quality of a
university. You may have your buildings, you may create
your committees and boards and regulations, you may pile
up your machinery of discipline and perfect your methods
of instruction, you may spend till no one can approach you;
yet you will add nothing but one more trivial specimen to
the common herd of American colleges, unless you send
into all this organization some breath of life, by inoculating
it with a few men, at least, who are real geniuses . . . Like a
contagious disease, almost, spiritual life passes from man to
man by contact . . . We are only beginning in this country,
with our extraordinary American reliance on organization, to
see that the alpha and omega in a university is the tone of it,
and that this tone is set by human personalities exclusively."
Thus William James, addressing the administrators of Stan-
ford University in 1906.

A real genius himself, James was setting his sights too high
for any but the chosen few among the great universities.
But if we replace the word "real genius" by "real scholar,"
his remarks will fit any university worth that name. The
real scholar is a man deeply rooted in the world of the mind,
capable of transmitting spiritual life from man to man. He
may be a revolutionary founder and innovator, or a humble
worker in some small, lost field; he may be prolific or dry
of written output: what ultimately matters is whether he
has that human personality that "sets the tone of a university." In an era of mass education, the real scholar may seem
a misfit in his institution. He may be a prime irritant, re-

served, unyielding, stubbornly fighting for ideals out of
reach, scornful of what others consider satisfactory. Or else
he may be endowed with the rare gift of diplomacy, doing
by sweetness what others try to do the hard way. Pleasant
or difficult, the scholars are what makes a university. They
are its roots deep down in the good earth whence the sap rises
into the tree.

As Robert Preston Brooks is "relinquishing his fifty years
connection with the University of Georgia, as boy and man,"
to quote his own words, buildings are going up all over the
campus, and the mighty steel skeleton of a great new library,
symbol of vigorous growth, is towering over the school where
he taught. It stands upon the ground where the Hills and the
Barrows, the Morrises and the Bococks used to walk, the men
who "sent the breath of life into all this organization." Preston Brooks is one of their kind. When all is said and done, this
remains.

PART ONE

HISTORICAL STUDIES

1

Race Relations in the Eastern Georgia Piedmont

[1911]

Published under the title "A Local Study of the Race Problem" in the Political Science Quarterly, Vol. 26 (June, 1911), pp. 193-221. Abridged.

THE NORTHERN LIMIT OF THE ANTE-BELLUM COTTON BELT in Georgia was the tier of counties extending from Elbert on the Savannah River in a southwesterly direction to Monroe county and thence westward to Troup county on the Alabama line. North of that line, some cotton was produced, but its culture was not the dominant agricultural interest. This fact determined the character of the population north and south of the line.

The present study is confined to the counties of the eastern Piedmont region or metamorphic section of Georgia. The soil of all this section is similar in character, consisting of red and sandy lands, with a firm subsoil of red clay. The counties under investigation fall into two distinct categories.[1] The line of demarcation between them is drawn according to the numerical preponderance of negroes in the southern group and their numerical inferiority in the northern group, both in ante-bellum times and at the present day.

The southern counties, or "black counties" for short, are typical of the cotton belt with its large plantations, numerous slaves and exploitative soil culture; while those of the north-

---

[1] For the boundaries of the two groups of counties see map on p. 29.

ern group, the "white counties," are representative of those districts which did not attract the large planter and in which farming was and is relatively intensive and diversified.

HISTORY OF THE BLACK COUNTIES[2]

The land that is now cut up into Wilkes, Lincoln, Elbert, Oglethorpe and other counties was settled, in the latter part of the eighteenth century, by some of those Virginians and Carolinians who were pressing southward and westward in search of new lands. Tobacco raising was the principal industry of these people, and the soil of the older commonwealths was becoming impoverished. Wilkes county[3] was the name given to the land occupied by the immigrants; and so rapid was the movement of population that when the first census was taken it revealed the fact that, of the 82,000 Georgians, 36,000 lived in Wilkes alone. The Carolinians who came to Georgia at that time were, as a rule, backwoods, frontier people; but the Virginians, who constituted the larger number and included the more important element— the men who were in the main responsible for the development of this section of the state—were not of the pioneer class. They measured up to the current standards of culture. They transplanted to Georgia soil the Virginian civilization, bringing slaves, stock, cattle, household goods and books. One of the ante-bellum governors of Georgia has left an interesting account of the Virginian families, closely related by numerous intermarriages, who settled in the Goosepond district, now in Oglethorpe county, on Broad River.[4] They raised tobacco as a money crop, but diversi-

[2] This group comprises Columbus, Warren, Hancock, Putnam, Morgan, Greene, Taliaferro, Oglethorpe, Wilkes and Lincoln counties. McDuffie county was so recently laid out (1871) that it had no separate history. [The proportion of Negroes in these "black counties" rose from about 40 per cent in 1800 to 70 per cent in 1900. It has since then dropped to less than 60 per cent. *Ed.*].

[3] See map in Twelfth Census, "Century of Population Growth," p. 69, showing changes in county lines. This map is inaccurate: Columbia county should not have been included in Wilkes, nor was Elbert ever a part of Franklin, having been cut off from Wilkes in 1790.

[4] Geo. R. Gilmer, *Georgians, passim.*

fication of farming was the rule. Practically everything used was produced on the farms. Though slave owners, the immigrants were not large planters—their servants were few in number and their estates were not extensive.

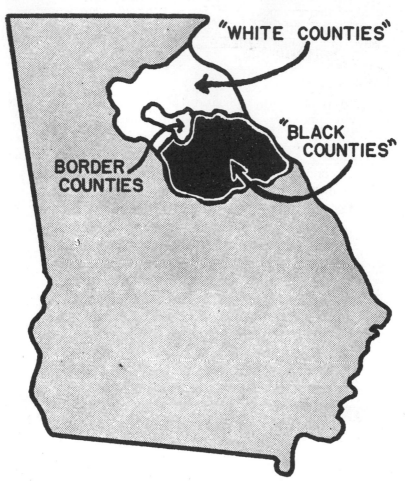

"BLACK" AND "WHITE" COUNTIES IN THE EASTERN
GEORGIA PIEDMONT, 1910

The "Border Counties", Elbert, Clarke and Oconee, represent a shading-off of the characteristic population features of the two groups.

The invention of the cotton gin revolutionized this simple economic régime. Cotton culture on a large scale superseded the diversified farming and tobacco raising of the early days. Those who had the means enlarged their holdings into many-acred farms; the people of lesser economic efficiency were bought out, and retired to less desired lands; slaves increased enormously in number and in price. In a remarkably short time what is known as the ante-bellum system was established in the section.

From 1800 to 1820 the number of slaves doubled, while the white population remained practically stationary. By 1820 the blacks outnumbered the whites, and they have ever since maintained the lead. This development is typical of the economic history of the cotton-planting districts. It was the universal belief that cotton could be most profitably produced on a large scale, by slaves in gangs. Farming being extensive and exploitative, there was an ever-increasing demand for lands and slaves. These two essential factors of production the poor man could not command. Conditions were against the small farmers, and the plantations tended to absorb their holdings. Not all of this class were dispossessed: there were always small farmers, but they were usually not prosperous and formed an unimportant and neglected element of the population.

At each census year after 1820 the white population in the black-belt counties showed a decline. Part of the loss was due to the departure of the small farmer in search of cheap lands, part to the movement of planters to fresher fields. Commercial fertilizers were unknown, and it was cheaper to move on to new land than to spend time and money in the effort to conserve the soil. The number of slaves fluctuated after 1820, in response to market conditions, but tended to remain stationary. The natural increase probably equaled the loss occasioned by the westward drift of planters. The noticeable break in 1840 was due to the crisis of 1837. For several years thereafter the planters made little demand for slaves. With flush times in 1848-1850, the domestic slave trade again became active. The acreage per planter and the average holding of slaves steadily increased from 1820 to 1860, as the plantation régime tightened its grip on the black belt.

HISTORY OF THE WHITE COUNTIES[5]

In the counties of the northern group there was little of the extensive cotton planting that had become characteristic of the black belt. The land in that part of Georgia was not in demand, as it was believed to be infertile. A trustworthy authority, writing in 1849, said of Jackson (which is now considered a good county) that "much of the soil is unproductive."[6] This statement was repeated verbatim as late as 1901.[7] Most of the counties in this northern group were once a part of Franklin county. This huge tract of land was acquired from the Cherokees and Creeks in 1783. The legislature threw open the land for settlement,[8] giving land practically free to all actual settlers. The country filled fairly rapidly, with an excellent class of immigrants of Scotch-Irish descent. They came principally from South Carolina, and were a people noted for "thrift, plainness and independence."[9] The newcomers were of the small farmer class and did not develop into wholesale cotton planters, as did their southern neighbors. Slaves were never numerous in this region. Accustomed to work with their hands, these immigrants settled down to careful, relatively intensive cultivation of the soil, and their land did not become exhausted. Lying outside of the zone of lands sought by the planter,

[5] The group comprises the following counties: Hart, Franklin, Banks, Hall, Forsyth, Gwinnett, Jackson, Madison, Walton. [The proportion of Negroes in this group rose slowly from about 16 per cent in 1800 to 25 per cent in 1860 and remained stable until about 1920, then dropped back to about 16 per cent. *Ed.*].

[6] White, Statistics of Georgia, p. 499.
[7] Department of Labor, Bulletin No. 35, p. 731.
[8] Watkins, Digest of Georgia Laws, p. 291.
[9] G. G. Smith, Story of Georgia, p. 152.

these counties received the overflow of the non-slaveholding
class from the cotton-belt counties of Oglethorpe, Wilkes
and Lincoln. Some slaveholders also moved in, but they
were of comparative unimportance amid the far more numerous small farmers.

It is clear, accordingly, that in ante-bellum days sharply
contrasted systems of economic and social life obtained in
these two groups of counties. The southern group was occupied by great planters, who lived in colonial homes, cultivated broad estates with numerous slaves, sent their sons
to college and concerned themselves with state and national
politics. The slaves, worked in gangs by overseers, learned
nothing of economy, management or conservation of the
soil. In the northern group, on the other hand, the farmer
personally performed the farming operations, raised his own
foodstuffs and managed his small place with care and fore-
sight. His few slaves worked by his side in the field, and
one can fancy them absorbing by imitation something of the
master's carefulness.

CONDITIONS SINCE THE CIVIL WAR

The emancipation of the slaves inflicted a far heavier loss
upon the planters of the black-belt counties than upon the
farmers of the other group, for slaves constituted the bulk
of the planter's wealth. His whole economic order shattered,
without operating capital or credit, disgusted with the difficulty of working as wage-hands the freedmen with their
fantastic ideas of liberty, the planter sold much of his land
to the blacks on easy terms, abandoned the remainder to
negro croppers and tenants, and moved to town. The land
was thus largely given over to the blacks, who, after the
novelty of freedom had in a measure worn off, settled down
to unintelligent cotton planting. Vast tracts went out of
cultivation. Lacking the guidance of white neighbors, the
negro naturally remained in ignorance of the progress of agricultural science and learned nothing of the use of labor-

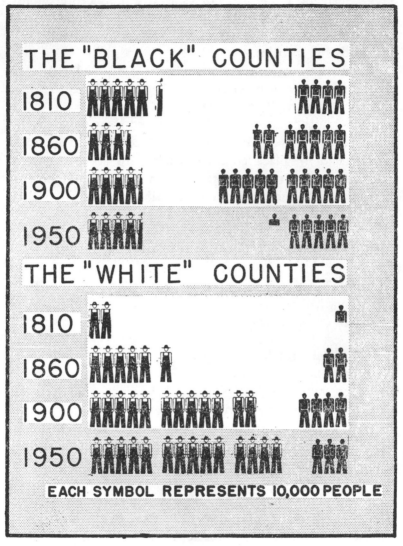

RACIAL CHANGES IN THE EASTERN GEORGIA PIEDMONT,
1810-1950

Between 1810 and 1910 "the white counties have grown whiter, and
the black counties blacker." (p. 34)

saving machinery. He had not as a slave practiced economy, and now as a free man he lived from hand to mouth. The productiveness of the soil was of course impaired and farming lands fell in price.

Since 1860 these conditions have tended to become accentuated. In the black counties the ratio of blacks to whites steadily increased between 1860 and 1900, whereas in the white counties, the whites have increased their numerical ascendency. In other words the white counties have grown whiter, and the black counties blacker. In every county in the black group, the white population was less in 1900 than in 1800, while the black element had increased from three to four hundred per cent.

Turning to the white group, in every county the whites have doubled in numbers and in some counties have increased from four to five hundred per cent since 1800. The black percentage in this group has risen from 16 in 1800 to 24 in 1850 and has remained rather stable from then on until 1900. See chart on page 33.

Southward Movement of Mountaineers

During the last ten or fifteen years a significant change has been taking place in these black-belt counties. The large amount of vacant land and its cheapness have attracted an ever increasing number of mountaineers from the northernmost tiers of counties to the plain. The large estates of the black counties are being cut up and sold to these mountain people. This fact doubtless accounts for the upward tendency of the white element of the population in Morgan, Greene, Oglethorpe and Wilkes counties. In the other counties of this group the white population is falling off or is remaining stationary. Particular inquiry on this point was made in Oglethorpe county, and the following interesting letter was elicited from one of the oldest and most prosperous citizens of the county:

The differences between the races here in Oglethorpe are growing more intense and troublesome. A few years ago in Oglethorpe the negro was the laborer and the white men were "bosses," generally, and workers, incidentally. That has all changed now, and the two races are coming into close competition as renters and day laborers. The negro has almost gone out of certain sections of our county, whites have filled in and are doing the work. . . . In the last few years some of our largest farms have been almost depopulated by the negroes' scattering to cities; and the counties above us, having increased in whites until they began to be crowded, and lands in those counties having gone up, these people, hearing of cheap lands in Oglethorpe, came down in great numbers and began to hire our people. Those that were able began to buy land, so that land which was ten dollars per acre is now twenty-five and thirty dollars. Some of these people are very satisfactory and make good citizens. Others from the mountains, never having worked very much, do not want to be confined very closely and do not exactly fit in the cotton fields, which demand much work. I am still holding many negro families, but at some loss last year and this, by reason of the fact that they are getting out of my control and influence. They do nothing but make a crop, and I have to furnish all their supplies and costly mules, which they abuse in spite of all my caution. The day of cheap labor is over, and even if it could be had it is unreliable and unmanageable. It seems that the larger farmers of Oglethorpe will be compelled in self-defence to sell their lands, because the lawful per cent on the price the lands will bring will be far more profitable than what the farmer can get from renters and croppers.

There are in Oglethorpe county three settlements of these mountaineers: one on the western edge, another in the northwestern part of the county and another on the eastern edge.

Supplementary to this movement of mountain people, many farmers from the white group of counties are moving into the black group. Two generations ago the fathers of these men were going in the opposite direction, from the

high-priced lands of the black belt to the cheap soil further north. To-day, the skillful and careful working of
small holdings by white labor in the white counties has enormously enhanced the value of the land. On the other hand,
the negro farmers of the black-belt counties have exhausted
the land in some localities and have caused its deterioration in others. Hence, the descendants of the men who
fifty years ago moved north are now coming back and
buying at a low figure the very land which was once too
valuable for their fathers to hold; and by the liberal use of
commercial fertilizers and leguminous crops they are building up the soil to its former state of excellence. This
improvement is primarily the direct result of these im-
migrations; in the second instance, it indicates the effect
of competition on the negroes.

The remainder of this paper is the result of an investigation undertaken to ascertain whether or not the diverse history of the two groups of counties and the extreme varia-
tion in the proportion of blacks to whites are in any way
reflected in the present economic condition of the negroes.

The Present Economic Status of the Negroes in the White Counties and in the Black Counties[10]

It is commonly believed in the South that negroes are most
prosperous where they are few in number as compared with
the whites. The Census supports this view as regards ownership of land: "In the Gulf states like Alabama the proportion of owners among negro farmers is largest in those
counties where two-thirds or more of the farmers are white,

---

[10] The Census of 1900 furnishes data for a detailed comparison of conditions
in the white counties and the black counties here discussed. The effect of a
predominantly white population in the northern group is seen in the superior
yield per acre of the staples, cotton and corn, the higher value of land, improvements and stock, and the greater diversification of crops. In the white counties the average production of cotton per acre under cultivation was 174.9; in
the black counties, 143.2 lbs. In the white counties, again, the average production of corn per acre was 10.2 bushels; in the black counties, 7 bushels. *Cf.*
Twelfth Census, vol. v, table 19, and various tables in vol. vi.

and smallest in the counties where two-thirds or more of
the farmers are black."[11] The two groups of counties in
Georgia here under examination afford an opportunity to
test the correctness of this statement. The comparison has
been extended, however, beyond the possession of land:
it is made to include also stock, farm tools and machinery,
household and kitchen furniture.

Farm statistics afford a rather striking confirmation
of the Census observation. As the percentage of blacks increases, the percentage of land owners among them tends
to decrease. The percentage of landowners among negro farmers is 8.76 in the white counties as against 5.10 in the black
counties. Further, the *per capita* wealth of the negroes in
the white counties is $8.64 higher than in the black counties.
When multiplied by eight or ten, to get something like a
truthful figure, the difference is a material one. The land
in the northern group was returned at a higher rate than
that in the southern; the negroes of the white counties make
a better showing in the matter of household and kitchen
furniture—evidence of a higher standard of living—and in
the possession of tools and machinery. The only point in
which the figures are in favor of the negroes of the lower
group is in the matter of stock. As will appear later, the bulk
of negro farmers in the black counties are "renters," while
those in the northern group are "croppers." A renter furnishes his own stock. Careful inquiry in person and by letter leads to the conclusion that the stock nominally owned
by renters belongs in the vast majority of cases to some
white man, having been bought on time. The amount of stock
to which the negroes in the black counties have clear title
is beyond doubt far smaller than appears on the surface.
The same condition applies to some extent in the other counties, but not so widely, as there are few renters in the northern group. Where a negro owns his land, his possession of

[11] *Ibid.*, Bulletin No. 8, p. 98.

stock is usually real possession. Landowning negroes, in the
opinion of their white neighbors, make good citizens.

THE SYSTEMS OF FARMING

The most striking contrast between the white and black
counties is in the important matter of land tenure. In addition to ownership, there are two widespread systems of
tenure, known as the "cropping" system and the "standing
rent" system. The Census groups together as "cash tenants"
those tenants who pay a cash rental for the use of the soil
and those who pay a fixed amount of the crop. In Georgia
practically no tenants pay actual cash, so that in this state
the term "cash tenants" means "standing renters."

Statistics show that the cash-tenancy system is spreading
in Georgia and that the cropping system is declining.[12] This
tendency has usually been interpreted as indicating economic
progress,[13] the emergence of the blacks from "what was
virtually the old slavery system under another name," as Du-
Bois described the cropping system, to a higher position.
Under the cropping system the landlord furnishes everything—land, house, stock, seed—and takes half the product
of the year as rent. He also commonly feeds the cropper
and deducts the charge for supplies from the negro's share;
or, in lieu of furnishing him from a commissary, the employer
"stands" for the cropper at the neighboring merchant's store.
The characteristic feature of this system of farming is
strict supervision by the landlord over the operations of the
farmer. In reality, the cropper is a day laborer, without responsibility except for the day's work. If through adverse
seasons his crop is a total failure, he remains under no obligation to the landlord. The employer takes all the risk. The
profits depend on the seasons, the prices, and the amount
and character of the supervision the landlord exercises. In

---

[12] E. M. Banks, Economics of Land Tenure in Georgia, pp. 88, 89.
[13] *Cf.* Taylor, Agricultural Economics, pp. 261-270, for an excellent discussion
of share tenancy and cash tenancy.

point of organization, this system resembles the ante-bellum plantation. Usually, almost invariably, indeed, croppers are found settled on small farms surrounding the residence of the landlord, the cabins close enough to permit the croppers to come in the morning for the stock without undue waste of time. The outlying portions of the plantations, situated at such distance as to make close supervision impracticable, are commonly occupied by standing renters.

Under the standing rent system, the farmer pays a definite amount of the crop as rental, say one thousand pounds of lint cotton per horse farm of thirty acres. The landlord furnishes only the land and house. The negro supplies his own mule and feeds himself, if he can get credit. In this matter custom varies. Very often the landlord is obliged to "stand" for the renter before the merchant will extend credit; in other cases, the negro is considered as good a risk as a white man —all depending on the individual. Competition among the country merchants is becoming so strong that credit is frequently extended to the average negro without the personal endorsement of the landlord. In such cases the merchant takes a second lien on the crop, as well as a mortgage on any chattels possessed by the tenant. There is a large element of risk in such business, and the merchants exact from the tenants a high rate of insurance.

The theoretical advantage of renting is that, after providing for the payment of rent by planting a certain proportion of the farm in cotton, the farmer is free from the control of the landlord and becomes an *entrepreneur* instead of a laborer. If the white or black standing renter be a man of exceptional intelligence and judgment, he has an opportunity to diversify his farming, and by producing foodstuffs he can be independent in large measure of the merchant. Unfortunately, the common run of negroes lacks the qualities that would enable them to use advantageously the freedom of the renting system. They do not diversify crops. Professor J. F.

Dugger, director of the Alabama Polytechnic Institute experiment station, says in a recent issue of *The Progressive
Farmer*:

> So far as the writer knows, there is no country in the world
> dominated by Caucasians and equal in civilization to America,
> in which land is cultivated in as careless and inefficient a
> manner as are the rented cotton fields of many planters in
> the southern states. If the next census should classify the
> yield per acre by negro renters as separate from the general
> average of all farmers, I doubt whether the yield of the
> (renting) farmer would be half of that obtained by the aver-
> age man working his own farm. If this assumption is true,
> that the renting system, as more generally practiced, reduces
> the productive capacity of the land by half and the final
> profit of the landlord and tenant by more, then it follows
> that the system should either be abandoned as soon as pos-
> sible or else reconstructed.[14]

In the opinion of practically every planter consulted, the
standing rent system is bad for both landlord and tenant;
and the consensus of opinion is that the negro prefers this
system, not so much with the view of bettering his condition,
as for the purpose of escaping the supervision of the landlord.

For the purpose of the present study it is fundamentally
important to note that share tenancy or cropping overwhelmingly predominates in the white counties; while in
the black counties standing renting is the prevalent system.
There are no exceptions to the rule in the white counties;
in the other group, however, Morgan and Greene form
exceptions. If the standing rent system marks a step forward
in economic evolution, as is generally contended, it would
be reasonable to expect the general well-being of the negroes
in the black counties under consideration to be superior
to that of the blacks in the northern group; but it is evident
that such is not the case. When it is remembered that during
Reconstruction times the conditions in the black belt were
very favorable for the acquisition of property by the negroes,

[14] *The Progressive Farmer*, Raleigh, North Carolina, December 10, 1910.

it is the more remarkable that the blacks of the northern group have more than held their own and, in the important particular of land ownership, are considerably in the lead. These facts have led the investigator to question the validity of the opinion that the standing renting system indicates advancement. The truth is that cropping tends to prevail in those communities where the landlord lives on his plantation and gives his whole time to the work of supervision. Unless closely supervised, the negro will not work steadily, nor take care of the stock, nor keep up the terraces, hedges, and fences, nor even take proper care of the crop at harvest.

OGLETHORPE AND JACKSON COUNTIES

In order to bring out clearly this important matter of land tenure, a special inquiry was made in two counties adjoining Clarke, the residence county of the writer. These counties were not chosen as being extremes of their respective groups. (Oglethorpe is, however, a somewhat extreme type.) The choice was made because the two counties are easy of access by railroad and bicycle. Furthermore, both counties are old and are historically contiguous—Clarke having been a part of Jackson, and part of Clarke having been added to Oglethorpe. That is to say, the only difference between the counties is their separate economic development. Another advantage in selecting these two counties is that a number of planters living in Athens (Clarke county) own plantations in Oglethorpe and in Jackson and are thus in a position to speak with authority about comparative conditions in the two counties.

Much of the Oglethorpe county farming land is still in large plantations owned by absentee landlords, who reside in Athens, Crawford, Lexington and other towns in the vicinity. The owners, usually engaged in other forms of business, are unable to be on the ground to watch the farmers. Hence the cropping system is impracticable, and the owners

are driven to the alternative, the standing rent system. In
Jackson county, on the contrary, the bulk of the farming
lands is owned by relatively small proprietors, who live on the
land. That 77 per cent of the Jackson negroes are croppers
and only 14 per cent standing renters means that the Jackson county landlords are in a position to give the necessary
supervision to the blacks and, where they can induce them
to work as croppers, prefer this system. The backwardness
of the Oglethorpe negroes and of the agricultural conditions
in general in that county may be attributed largely to the
fact that the absence of white landlords makes impossible the
cropping system. The absentee ownership, with the land
left to renters, is characteristic of the black-belt counties,
with few exceptions. The writer knows, for instance, of a
5000-acre farm in Warren county—one of the lower group
under examination—the owners of which live in Athens, visit
the place only twice a year and have no overseer in charge.
Standing renters occupy the soil.

The negro's success seems to depend directly on the close-
ness of contact between him and an intelligent white guide.
The cumulative evidence of observation and of testimony
by landlords is conclusive on this point. It often happens
that on the same plantation are found closely supervised
croppers and unsupervised renters. There is no mistaking
the crop of the cropper. The effect of capable supervision
is seen in well-kept terraces, first-class crops of corn and
cotton and the presence of workers in the field.

The landlords of both counties bear out the Census statement, that standing renting is increasing and cropping declining; and they feel that this tendency represents a retrogression in agriculture.

Apart from absenteeism, which practically necessitates
the standing rent system, there is another factor in this movement, namely, the growing aversion on the part of the negro
to supervision. He desires his movements to be absolutely

unrestricted; and he does not see that this personal freedom often entails economic dependence. In fact, a hardworking cropper has a better chance than the renter of coming into ownership of land and thus reaching the goal of peasant proprietorship. The Twelfth Census (Bulletin 8, p. 89) makes this general statement: "Those states with a relatively large percentage of owners . . . have in nearly all cases fewer cash tenants, or renters, than share tenants, or metayers (croppers), showing that it is as easy to pass directly from share tenancy to ownership as to stop at the intermediate stage." A more reasonable inference would have been that it is easier to pass from share tenancy to ownership than from standing renting to ownership.

Of the many stories picked up in the course of several visits to Jackson and Oglethorpe counties, two are given to illustrate this point of supervision. Negroes frequently get hopelessly in debt to their landlords. In order to extricate themselves they go to a neighboring planter and borrow enough to square up with the creditor, promising to become tenants to the lender and work out the new debt. So great is the competition for laborers that planters take on hands under such circumstances and are glad to get them. Mr. H., of Jackson county, advanced a negro, Ben, money to meet such an emergency. The first year Ben was put on a small farm near the house of the owner. He proved to be a good man and paid about half of his debt with the proceeds of his crop; the second year he not only paid the balance but had a margin to his credit. The third year, Mr. H., seeing that he had found a valuable man, put Ben on a farm some six miles distant and did not exercise the same close supervision as theretofore. The result was a complete failure.

Mr. S., of Oglethorpe county, had a negro working as a renter. At the end of a certain year the output was three bales of cotton. The following year, Mr. S. undertook an experiment in supervision. He took the negro as a cropper on the same land, and, by directing his work and keeping him at it, secured from him an output of twelve bales. When the darky's attention was called to the difference between his first and second year's profits, he expressed the opinion that he would have made sixteen bales if the landlord hadn't "pestered" him so much.

Negro Schools of Jackson and Oglethorpe

In discussing the various aspects of this subject with a number of farmers who have in recent years moved from Jackson county to Oglethorpe, and with several planters who own and operate places in both counties, it was found to be the general opinion that the Jackson county negroes are more intelligent and business-like than those of Oglethorpe. This fact he attributed partly to the closer contact between the races in Jackson, where two-thirds of the population is white; and partly to the influence of the public schools. In the largely white communities the school facilities are better than in the districts where the whites are less numerous. The reason for this is that in the white communities the public-school fund is supplemented by local taxation. Where such a supplementary tax is levied, blacks as well as whites participate in the improved school facilities, though the former pay only a very small part of the extra tax. Furthermore, the interest of the negro in education increases as we proceed from the practically all-black communities to those where the negro is an inconspicuous factor. It will be suggestive to quote here from a letter received from the county school commissioner of Oglethorpe county:

> In some sections of our county, negroes constitute about ninety per cent of the population, and in these sections they take very little interest in schools; will not send their children and will not pay the teacher anything. In other sections, where they constitute less than fifty per cent of the population, they send to school better and will pay teachers from ten to twenty-five cents per month for each pupil.

In Jackson county sixteen districts levy a special school tax and the school buildings and equipment have been greatly improved. In Oglethorpe only three districts have voted the tax. Oglethorpe's shortcoming is due to the preponderance of the black population. The white people take the position that they prefer to deny their children increased school facilities (the public-school term lasts only from five to seven months) rather than pay for similar advantages for so disproportionate a number of blacks. That the blacks of Jackson have been materially assisted in this matter by the special tax is evident from the fact that there is in this county one teacher to every 68 colored children of school age, while in Oglethorpe the ratio is one teacher to every 85 pupils. Salaries are uniformly higher in Jackson.[15] In Jackson 14 school buildings belonging to the board of education are valued at $12,000,[16] while in Oglethorpe 21 such buildings are valued at $6,000. In Oglethorpe 36 buildings not belonging to the board of education are returned at $3,000. The negro children in Jackson ordinarily remain in school longer than in Oglethorpe.

GRADES OF BLACK PUPILS[17]

	FIRST TO THIRD	FOURTH AND FIFTH	SIXTH	SEVENTH
Jackson	904	760	140	29
Oglethorpe	2000	300	100	50

In the first three grades, it will be noted that the Oglethorpe children outnumbered those of Jackson by two to one, but in the fourth and fifth grades the ratio was reversed. Only 2.5 per cent of the Oglethorpe pupils reached the seventh grade, while 3.2 per cent of the Jackson pupils carried their education to that point—a deplorable showing for both, it must be admitted.

---

[15] Reports of the State School Commissioner, 1908, table 1.
[16] *Ibid.,* table 3.
[17] *Ibid.,* table 8.

Testimony of Landlords in Jackson and Oglethorpe

After personal conference with as many leading planters and merchants as could be conveniently interviewed, a series of questions on the general cause of the prevalent labor troubles was prepared and mailed to a carefully selected list of a score or more farmers in each county. The most interesting feature of the answers was that the Jackson county planters replied in the briefest possible manner, in many cases with a single word, while a number of Oglethorpe landlords not only answered the questions by filling out the blank enclosed but wrote separate letters of from five to ten pages. This fact indicates that conditions are worse in Oglethorpe than in the other county. The following is typical of the letters from Oglethorpe:

> I think, without some change for the better (and I see no sign of it), the mountaineer will soon have replaced the negro. The younger set think of nothing but gadding about, baseball, hot suppers, church fights and the city court. The quick-thinking farmers of this county are dropping the negro as fast as they can and filling his place with white tenants. I have always had negro tenants and have been a staunch friend to the negro. Have families on my lands that have been with me from six to twelve years, but as the old ones die out the younger set do not take their places. They join the numerous orders and the church, and when they have finished the rounds of the secret orders and the churches, there is no time left for work, and the crop is not worked. The above is the general rule, with very, very few exceptions.

Four Jackson county landlords put themselves on record as believing that the negroes were progressing, and three planters reported no scarcity of labor due to migration of the blacks. In is interesting to note that all these favorable replies came from the northern half of the county, in which the proportion of blacks to whites is smaller than in the southern half. Only two Oglethorpe planters gave encouraging reports. One of these correspondents lives in the same section of the county from which the letter in regard to the coming of the mountaineer was written; the other lives in Arnoldsville, where is located the largest settlement in the county of recent immigrants. While this is insufficient evidence from which to draw conclusions, it suggests that the pinch of competition is beginning to be felt by the negroes.

On the whole the majority of the writers are pessimistic in regard to the present and the future of the negro. It is said in many letters that the younger generation is rapidly becoming unmanageable. The trouble seems to be a deep-seated dislike of control and discontent with farming life and conditions. The tendency is strong to wander from plantation to plantation and to the towns. Various causes, economic and social, are offered in explanation of this condition of things. In Georgia this is an era of unprecedented activity in the opening-up of new and the reviving of old industries—construction of railways (including street railways in the towns), erection of public buildings, paving, installation of waterworks and other civic improvements. The supply of labor for these industries is inadequate, and the result is an exodus of the negroes from the country to the towns and cities. In these employments good day wages are paid in cash, whereas on the farm, except for occasional advances, payment comes at the end of the year—if, indeed, the tenant finds himself entitled to a balance. So high is the price of labor and so low the negro's standard of living, that three days' work in town or on the railroad affords him subsistence for a week. He then usually prefers to rest the remainder of the week. The city of Atlanta has recently taken severe measures to rid the streets of vagrants. Most of them are said to be negroes with money in their pockets.

It is also doubtless true that the systems of farming already described make for discontent in the country. Under both systems, landlords are inclined to insist on the planting of cotton to the exclusion of other crops. To this rule there are gratifying exceptions; but in general the tenant is not sufficiently encouraged to produce corn, hay, hogs, cattle or poultry. All his energies are expended in making cotton. Foodstuffs come from the merchant. The credit system and the lack of diversification in farming are fatal to the negro, and, indeed, to the white farmer.

While such forces as these are at work, the migrations of the masses of negroes are not by any means entirely in response to such stimuli. It has been shown time and again that negro tenants will, wholly without grievance, leave places in which they have advanced from poverty to comparative comfort[18] simply because they "jest want a change." The blacks are naturally easy-going and improvident. They need the stress of competition and the presence of examples of industry. One of the ablest leaders of the race says: "In nine cases out of ten where a negro in the South is found owning property, he has had an individual white man or a group of southern white men to help guide and encourage him in this respect."[19] The black man's powers of imitation are great; and where his energies are properly guided and he is encouraged to practice self-restraint and prudence—taught to defer present enjoyment for future good—many a black man has become a prosperous and upright citizen. But the population of the southern states is so small and the proportion of blacks to whites so great that, under the present conditions, it is not surprising that the progress of the negroes is slow and that in some sections there appears to be no progress. The greatest need seems to be the increasing of the proportion of whites to blacks. This end might be reached in two ways: first, by the emigration of negroes to other and predominantly white sections; second, by attracting white immigration to the South. The first of these modes of remedying the situation seems unlikely to

[18] A. H. Stone, Studies in the American Race Problem, *passim.*
[19] Booker T. Washington, in *Atlanta Journal*, January 13, 1910.

affect the masses of the negroes; the second holds out promise of greater influence. The profound industrial and agricultural revolution through which the South is now passing
will inevitably draw immigrants. The movement has, in
fact, already begun; and while some southerners are at present unconvinced of the desirability of immigrants, the advantage of an abundant labor supply will doubtless in time
overcome their objections, which are superficial and in
some instances, unreasonable. The establishment of a small
proprietor class should prove a great incentive to the negro,
pointing out to him the goal to be reached as the reward
of industry.

2

The Agrarian Revolution in
Georgia, 1865-1912
[1914]

Abridged from the Bulletin of the University of Wisconsin, *No. 639, Madison, Wisconsin, 1914, 129pp. (History Series, Vol 3, No. 3, pp. 393-524).*

PART 1: DESTRUCTION OF THE OLD PLANTATION SYSTEM

GENERAL CONDITIONS IN GEORGIA, 1865-1870

THE UPHEAVAL OF THE SIXTIES, WHILE LEAVING UNTOUCHED no phase of economic and social life in Georgia, necessarily accomplished its profoundest work in connection with the agricultural interest since more than three-fourths of the population were engaged in farming. Agriculture, along with all other industries, suffered from the destruction of capital and loss of credit entailed by the war, to say nothing of the disastrous aftermath of Reconstruction. Peculiar ills, however, affected the planting element, such as an almost total failure of crops in 1865 and 1866; labor difficulties, due to the negroes' misconception of the meaning of liberty; and the extraordinary mobility of the population, making it difficult for the Georgia planter to secure labor.

The outlook was distinctly discouraging to the farmers when they returned home in the spring of 1865. During their absence in the armies, the farms had been allowed to run down. Ditches had filled, their banks had grown up with

bushes and briers, fences were falling, gates and bars were out
of repair; "the teams were ruined by old age and hard usage,
and by the constant military impressment system, both officially and without authority, by day and by night,"[1] the
farm equipment of plows, hoes, and harrows was worn out.
The laborers were thoroughly demoralized. Cotton was extremely high and everybody turned at once to cotton planting. Good seed were not to be had. The soil was badly prepared and inadequately cultivated; the harvest was a failure,
both in 1865 and 1866.

So widespread was the distress following the crop failures
that thousands of Georgians must have perished from starvation but for the timely aid of the government. The Federal
authorities opened a food distributing office in Atlanta in 1865.
Thirty-five thousand persons in the counties around that city
were dependent upon public aid during the winter of that
year.[2] The destitution continued in 1867, but in 1868 conditions had improved, and there was no general issue of food
by the Federal government that year.[3]

Farmers who had mortgaged their property to obtain
stock, implements, and food with which to make crops were
now in desperate straits. Notwithstanding the high price of
cotton, the total failure of crops made it impossible for them
to meet obligations. Foreclosures were numerous. The debtor
class, always ready to demand legislative aid, secured the passage of homestead and exemption acts, removing from the
reach of creditors a certain amount of property. Early in
1866 a bill of this sort was vetoed by the governor and the
House refused to join the Senate in passing it over the veto;[4]
but the movement was a popular one, and the Constitutional
Convention of 1868 put into the new constitution an article
directing that a homestead of realty to the value of "$4,000 in

---

[1] *Southern Cultivator* (Athens, Ga.), July, 1867.
[2] *Annual Cyclopedia*, 1865, p. 392.
[3] 40 Congress, 3 sess., *House Executive Documents*, 3, No. I. p. 1044.
[4] Georgia Legislature, *Senate Journal*, 1865-1866, pp. 598-599.

specie, and personal property to the value of $1,000 in specie, be set aside for each head of a family. . . ."[5] Foreseeing the popular ratification of this constitution, creditors began rapidly to foreclose mortgages. The cry of oppression was raised and General Meade, then military governor, was induced to declare the acts of the convention binding until passed on by the people.[6]

The Negroes' Misconception of the Meaning of Liberty

Since the abnormal conditions which characterized the transition from the old to the new regime gave, in a measure, to the readjustment of race relations the direction it finally took, it becomes necessary to consider the freedman's conduct in his new status. This was, of course, the most interesting and important of contemporary problems. Opinions as to the negro's capacity for exercising the privileges of freedom vary with the personal and sectional bias of the observer. Southern farmers were, on the whole, convinced that his utility as a laborer had been permanently destroyed. One of the military governors of Georgia, General Pope, was much impressed with the progress the blacks were making. In an official report he expressed the opinion that within five years the bulk of the intelligence of Georgia would be shifted to the negroes. The matter seemed otherwise to a special agent of the American Union Committee, who made a journey through Georgia in 1866. He reported that the negroes as a class "appear to be idle, vagrant, thieving and licentious. They congregate about cities in hosts. A great many live on the resources of the Bureau for Refugees and Freedmen, a great many on small short jobs and pilfering, a few on constant manly labor. . . . I found their general idea of freedom to be, naturally enough, idleness and license."[7]

[5] Irwin, D., *Code of Georgia Laws*, 1873, p. 925, Sec. 5135.
[6] 40 Cong., 3 sess., *House Ex. Docs.*, 3. Pt. I, No. I, p. 75.
[7] *DeBow's Review*, May, 1866.

On many plantations operations went ahead with scarcely any interruption.[8] Planters called informal meetings of the freedmen, explained in simple terms their new condition and offered employment at the current rate of wages to all who desired to remain. After wandering off a short distance simply to assert their freedom, many negroes returned to the familiar surroundings and took up their former labor. Those planters who had been most considerate of their slaves experienced the least trouble in employing them as freedmen. This peaceful readjustment seems to have been common during the period of the Johnson government, although it was in many cases disturbed by the political troubles accompanying the congressional reconstruction.

Repressive Legislation, Vagrancy, Apprentice Laws

On the other hand, there was a large element of the freedmen who did not follow the course just outlined. The widespread belief that the plantations of their former owners would be divided among the ex-slaves at Christmas, 1865, acted as a deterrent to steady industry.

Vagrancy and lawlessness in the towns increased to such an extent as to threaten the stability of society. The correspondent of *The Nation* wrote from Macon that the presence and conduct of negro troops were responsible for a large part of the disorder.[9] Agricultural operations almost ceased in some sections. Governor Jenkins in 1867 attributed the crop failures of the past two years in part to the indisposition of the negroes to work. Some sort of repressive measures were necessary. In 1866 the legislature passed laws intended to check vagrancy. One law dealt with vagrants of age, authorizing imprisonment, upon conviction, for a year or permitting the county court to bind the vagrant to

---

[8] Leigh, Frances Butler, *Ten Years on a Georgia Plantation Since the War* (London, 1883), pp. 14 and 21. *Southern Cultivator,* April, 1866, quotes Macon (Ga.) *Telegraph.*

[9] *The Nation,* Oct. 5, 1865.

some person for twelve months.[10] At the same time an apprentice act was passed, providing for the binding out until the
age of twenty-one of negro minors whose parents were unable to support them. The master was bound to teach the
apprentice some useful occupation, furnish him with wholesome food and clothing, teach him habits of industry, hon-
esty, and morality, cause him to be taught to read English,
and govern him with humanity, "using only the same degree
of force to compel his obedience as a father may use with
his minor children."[11]

No one with any knowledge of negro characteristics can
now question the wisdom of such acts, but in the inflamed
condition of public opinion in 1866, the laws were widely denounced. It is significant that the Freedmen's Bureau itself
recognized the necessity of an apprentice act. Bureau agents
in all counties were authorized to bind out minors of both
sexes until they were of age. Such contracts were legalized
by the legislature.[12]

Arson, burglary, and horse stealing became so prevalent as
to lead the legislature to impose the death penalty for these
crimes.[13] Minor offenses, such as carrying weapons, driving
overseers from plantations, resenting the exercise of legitimate
authority, and general disrespect to employers, were rife.[14]
Petty misdemeanors, formerly punished by slave owners, now
came before the courts, and it became necessary to reduce the
penalty attaching to larceny in order to make the punishment
more in accord with the untutored condition of the freedmen.
The lessening of the penalty for minor infractions of law, in

connection with the heightening of the punishment for arson and burglary at night, were admirably suited to existing conditions.

The flood of convicts under the new laws was so great that the central penitentiary was speedily overtaxed. In 1869 the leasing of convicts to private individuals and corporations was begun, a system which developed many objectionable features, although vested interests prevented its abolition until 1908.

In general, the policy of the congressional radicals fostered and encouraged political rather than industrial activity on the part of the blacks, and thus tended to prevent a speedy and satisfactory readjustment of the labor situation.

Interstate and Intrastate Population Movements

In comparison with the middle western states and some of the eastern states, the population of Georgia was relatively stable in the years immediately following the War. But it is easy to overemphasize this tendency to stability. The absence of free government land and the prevalence of political and social troubles rendered Georgia unattractive to immigrants. Such population movement as there was confined itself to migration away from the state, and to removals of Georgians from North and Middle Georgia to the southwestern part of the state.

The counties of extreme South and Southwest Georgia were receiving the bulk of the people leaving the old slave counties. The shifting of the negro population produced striking changes. In forty-one counties there was an absolute loss of negroes between 1860 and 1870. These counties lay in three distinct sections. The first was the mountainous region of extreme North Georgia. There had never been many slaves in this region, as it was unsuited to agriculture of the sort that made slavery profitable. The freedmen, therefore, migrated to the rich cotton lands further south. The second section was the old cotton belt, in which the lands were worn, the per acre production of cotton low, and consequently wages below the level of the newer regions. The third section that was losing its negro population was the seaboard. There the labor of the slaves had been most arduous on the rice plantations. The negroes refused to do the heavy ditching and banking, and the rice plantations fell into ruins.

Nearly all the counties that received heavy accessions of negroes lay below the fall line of the rivers.[15]

Another noteworthy fact is that the cities of Georgia attracted many negroes during the decade. The increases ranged from 50 per cent in Richmond County (Augusta) to over 400 per cent in Fulton County (Atlanta).

The effect of these movements of the black population was a thorough disorganization of labor in the older cotton belt, and, in the cities, the introduction of a disorderly and idle element, for whose control the statutes already mentioned were intended.

The available statistics shed no light on the movement of population away from the state. But survivors of the time say that the westward migration was marked, and in the notes of tourists one often comes across such statements as this: "There is a constant drain of emigration from the poorer districts of Georgia. . . . Hundreds of poor Georgians, unable to make a living from the wornout soil, under the new order of things, fly to Texas."[16]

The freedmen, however, were undoubtedly a much less stable element of the population. In 1866 the Comptroller General reported that "the state has lost over one hundred thousand producing laborers since 1863,"[17] a fact which he attributed to westward migration and increased mortality among the negroes. A report of the United States Department of Agriculture contains the statement that between

[15] See map on p. 91.

[16] King, E., *Great South* (Hartford, 1874), p. 366.

[17] Georgia Comptroller General, *Report*, 1866, p. 17.

1865 and 1868, 139,988 Georgia negroes had moved west.[18] "For some time," the report states, "the average number [of negroes] passing through Atlanta has been 1,000 daily." The Freedmen's Bureau agent made note of this migration in the report for 1867.[19] In that year, the average yearly wage paid for farm labor, including rations, was $125 in Georgia, $149 in Mississippi, $150 in Louisiana, $136 in Arkansas.[20] The negroes were moving, therefore, in response to an economic demand.

THE FAILURE OF THE PLANTATION SYSTEM

The ante-bellum "plantation" implied large-scale production of a staple crop by forced labor. The success of the system as a productive enterprise lay in the ability of the plantation manager to organize and direct the labor of slaves, over whose movements he had complete control.

The problem confronting the planter in 1865 was to preserve the maximum degree of control over the laborers consonant with their changed condition. The best chance of securing this control seemed to lie in maintaining in most of its essentials the plantation organization. Of what use was the brawn of the masses of freedmen, utterly ignorant and penniless, if dissociated from the intelligence and skill of their former owners? Let everything proceed as formerly, the contractual relation being substituted for that of master and slave, wages taking the form of money payments instead of consumer's goods, and the laborer's freedom of movement being recognized. With such ideas as these the planters began life anew in 1865. There was no thought of abandoning the direction of labor; all the experience of Georgia cotton producers had taught them that negro laborers would work regularly and efficiently only under the supervision and control of employer or overseer. The plan-

---

[18] U. S. Department of Agriculture, *Yearbook,* 1868, pp. 573-574.
[19] 40 Cong., 2 sess., *House Ex. Docs.,* i, No. I, p. 675.
[20] U. S. Department of Agriculture, *Yearbook,* 1867, p. 416.

tation was the established form of organization and it was natural that the planters should try to perpetuate it. In 1865, therefore, in a great number of cases all the externals of the former regime were continued: the negroes lived in "quarters," went to the fields at tap of farm bell, worked in gangs under direction, and were rationed from the plantation smokehouse, the charge for food being deducted from the wage. A money wage was usually paid in 1865 and 1866, payment being weekly, monthly, or yearly, according to contract.

Though no definite statement can be made as to the proportion of the planters who attempted to reestablish the plantation system, the evidence indicates that the effort was widespread. The high price of cotton in 1865 and 1866 was a mighty stimulus to cotton production. Every planter who could assemble a force of laborers went feverishly to work. The result of the operations of 1865 was a bitter disappointment. In spite of the abnormal price of the staple, heavy losses were sustained. It was impossible to get cash to pay wages, for money was simply nonexistent in Georgia.[21] The wages fixed by the Freedmen's Bureau were unreasonably high.[22] The labor was worthless in the absence of power to compel attention to duty. The negro saw no reason why he should not stop work to go fishing; he was willing to sacrifice his wages and was unconcerned about the state of the crop.[23] The charge of unreliability was made against the negroes in practically every issue of the *Cultivator;* if paid on Saturday, they were as likely to be absent as present on Monday.[24]

After the experience of 1865, the editor of the *Cultivator* suggested the substitution of the share system, hoping that the planter might in this way enlist the self-interest of the

---

[21] *Southern Cultivator,* July, 1865, editorial.
[22] *Ibid.*
[23] *Ibid.,* December, 1865.
[24] *Ibid., July,* 1866, letter from Greene County.

negroes in the farming and thus check their roving pro-
clivities. There was no suggestion that this change would in
any way impair the owner's control over the labor. Thus,
while advocating the share arrangement, the editor said:
"There is little hope that this or any other plan will succeed, under any other oversight than the planter's own eye."[25]

It seems that in 1866, on the whole, the negroes improved
as laborers.[26] The Freedmen's Bureau was exercising pressure
on them, and they had by that time learned that the expected
division of lands would not take place. Planters continued
to operate the plantation system, though still with discouraging results.

Migration Causes Scarcity of Laborers

Competition for laborers was one of the most important
reasons for the great changes in the farming system, subsequently to be described. The movement of the negroes
became more general in 1866, and the conviction was growing
that a new system must be inaugurated.[27] So pronounced became the scarcity of laborers in Middle Georgia, the region
from which the greatest exodus of negroes occurred, that
radical changes in agricultural organization were suggested
and carried out. Large plantations in that region lay idle
for want of laborers.[28] The planters were confronted with
the alternative of totally abandoning their plantations or of
taking laborers on their own terms. Some planters under
this pressure rented their lands outright to negroes. The editor of the *Cultivator* came out frankly in the November, 1867,
issue with a statement that "under the present state of affairs,
experience of the past two seasons has demonstrated that
plantations on an extended scale, with free labor, cannot be
made profitable. The first change that must occur, and

[25] *Ibid.*, December, 1865.
[26] *Ibid.*, April, 1866, quotes Macon *Telegraph*.
[27] *Ibid.*, letters from Schley and Columbia Counties.
[28] *Ibid.*, March, 1867. Letter from Warren County.

which will eventually prove beneficial, is the subdivision of landed estates." Certain recommendations constantly recur in communications from leading agriculturists of the state, namely, contraction in amount of land used, more intensive culture, manuring, and use of improved implements and commercial fertilizers. The dominant idea underlying these suggestions was the economizing of labor.[29]

Opinion was rapidly shifting by 1868 in favor of abandoning the old system. Letters still appeared in the *Cultivator* advocating the plantation arrangement, but letters of opposite tendency were more numerous. In January, 1868, a long and interesting communication appeared under the caption "The Question of Labor," unsigned, but by a Middle Georgia planter. He advised the retention of the plantation system, maintaining that the trouble in the past two years had arisen from the excessively high wages and the unreliability and instability of labor. He ended with a plea that all pull together and regulate wages. "Don't go out to look up hands by any means. Let them hunt homes and they will not be so arrogant and self-inflated. Dictate your own terms to them . . . Let a certain price rule the land throughout." Other planters expressed views diametrically opposed to these. For instance, the May, 1868, *Cultivator* prints the following: "I am satisfied from my experience and close observation for the past two years, there is but one correct mode of working our present labor (which I think is the best in the world), and it is simply this. Let each family work by itself, in separate fields or farms. This is much easier and I think far better than the old plantation style of working all together." On the seacoast matters were in a desperate condition.[30]

The supply of negroes available as wage hands was even less adequate in 1869 than during the preceding years. The West was still drawing away many negroes. But by this

[29] *Ibid.,* November, 1867. Letter from Floyd County.
[30] Leigh, *Ten Years,* pp. 128-129.

time a new complaint became general, namely, that planters were renting their lands to negroes. It is to be carefully noted that migration and renting had exactly the same effect on the planter who was trying to maintain the plantation system. The presence of large numbers of renters indicated that many planters had given up the struggle and abandoned their holdings to negro renters. The case was excellently put by a Burke County planter:

> . . . some of the landowners have rented lands to negroes, to farm upon their own responsibility. This is certainly ruinous to the general interest. Those who rent their lands to negroes, never realize any profit, and the negroes never make a support, hence, they steal all the stock within reach —have all the loafing vagabonds in the community around them. *It takes an immense quantity of labor from under the direction of the skillful farmer* . . .[31]

The significant words have been italicized; it was the escape from skillful direction that was unfortunate from the standpoint of production and conservation.

The supply of labor was said to be steadily diminishing this year also in Southwest Georgia.[32] Of course, the constantly increasing tendency of negro women to withdraw from field work accentuated the scarcity of labor.

Clearly, the plantation system was tottering in 1869, in large measure on account of the inability of planters to secure the necessary labor. Had the blacks been willing to work as hired day laborers, it is probable that the plantation would have been widely preserved, for those planters who were efficient managers and were able to find laborers succeeded in maintaining themselves under the new conditions. There were more of such cases than has been supposed. The most active and determined planters, with ranks recruited from the former overseer class, continued very much on the former lines. Indeed, there has never been a time up to the present when

---

[31] *Southern Cultivator,* February, 1869.
[32] *Ibid.,* Article copied from Cuthbert *Appeal* (Randolph County).

excellently ordered and successful plantations have not existed in the black belt counties. Only the most vigorous men succeed in the planter's role. A convention, presumably of such men, held in Atlanta in 1869, was unanimously of the opinion that the old system was the best.[33] Nordhoff, in 1875, observed that the best planters in Georgia preferred the wage system.[34] But the conditions of success were hard—too exacting for the general run of the ante-bellum type of planter. Even where laborers were to be had, the task of supervising their efforts was one requiring almost superhuman endurance and talents of a high order.

It was a hard matter to find men who were willing to work as overseers. With such capacity for work, and plenty of land to be had at nominal prices, they quickly set up for themselves. The fathers of some prominent citizens of Georgia today were once overseers on slave plantations. The reward awaiting their skill and industry was great and they seized the opportunity. Those planters who were less proficient in the art of managing negroes, whose methods were slack and who did not stay constantly on the plantation, were forced out of business.

The Economic and Social Forces Which Destroyed the Plantation System

It should be evident from the foregoing that in trying to maintain the system of large scale production with closely supervised labor, the planters, as a class, were fighting against economic and social forces much too powerful for them to overcome. The first in importance of these forces was the repugnance of the negroes to supervision and their determination to escape it, coupled with an abundance of very cheap land to which they might resort as tenants. Secondly, the negroes largely controlled the situation in Georgia by

---

[33] Milledgeville (Ga.) *Southern Recorder*, February 9, 1869.

[34] Nordhoff, Charles, *Cotton States in the Spring and Summer of 1875* (New York, 1896), p. 107.

virtue of the urgent demand for cotton-producing labor, intensified by the call of the western cotton belt for labor from the East. In the third place, the maintenance of a wage system necessitated the use of considerable sums of cash, and few planters could obtain ready money. To meet this difficulty, lien laws were enacted, by which supplies could be obtained from merchants on the execution of a lien on the coming crop. These laws were at first intended to permit only planters to give crop liens, but subsequent modifications extended the privilege to tenants, so that the lien laws facilitated the escape of the negroes from the supervision of the landlord, though substituting a more exacting master, the merchant. These considerations require further elaboration.

It was natural that the negro should desire to control his own movements. His crude conception of freedom was summed up in his release from physical restraint. Rarely beyond the confines of the plantation as a slave, now that he was at liberty to travel, the desire to wander was irresistible. Of course, the plantation system of free hired labor meant almost as much restriction as did slavery. If the negro expected to receive a daily or weekly wage, he had to work every day and work as directed. From daylight to dark was the universal rule on cotton plantations. Where no alternative of working for a share or of renting presented itself, the freedman attempted to preserve his liberty of movement by refusing to hire for a year. He greatly preferred to contract for a week or a month, and in many cases would not contract for more than two days in the week.[35] The presence of the overseer became extremely irksome to the negroes, even where the control was very liberal.[36]

There was, however, no reason why the negroes should remain in the status of wage laborers. They were in a position

---

[35] U. S. Department of Agriculture, *Yearbook,* 1866, p. 573.
[36] Barrow, in *Scribner's Magazine,* April, 1881.

to make terms for themselves. Each year after 1865 found
the planters more and more convinced that they would be
unable to preserve the plantation organization. In order to
keep the negroes from abandoning the older cotton belt
in Georgia for the fertile West or the new Southwest corner
of Georgia, it was necessary that wages should be fixed to
meet the opportunity element which the negro demanded,
or retain him by changing his status to that of tenant, or
quasi-tenant. That the difference in the wage offered in
Georgia and other cotton states was material is seen from
the fact that wages in the South in 1867 ranged from $100
to $158 (Georgia: $125), while the wage level in 1868 was
considerably lower, ranging from $83 in Georgia to $130.
The break between 1867 and 1868 was sharper in Georgia
than in any other state, a fact which had immediate effect
on the labor situation there.

Out-of-State Demand for Workers

It is not to be supposed that the many ex-slaves would of
themselves have responded to such a fluctuation in the rate of
wages. External pressure of the most effective sort was supplied. Planters from the West came in numbers, hired gangs
of negroes, furnished transportation, and took them away
from Georgia.[37] The Freedmen's Bureau was most active in
this connection. It became a vast intelligence office, supplying
planters from all over the South with information as to
sources of labor. Through the exertions of the various Com-
missioners of the Bureau, thousands of negroes were moved
from Middle Georgia. Very often the government paid transportation expenses. In 1866 the Assistant Commissioner for
Georgia reported that he was "overwhelmed by applications
for laborers," and that "the demand for labor and the price
paid for it are increasing every day."[38]

---

[37] Trowbridge, J. T., *The South*, 1866, p. 460.
[38] 39 Cong., 1 sess., *Sen. Ex. Docs.*, 2, No. 27, pp. 88-89.

Influence of the Freedmen's Bureau

By way of digression, it may be said that but for the interference of the Bureau, the negroes would have been at the mercy of their employers. Exercising under the Federal Law complete supervision over the contractual relations between the races, the officials required that contracts should be in writing and should not be considered binding unless approved by the Bureau. As the officials refused to approve contracts in which the rate of wages was lower than they thought fair, a general rise in wages followed. General Tillson reported that his supervision had increased wages from between two and seven to between ten and fifteen dollars per month.[39] A typical case of such interference was related by General Tillson to Mr. Trowbridge.[40] An Oglethorpe County planter had contracted with laborers at $75 to $100, with food and house, per year. The contract was set aside by the assistant commissioner on the ground that the planter could afford to pay $144, food, and house. After a lengthy argument, the planter submitted the following estimate of the result, should he pay $144 per laborer:

"Good hands will make 2 bales (of cotton) $300.00
     85 bu. of corn 85.00
                                                 —————
                                               $385.00

Expenses.

3 lbs. Bacon per week at 60c, 1 peck meal
    per week at 25c $44.20
Rent of cabin 10.00
Fuel 25.00
Wages 144.00
                                       —————— $223.20

Net profit per man $161.80

[39] *Ibid.*, pp. 89-90.
[40] Trowbridge, *South*, p. 492.

Extreme Competition for Labor

In the unsettled condition of labor, it became a common thing for negroes who had contracted with one planter to be enticed away by promises of higher pay elsewhere.[41] It was a matter more of chagrin than of surprise if one's entire plantation force disappeared over night. The negroes were entirely devoid of any conception of the binding nature of a contract, and the conduct of the whites in inducing them to break contracts quite naturally did not tend to enlighten them. Of course, legal action against the freedmen was useless. The Bureau attempted to stop the practice of enticing laborers by imposing fines. In 1866 the legislature made it a misdemeanor to entice another's servant, and it is interesting to note that a law to this effect has been in force ever since.[42]

The extremes to which Georgians were sometimes put in order to retain laborers is indicated in the following letter written by a Mississippi planter to Trowbridge:

> I determined to go to Georgia for the purpose of obtaining the requisite number of hands. I succeeded tolerably well, and could have hired many more than I needed had not the people induced the negroes to believe that we were taking them to Cuba to sell them. I award the palm to the Georgians as the meanest and most despicable class of people it was ever my misfortune to meet.[43]

The scarcity of labor has been canvassed at such length in order to emphasize the fundamentally important fact in the history of the changes that were to come, namely, the negroes' control over the situation. In the dilemma between abandoning farming or hiring negroes on their own terms, many planters chose the former alternative. Their idle plantations, available for the renter, only made it the more difficult for those not disposed to give up, to hire wage hands.

---

[41] 42 Cong., 2 sess., *House Reports of Committees*, "Georgia," 2, p. 758. Testimony of B. H. Hill before Ku Klux Committee.

[42] Legislature of Georgia, *Acts*, 1866, pp. 153-154 ; 1873, p. 20 ; 1882-83, p. 68 ; 1901, p. 63.

[43] Trowbridge, *South*, p. 498.

Those planters who desired to continue farming were forced to modify the system to suit the wishes of the negroes. The material fall in wages in 1868 in response to the break in cotton prices doubtless had its effect in increasing the negro's desire to escape from the old system. Not understanding the economic causes which fixed wages, and seeing the cotton still being produced, he was of the opinion that he was being defrauded.

Importation of Laborers Fails

The luxury of having their erstwhile owners compete for their services did not make for the economic efficiency of the negroes. General Tillson, a staunch friend of the blacks, was quoted in 1865 as saying that he was satisfied the negroes were not generally doing more than about half the work they might.[44] Dissatisfaction at their predicament of having to pay very high wages for very poor labor led planters to experiment with white laborers from Europe and the North. Irishmen were used on the coast to do banking and ditching on the rice plantations, work which the negroes refused longer to do.[45] In 1873 the Leighs imported English laborers, but they were a failure.[46] The effort to secure labor other than the negro was in line with the experience of other southern states. Coolie labor was favored in Mississippi and Louisiana. The press of the period was full of agitation over the subject of immigration. But the demand was from the planter class for laborers: one rarely sees in the literature of the time inducements held out to foreign or northern farmers. Small tracts of land on easy terms were not often the subject of editorials and communications. It was always the scarcity of wage labor that was stressed. Naturally enough, the effort to attract immigration on these terms was a dismal failure.

[44] Andrews, Sidney, *The South Since the War* (Boston, 1866), pp. 359-360.
[45] Leigh, *Ten Years*, p. 128 ; Phillips, U. B., in Documentary History of American Industrial Society, (Cleveland, 1910), *Plantation and Frontier*, II, pp. 181-182.
[46] Leigh, *Ten Years*, pp. 204-206.

It could hardly have been otherwise, when in the West the government was offering quarter sections of virgin land free to the actual settler, in a region where social conditions were much more favorable.

An intelligent non-southern contemporary observer said in effect that in the settlement of the relations between the white employers and negroes, negroes had whites at a great disadvantage. The demand for labor, emigration of negroes, absence of white labor, the possibility of the negro's living for practically nothing, a foolish lien law, all worked for the negro.[47]

The Crop Lien System

Probably no phase of southern post-bellum agriculture has attracted more attention than the credit system which has grown up around the lien laws. So early as December 15, 1866, the Legislature passed an Act permitting landlords to have by special contract in writing a lien upon the crops of their tenants for stock, farming utensils, and provisions, furnished for the purpose of making their crops, and providing that "factors and merchants shall have a lien upon the growing crops of farmers for provisions furnished and commercial manures furnished."[48] The word "farmer" here was not intended to include tenant farmers. In January, 1873, the law was extended so as to enable merchants to take crop liens from tenants also, but the following year the law was again changed so as expressly to deprive merchants of the right to take crop liens from any but the landlord.[49] The next year, however, the legislation against merchants taking liens from tenants was rendered practically null by an act permitting landlords to assign their liens for supplies, and providing that such assigned liens might be enforced by the assignees in the manner provided for their enforcement by landlords.[50]

[47] Trowbridge, *South,* p. 469.
[48] Legislature of Georgia, *Acts,* 1866, p. 141.
[49] *Ibid.,* 1873, p. 43; 1874, p. 18.
[50] *Ibid.,* 1875, p. 20.

These rapid changes in the law indicate a conflict between the planters and the merchants. Planters desired the exclusive right to take liens for supplies from tenants, because they could in this way regulate the expenditures of tenants, and would be justified in exercising supervision over their work in order to protect themselves from loss. Merchants desired to deal directly with tenants because they were easy prey and would buy everything in sight as long as the merchant would extend credit. Tenants preferred to deal directly with the merchants because it increased their sense of importance and enabled them to escape from supervision on the part of the landlord. The Act of 1875 may be regarded as a compromise measure, enabling those planters who were firm enough and sufficiently strong financially, to retain control over their tenants in the matter of supplies; and, on the other hand, legalizing the transfer of the supply lien in cases where the planters desired to escape from the bother of managing the negroes and were willing to abandon the whole business to the merchant.

Here again the difficulties of the planter desiring to preserve his organization were increased. In most cases where the landlord assigned his lien for supplies, thus practically abandoning control over his place, he moved to town and became an "absentee." Negroes at once began to abandon the well-regulated plantations in favor of the merchant-controlled absentee places. The result is simply and adequately stated in one of the letters in "Inquiries I:"[51] "Non-resident land holders rented their land, forcing those who resided on farms to adopt the rental system or no labor could be procured."

While the subsequent effects of the lien laws were bad, it cannot be doubted that, at the time they were enacted,

---

[51] *Inquiries I*, letter from Putnam County. (In the winter of 1912 a circular letter was addressed to a number of Georgia planters who had been engaged in agriculture in 1865. The twenty-one useful replies received were placed in the library of the University of Georgia under the title *"Inquiries I, 1912*, with reference to farming in Georgia immediately after the Civil War.")

they were a boon to the farmers. Only a very small minority of planters could borrow money from banks. The masses of cotton producers had no basis of credit except land, which was not a favored form of security with banks. Furthermore, in most cases the loan desired was small and credit for a year's time was needed—additional reasons why banking of the sort that then existed was of little help. The lien law provided a basis of credit in an emergency when no other relief was practicable. Had the conditions been favorable, the introduction of a cooperative agricultural credit system would have been the salvation of the farming class.

The small town merchant now became a factor in the farming situation. The great cotton factors of the cities were ruined, and the country bank took over the business of supplying the merchants with money. In the early spring, the farmers would call on the merchant, arrange for credit, execute a crop lien, sometimes with the additional security of a real estate or chattel mortgage. He would then procure supplies of tools, clothing, foodstuffs, and commercial fertilizers from time to time as occasion required, and settle the account from the proceeds of his crop at the end of the year.

Consequences of the Lien Laws

The lien laws greatly facilitated the transformation of the agricultural system. Two developments took place, both of which involved widespread abandonment of the wage system. One of these changes was the introduction of the share system. The majority of the planters refused to assign their liens for supplies to merchants. They got supplies directly from the merchants and used them to furnish their laborers with their minimum of subsistence, deferring a final settlement to the end of the year, when each individual laborer was paid the value of the cotton raised on the small farm allotted to him, less the cost of his keep. Both planter and laborer were willing to give up the money payments, the planter alarmed at the fall in the price of cotton, and the negro at the sharp drop in wages. Under this share arrangement, subsequently to be described at length, the planter did not by any means give up his right of supervision, but his control was weakened, for when the negro was received into what was virtually a partnership, he was able to assert himself to a greater degree than as a day laborer. Whatever loss from the point of view of production might have been entailed by this change was at least partly offset by the greater stability given to the labor, since the negroes necessarily remained on one farm for at least one year.

The share system may be called "quasi-tenancy," since under it the landlord retains a large measure of control over the labor. The second development was the introduction of real tenancy, or renting. In cases where the landlord would assign his lien for supplies, the tenants received their supplies directly from the merchant, and remained under no control whatever, their only connection with the landlord being the obligation to pay a fixed amount of rent, either in cash or in cotton. Under this renting arrangement, it was necessary that the tenant have sufficient capital to buy stock and tools, or be able to induce some one to "set him up." Those negroes who could do neither of these things became share tenants.

Yet another consequence followed the lien laws. The land-poor planters in many, many cases were willing to sell land at nominal prices to their ex-slaves or to white purchasers of the former non-slaveholding class. The sales were commonly on the basis of deferred payments. The lien laws enabled these new proprietors to stock their farms and operate on credit, with a good chance in prosperous times of paying off the incumbrances on their lands. Negroes in Georgia, in 1874, owned 339,000 acres of land,[52] most of which was doubtless acquired in the above fashion.

---

[52] DuBois, W. E. B., *Negro Landowner of Georgia,* in U. S. Department of Labor, *Bulletin,* No. 35, July, 1901, p. 665.

A New Class of Merchant Owners Rises

But many planters and small farmers were ruined by the lien laws. Exorbitant credit-prices were charged, and a bad crop would prevent the farmer from paying his account, which had to be carried over, with interest, to the following year. A succession of unfavorable seasons, a failure of the labor supply, or bad management, soon involved many hopelessly in debt. Wholesale execution of mortgages followed and landed estates passed into the hands of the town merchants.[53] These merchants combined the supply business with farming on the negro tenant plan, looking to the mercantile feature of the relationship for most of their profit. This system became widespread, and almost prostrated agriculture in the black belt.

DECADENCE OF PLANTATIONS: BEGINNINGS OF SMALL PROPRIETORSHIPS AND OF TENANCY

As has already been pointed out, scarcity of laborers willing to work for wages was one of the controlling factors in the failure of the plantation regime. This dearth of labor was due partly to migration, but also to the fact that there was an abundance of cheap land which former day laborers might acquire either as owners or renters.

Abundance of Land in Georgia at Low Prices

There was no public land in Georgia in 1865. The last land of this character had been distributed to citizens on the expulsion of the Cherokee Indians in the thirties. This is a fact of some importance, as the existence of free public lands in Alabama, Mississippi, Louisiana, and Arkansas attracted many of the more energetic Georgians; while the demand for labor at higher prices in the West was drawing off thousands of negro laborers.

---

[53] Banks, E. M., *Economics of Land Tenure in Georgia* (New York, 1905), pp. 49-50.

But of private land for sale there was plenty. Of the total acreage of the state, only 63 per cent was reported in 1870 as being in farms, and only 18 per cent was classed as improved.[54] That large section of Georgia known as the "Wiregrass country" had formerly been regarded as unsuited to agriculture, but the great demand for cotton, coincident with a remarkable development in the use of commercial fertilizers, brought this region into cultivation in the years following the war. Not only was this huge supply of land opened up, but there were also available many thousands of acres of improved lands in the older sections, now coming on the market with the breakup of plantations. A further supply of land was the "old field" or formerly cultivated land, abandoned in the exploitative processes characteristic of the ante-bellum period.[55]

Reliable data as to land prices are extremely scarce. In the general description at the close of the war, the feeling was that values were low. The lands offered in Georgia ranged from $1.00 per acre in the Wiregrass country to $100 in the neighborhood of cities. The general level of the price quotations was higher than would be expected in view of the unsettled labor conditions and the rapidly falling price of cotton. The highest prices were for "improved" farms in the oldest part of the belt. Unimproved lands could be had at much lower prices, and it was doubtless out of these unimproved areas that most of the new farms presently to be mentioned were carved.

Number of Farms No Indicator of Ownership

The sudden growth in the number of farms and the decrease in the acreage size of farms in the South have justly been regarded as among the most conspicuous results of the Civil War. The change was immediate and far-reaching in Georgia. Between 1860 and 1880, the total farm area in the

[54] United States Census, 1870, *Industry and Wealth,* p. 120.
[55] *Southern Cultivator,* July, 1865.

state declined from 23.6 to 23.0 million acres, but the number of farms more than doubled; hence the average farm size fell from 430 to 188 acres. A study of farms by size in 1860 and 1870 throws further light on the movement. In these ten years, half of the farms of more than 500 acres disappeared. The entire increase in the number of farms is found in the 20 to 100 acre group.

No certain answer can be given to the question to what extent this increase in the number of farms meant the spread of small ownership, on the one hand, and of tenancy, on the other. The United States Census published no statistics on land tenure until 1880. In that report (and the subsequent practice has been the same) farms were classified into three groups, namely, farms operated by owners, cash tenants, and share tenants. Since, on the one hand, a single owner may operate several distinct farms, and, on the other, many landlords do not farm at all, it is obvious that the number of farms operated by owners does not by any means represent the number of landlords.

Negroes Make Little Progress as Landowners

Estimates based on the scant data available make a very poor showing for the negro as a landowner in Georgia. While negroes composed, in 1900, one-half of the population of the state, they had taxable titles to only one twenty-fifth of the land.

The progress of the negroes in acquiring land did not seem at all satisfactory to their contemporary leaders. A conference of social settlement workers in Georgia and the South met in Atlanta in 1875, and went on record as follows:

> The outlook is not encouraging. Many of the negroes are making a noble and successful struggle against all their difficulties, without and within, but as a rule they are not acquiring homes and property, their enthusiasm for education is yielding to the chilling influence of their poverty, and their innate evil propensities, uncorrected by their

sensational religion, are dragging them downward. Numbers are becoming discouraged as to acquiring property.[56]

Further evidence that the development of small proprietorship among negroes was not striking may be found in the detailed investigation conducted by the Bureau of the Census in 1880.[57]

Rise in Number of Farms Explained by Tenancy

Banks' study showed that despite the large increase in the number of white landowners, the ratio between white landowners and white population was about the same in 1900 as in 1860, that is to say, about every other white family in the state owned land.[58] One is led, then, to suspect that the growth of small ownerships was not so widespread as has usually been supposed. By far the larger part of the increase in number of farms in the post-bellum period represents increase of tenant farmers. By 1880, 45 per cent of all the farms in the state were tenant farms.

A Typical Example of Disintegration: The Barrow Plantation

This growth of tenancy meant a weakening of control over agricultural operations on the part of the former managing class. The readjustment of the labor system in Georgia has been a process of decentralization, from complete control by employers of wage gangs to the regime of independent renters. An account of this process has been preserved for one of the large Oglethorpe County plantations.[59] For several years following emancipation, the force of laborers was divided into two squads, the arrangement and method of work being as in the ante-bellum period. Each squad was under an overseer, or foreman. The hands were given a share of the crop. As time went on, the control of the foreman became irksome to the negroes. As a consequence the squads were

[56] DuBois, *op. cit.*, p. 666, quoting from *American Missionary*, June, 1875.
[57] U. S. Census, 1880, VI, *Cotton Production*, Pt. 2, p. 174.
[58] Banks, p. 43.
[59] Barrow, D. C., in *Scribner's Magazine*, April, 1881.

split up into smaller and smaller groups, still working for a
part of the crop, and still using the owner's teams. This process of disintegration continued until each laborer worked
separately, without any oversight. The change involved great
trouble and loss. Mules were ill-treated, the crop was badly
worked and often the tenant stole the landlord's share. It
became necessary to abandon the sharing feature. The owner
sold his mules to the tenants, thereby putting on them the
burden of loss incidental to careless handling of stock. It
became impracticable to keep the cabins grouped when each
man worked on a separate farm, since some of the farms
were at a distance from the "quarters." New cottages were,
therefore, built scatteringly in convenient places near springs.
The negroes now planted what they pleased, and worked
when they liked, the landlord interfering only to require that
enough cotton be planted to pay the rent. As Barrow said,
"the slight supervision which is exercised over these tenants
[in 1880] may surprise those ignorant of how completely the
relations between the races in the South have changed."

In this instance the share arrangement was adopted from
the first. Had wages been paid for a year or two and then
the change to shares been made, the case would have been
typical of the history of the decentralization of agricultural
operations in Georgia.

The Share System Supersedes the Wage System

The rapidity with which the share system was adopted
is indicated by the statement in the Freedmen's Bureau report of 1868 that most of the contracts for that year were
for a part of the crop.[60] This was an exaggeration, but it
shows that there was a wholesale abandonment of the wage
system. The extent to which the movement had progressed
was first definitely known in 1880, when the Census showed
that 31 per cent of all Georgia farms were operated on the
share arrangement.

---

[60] 40 Cong., 3 sess., *House Ex. Docs.*, 3, No. I, p. 1044.

For a number of years after the introduction of this system of crop-sharing, there was no uniformity of practice as to what share should be given to the laborer. The share varied with the relative bargaining power of the parties, with variations in the fertility of the soil, and with the amount and character of the equipment furnished by the employer. At the present time in the Black Belt one rarely meets with any other basis of division than the half. Outside of that region, in sections where tenants are largely white, a "third-and-fourth" system is practiced.

Supervision of Labor Under the Share System

Of first importance in connection with the development of tenancy is the matter of supervision or control of labor. If the planter continued to work the share tenants in groups under strict supervision by himself or his representative, the plantation organization was not seriously impaired. Neither could the plantation be said to have disappeared when the tenants were given separate farms, provided the owner supervised their farming. But if the laborers were scattered over a large plantation and were allowed to escape from all control, the former organization cannot be said to have remained intact. The plantation, in fact, in such cases, became a collection of little farms, independently operated. At the present time, an unsupervised "cropper," as share tenants have come to be known, is almost never met with. The supervision of his operations is as close as the planter can make it, the right of control being based on the fact that the owner furnishes all the capital necessary to make the crop. Few men would now think of entrusting such capital to uncontrolled negroes, and such evidence as is to be found tends to show that this practice of supervision dates back to the inception of the share system.

There were, on the other hand, planters who tried the plan of unsupervised share tenancy. The Barrow plantation just discussed is a case in point. Maltreatment of animals and loss of crops resulted, and the share system was abandoned for renting. The Agricultural Department correspondent for Georgia said in 1876: "Many farmers [of Georgia] have been nearly ruined by neglect to exercise wholesome supervision of the farm economy, and waste and improvidence of share croppers. Some have benefited themselves and laborers by a judicious control."[61] A similar note occurs in a census publication of 1880.[62]

It seems clear from the evidence that unsupervised share farming was a failure; but it was impossible to impose restrictions on negroes who had been permitted to work on this system. The solution of the problem lay in a more complete separation of landlord and tenant, in other words, in real tenancy or renting.

Renting Commences

The practice of renting lands arose from a variety of causes. Many planters in the unsettled condition of labor did not care to attempt farming, and, unable to realize on their holdings, or unwilling to sell, turned over their lands to white and black renters, who, under the lien laws, could get their supplies from merchants, with or without the landlord's endorsement. Other planters, owning large bodies of land and desiring to continue operations, were able to secure a sufficient force of laborers to man only part of the plantation, and therefore rented the balance, rather than have it remain idle. Yet other planters, influenced by the new impulse towards popular education, moved to the towns to educate their children, and under such circumstances rented their lands, the only alternative to selling, since the wage or share system was impractical without constant oversight. But the most potent factor in bringing about the renting system was the

---

[61] U. S. Department of Agriculture, *Yearbook*, 1876, p. 132.
[62] U. S. Census, 1880, VI, *Cotton Production*, Pt. 2, p. 172. Letter from a Georgia correspondent.

negroes' desire for complete emancipation from control.[63] By reason of the scarcity of labor they were able to realize their wishes. When the movement was once begun, it grew with great rapidity, for as soon as the negroes who were working as day laborers or share hands saw the large degree of personal liberty enjoyed by those who had succeeded in attaining the position of renters, they speedily demanded like privileges, and, in a large number of cases, the planters were not in a position to refuse.

The workings of the share and renting systems will be discussed in the following chapter. The essential differences between the two systems may be briefly explained at this point. Under the *renting system* the landlord furnishes only the land and house. All supplies are furnished by the tenant. The landlord has nothing to do with the tenant's crop, no right of supervision as to the sort of crops grown or the amount of labor expended. The rental under this arrangement is commonly stated in terms of cotton, though outside of the Black Belt there is a considerable amount of cash renting.

Under the *share system*, the landlord supplies everything necessary to make the crop, except the manual labor, and the owner and tenant are in a sense co-partners in the undertaking. Since the landlord has undertaken all the risk, he claims the right of complete control over the tenant and the crop, just as in the case of a day laborer. It is this supervision that the darkies resent. It is a well-established fact that their profits under the supervised share system are usually far higher than they can make as independent renters. Profit, however, is a secondary consideration.

In 1880 more than twenty per cent of all the Black Belt farms were being operated on a renting basis, by far the larger part of the renters being negroes. By that time, all the forces which determined the post-bellum history of agricultural labor in Georgia were in operation.

---

[63] Industrial Commission, *Report*, X, p. 487. Testimony of F. M. Norfleet.

CONTRASTING TYPES OF TENANCY:
CROPPING AND RENTING*

The table below presents the facts upon which the following discussion of cropping and renting will be based. It
shows the development of the various classes of farmers for
the census periods 1880-1910:

Year	Total Number of Farms	FARMS OPERATED BY					
		Owners		Cash tenants		Share tenants	
		Number	Pct.	Number	Pct.	Number	Pct.
1880	138,600	76,500	55	18,600	13	43,600	32
1890	171,100	79,500	46	29,400	17	62,200	37
1890	224,700	81,600	40	58,800	26	75,800	34
1910	291,200	100,200	35	82,400	28	108,600	37

These figures are for the whole state of Georgia; they
will be more suggestive when broken down by races and
sections of the state. However, certain well-defined and constant movements are revealed by these overall figures.

In the first place, there has been a regular and large increase in the total number of farms throughout the period,
the increase being more rapid than the growth of population. This increase is principally due to the steady disintegration of large plantations, a movement which is still going
ahead with unabated vigor.

A second cause of the increase has been the bringing into
cultivation of new land in South Georgia with the gradual
disappearance of the pine forests.

The percentage of Georgia farms operated by owners has
declined from 55 in 1880 to 35 in 1910. This fact has been
misunderstood, wide currency having been given to the idea

---

*This chapter and the rest of this study are largely based on the following
unpublished and hitherto unused material: (1) *Plantation Schedules, 1911,* and
Reports on Georgia Plantation Districts, 1911, now in the University of Georgia
Library. These data originated in connection with the effort of the Census of
1910 to obtain information on the modern plantation system. This writer, assigned to the state of Georgia as a special census agent, spent three months in
the summer of 1911 on this task and collected the large amount of fresh material contained in these schedules and reports. (2) *Inquiries II, 1902,* being
the replies to an investigation of tenancy prepared in 1902 by the U. S. Department of Agriculture. (3) *Inquiries III, 1906,* material resulting from a valuable
inquiry conducted in 1906 by the Department of Rural Economics at the University of Wisconsin.

that it has meant the growth of tenancy at the expense of owner-operated farms. This, however, has not been the case. Small ownership has been steadily growing, not declining, during the four decades since the Civil War. The spread of tenancy has not involved a decline of owners. For instance, suppose that on a given farm twenty hired laborers were employed. The Census would record this unit as one farm. Now, if by the time the Census enumerators visited that farm again, the twenty laborers had become share tenants, using the same land and working as formerly under the eye of the owner, the essential economic unity of the plantation having remained unimpaired, the farm would be reported not as one operated by the owner, but as twenty operated by share tenants. Clearly there is a fallacy in supposing that such a change as this has in any way affected the number of farms operated by owners. It is to be remembered that the large majority of tenants are just such share tenants.

Fifty per cent of the white farmers in the state own their farms. The percentage of farmers working their own land is lowered by reason of the small percentage of negro farmers who own their land, and in the view of the writer it would be a social advantage if the number of negroes operating their own land were reduced and the less efficient class of negro owners should resume their former positions as day laborers.[64]

Though share tenants have only about maintained their relative position since 1880, cash tenants have increased at a very rapid rate, from 13 per cent in 1880 to 28 per cent in 1910, or from less than 20,000 to more than 80,000 in thirty years. Herein lies the only disquieting feature of the change. To the extent that these cash tenants are irresponsible negroes without capital and intelligence, the growth of cash tenancy is a distinct evil. It is, on the other hand, an evidence of progress

---

[64] Hoffman, F. L., *Race Traits and Tendencies of the American Negro*, in American Economic Association, *Publications*, XI, 1896.

in the case of those efficient white and black men who are
qualified for the higher economic position.

The Difference Between Share and Cash Tenancy

It is necessary to draw a clear line of demarcation between
the two forms of tenancy. Cash tenancy usually represents
an economic advance over share tenancy. The common practice in the country-at-large is for the young man without
capital but with ambition and energy to begin life as a share
tenant. Under this system he incurs little risk. The necessary
land and capital goods are supplied by the landlord who
actively manages the undertaking. The combination of self-
interest on the part of the share tenant and the entrepreneurial
efficiency of the landowner, usually an experienced farmer,
form an excellent arrangement.[65] When the share tenant has
accumulated sufficient capital to stock a farm and has acquired the skill and experience necessary to successful farming, he strikes out for himself as an independent renter. He
is now in a much more advantageous position, because after
the payment of a fixed rental per acre, all of the increment
of product due to his superior managerial efficiency goes to
himself, whereas the share farmer must pay proportionately
more rent as the product of his industry increases.[66] More
careful culture and more constant industry may normally
be expected of cash tenants. From the standpoint of social
production, the cash system is preferable, because it makes
for a more perfect utilization of the land; indeed, one of the
difficulties attaching to the cash system is the tendency of
the farmer to force the soil in the effort to extract from it the
maximum yield during a given tenancy.[67]

The same qualities being necessary for the cash tenant as
for the landowner, success as a cash tenant often means an

---

[65] Taylor, H. C., *Agricultural Economics* (New York, 1911), p. 263.
[66] Carver, T. N., *Principles of Rural Economics* (Boston, 1911), p. 232.
[67] Taylor, *op. cit.*, pp. 269-270; Carver, *op. cit.*, p. 232.

easy transition to landownership. Experience has shown that this evolution may be expected.

The above considerations do not apply in the case of the negro element of tenants in Georgia. In that state, share tenancy implies close supervision on the part of the owner; cash tenancy, freedom from such control. It has been well said that the passage of the negro from the former to the latter class "marks not his greater ability but his greater opportunity to declare his independence from the close supervision of the landlord." It is the escaping from supervision, not the large opportunity of profits that the negro has in mind in shifting from the position of wage earner or share tenant to renter. The history of the normal negro agricultural laborer is about as follows: He begins as a youth working for wages. As soon as he has a family that can be utilized for field work he becomes a share tenant. Under the semicompulsion of this system, he makes good profits, and, if he has any capacity for saving, can in a short time buy a mule and a few tools, and set up as a renter. So great has been the competition for laborers and so completely have the negroes had the upper hand in this matter, that negro wage earners and share hands have in many instances been able to achieve an independent position even without having to save the small amount necessary to stock a renter's farm. Being, in the mass, of low efficiency, the cash tenant begins getting in debt the first year; after two or three years, everything he has is taken for debt, and he returns to his former position of day laborer or share tenant.

Sometimes the share tenant uses his profits to make an initial payment on a piece of land and becomes a small proprietor. His experience as a landowner is often similar to his experience as a renter.[68] He struggles on from year to year, making a miserable living, being able to exist solely because of his deplorably low standard of life, using the least ef-

---

[68] *Inquiries, II,* 1902, Letter from Upson County.

ficient stock and implements and the most antiquated methods of cultivation. It is little short of miraculous if he maintains himself, for it is a struggle against all the tendencies of the time. He is the marginal farmer, and with the increasing value of land that must follow a rapidly growing population, the likelihood of his surviving seems small.

Successful and Unsuccessful Types of Negroes

There is an element of negroes who are prospering as renters and landowners. In the investigations of 1911, the writer made it a rule to ask every planter whether he knew of cases of successful negroes and found no planter who could not mention by name such cases. These negroes are the hope of the race, because they are a standing refutation of the belief held by many persons that the negro is incapable of advancement. No claim is here made that negroes are not progressing. Such a claim would be idle in the face of the fact that in 1910 they were assessed for taxation in Georgia on $32,234,047 worth of property, including 1,607,970 acres of land.[69] The point on which insistence is made is that the mass of the race are wholly unfit for economic independence, and that they are sacrificing their best chance for well-being in seeking too rapid a divorcement from the tutelage in industry through which they should pass. The economic motive that urges men of other races to labor is weak in the negro race.[70] Any influences which would tend to increase his wants are to be welcomed. He needs larger desires and the pressure of competition for work. However slovenly his work under the conditions that have existed for nearly a half century, he is assured of a living, mean though it be, and this is sufficient. He feels no necessity for greater industry, and hence will not work unless encouraged to do so by the presence of some supervisor.

---

[69] Georgia Comptroller General, *Report,* 1910, Table 17.
[70] Hammond, *Cotton Industry,* p. 186.

Planters Resent the Growth of Renting

In the preceding chapter it was shown that from the beginning of the share system some planters exercised supervision, and that those who did not became involved in failure. Gradually all share tenants who could be retained were placed under supervision and those who refused to acquiesce in the arrangement took the further step and became renters. In this way the landlord either recovered his manifest right to safeguard the property necessary to operate a share system, or, by renting out the land, tended to escape from responsibility as to the capital goods required.

Planters have been virtually unanimous during the entire post-bellum period in resenting the growth of renting. They feel that where the laboring class is of such a low order, complete control should remain in the hands of the capitalist class. They know that skill, industry, knowledge, and frugality are essential to successful farming, and they know that negroes in general lack these qualities. The indictment against the renter is overwhelming. Of the twenty-two letters received in "Inquiries III," one letter may be reproduced as the type of them all.

> The renter being independent, obligated for so much rent, is in ninety-nine cases out of a hundred, left to his own pleasure and judgment; the result of which is, the farm on which he works is consistently going down, houses get out of repair and rot down; fences are burned, as it is easier to move them than to split wood; ditches are allowed to fill up; grass and shrub bushes constantly encroach on the open land, and, in fact, in all parts of Georgia where the rent system is allowed, it is a saying that the negro renter's foot is poison to the land.[71]

A Screven County planter,[72] operating 16,000 acres with one hundred and forty-two share tenants, in 1910 performed the following experiment with a view of demonstrating to

---

[71] *Inquiries III*, 1906, Letter from Muscogee County.
[72] *Plantation Schedules*, 1911, No. 10.

the tenants the superiority of the share arrangement. A sixty acre tract of land of uniform grade was selected and divided into two farms. This land was turned over to one of the "two-horse" tenants under an arrangement by which the two tracts were worked with the same animals and tools, and a like amount of fertilizers. The only point of difference was that on one of the farms the tenant worked according to his own ideas, on the other he followed the directions of the manager. The supervised farm produced twenty-two bales of cotton, the other twelve. Nevertheless, the negro left the plantation at the end of the year because the manager refused to allow him to stay as a renter. No stronger evidence could be produced that share farming is better for landlord and tenant, and that profit is a secondary consideration with the tenant.

Scores of such cases are recorded in *Plantation Schedules.* In nearly every case the share tenant admits making more profits under the share system, but utterly denies that the owner's direction is responsible for the result.[73] The superior profits are attributed to the fact that croppers are put on better grades of land and that more fertilizers are used. Several tenants were found who admitted the advantage of wise direction. On one plantation visited, a mulatto was acting as foreman. This man without hesitation stated that the mass of negroes were not qualified for independent renting, and that they desired to rent principally for the reason that as renters they had the unrestricted control over a mule to ride on Sundays.[74]

The Share Tenant Really a Day Laborer

Viewed in the proper light, only one form of tenancy exists in Georgia, namely, renting. The share tenant is in reality a day laborer. Instead of receiving weekly or monthly wages, he is paid a share of the crop raised on the tract of

[73] *Ibid.,* No. 7. Similarly No. 39.
[74] *Ibid.,* No. 16.

land for which he is responsible. Absolute control of the crop remains in the hands of the landlord. He deducts all charges for support of the tenant, and turns over the balance to the cropper. It is true that the typical wage method of working in gangs gave way on the whole to individual holdings, but this change did not eliminate supervision. Instead of standing over the gang of laborers constantly, the owner or his representative now rides from farm to farm, watching the state of the crop, deciding on the method of cultivation, requiring the tenant to keep up the property, and above all enforcing regularity of work. Supervision was to some extent weakened by the change, but it is questionable whether in a free-negro regime the slackening of discipline materially affects production. The wage hand was an uncertain factor in that he was liable to disappear on any pay day; the cropper is obliged to stay at least during an entire year, or forfeit his profits. This steadiness imparted to the tenant by self-interest doubtless compensates for the slight relaxing of discipline. Indeed, the share system is not altogether incompatible with gang labor. Many planters hold that in large-scale production of cotton the really crucial point of difference between the share and renting systems is in connection with the preparation of the soil. When the plantation is organized on a share basis, the planter furnishes heavy plows and harrows and strong teams, and all the share farms are prepared just as if they were one farm, laborers and teams going in gangs straight over the plantation, regardless of the individual holdings. In this way every portion of the plantation receives similar treatment. Division into individual holdings is made after preparation and planting. Furthermore, as the croppers are under full control as to their time, they are sometimes worked in gangs during the cultivating season. For instance, if the manager sees that the crop of one of his share tenants is being neglected, he may send a gang of other croppers to put things to rights, charging the extra time

against the negligent cropper's half of the crop. This sort
of cooperation is not practicable with renters. In the first
place, the planter does not have control of their time. In the
second place, renters' work-animals and tools are of varying
degrees of efficiency, many tenants owning only the most
wretched stock and implements. It would not be fair to combine poor animals with good ones and give the inefficient
renter the benefit of the services of the equipment of the
efficient men. A third difficulty is that renters are independent and differ in their ideas about farming, for example, about
the amount of fertilizers that may profitably be used.

When it is once realized that the share system finds place
only on plantations under close supervision, that the share
tenant is really a day laborer, and that his holding is not a
farm but a section of a well-ordered unit, it should be manifest that there is little cause for alarm on account of the decline in the percentage of farms operated by owners, and the
growth of tenancy in Georgia.

Georgia Law Holds That Sharing Is Not Real Tenancy

The law of Georgia sustains the position that the share
tenant is only a day laborer and not a real tenant. Of course,
the law simply crystallizes the economic facts as they have
worked out. In 1872, the Supreme Court in the case of Ap-
pling *vs.* Odum held:

> There is an obvious distinction between a cropper and a
> tenant. One has a possession of the premises, exclusive of
> the landlord, the other has not. The one has a right for a
> fixed time, the other has only the right to go on the land
> to plant, work and gather the crop. . . . *The case of the
> cropper is rather a mode of paying wages than a tenancy.*
> The title to the crop subject to the wages is in the owner of
> the land.[75]

This view was reiterated in 1878 when the court held that
"where one is employed to work for part of the crop, the

---

[75] 46 *Georgia Reports*, pp. 584-585. Italics added.

relation of landlord and tenant does not arise."[76] Ten years later the court defined with great clearness the position of the share hand:

> Where an owner of land furnishes it with supplies and other like necessaries, keeping general supervision over the farm, and agrees to pay a certain portion of the crop to the laborer for his work, the laborer is a cropper . . .[77]

It should now be clear that in economic significance, and in their practical and legal aspects, renting and share tenancy are as wide apart as the poles. The cropper is a day laborer, works under constant direction, has no exclusive right to the premises or title to the crop he produces. The renter, on the other hand, is a real tenant. The court has explicitly held that the landlord has no right to enter on the tenant's farm against his will to interfere with the crops.[78] The tenant has exclusive possession of the premises for the time being and entire control over his crops. It is scarcely necessary to point out that the reasoning behind this distinction is that, in the case of the cropper, the landlord is the sole capitalist and entrepreneur. Everything necessary to make the crop is supplied by him; while, in the case of the tenant, a fixed rental per acre is paid the landlord, and the landlord's connection with the tenant's farm ceases there.

PART II: THE FIVE NATURAL REGIONS: ECONOMIC AND TENURE MOVEMENTS

THE MOUNTAIN COUNTIES AND THE UPPER PIEDMONT

In the preceding discussion, Georgia has been treated as a unit, although developments have not been uniform throughout the various sections of the state, which differ widely in climate, soil properties, and health conditions. The physiogra-

---

[76] 61 *Georgia Reports*, p. 488.
[77] 80 *Georgia Reports*, p. 95.
[78] 75 *Georgia Reports*, p. 274.

phy of these areas has determined their historical development and the character of their population. The state falls into five natural divisions: the Mountain Region, the Upper Piedmont, the Black Belt, the Wiregrass Country, and the Coast counties.[79]

The Mountain counties are treated as a separate region because they are insignificant in agriculture; and they are therefore given passing notice. The Coast counties have been separated from the Wiregrass region because these two sections are totally dissimilar in the character of the population and the status of the agricultural classes. Historically, the Coast counties are of prime importance. They were, however, not included in the investigation of 1911 and the present writer knows little at first hand of conditions there.

THE MOUNTAIN COUNTIES

The southern extremities of the Appalachian chain run across the northernmost tiers of Georgia counties, the Blue Ridge in the northeastern corner and a number of ranges in the northwestern corner. The Blue Ridge section includes ten of the counties of this Group. The valleys of the Blue Ridge vary from 1,600 to 1,800 feet above sea level, several of the peaks running over 4,000 feet in height. In the northwestern part of the Group, the valleys range from 600 feet upwards, while the highest peaks are about 2,500 feet above sea level.[80] The lower counties of the northwestern section, Floyd, Polk, and Bartow, are important in agriculture and are included in the second group.

The soil of the northwestern counties is largely limestone, well suited to cereal production. The Blue Ridge counties are metamorphic, and here the fruit and vegetable industries have grown to important proportions. The mineral wealth of the Mountain counties is great and is now being developed.

[79] For the boundaries between these regions, see the map on p. 91.

[80] Georgia Department of Agriculture, *Georgia Historical and Industrial,* 1901, pp. 36-40, 148; U. S. Census, 1880, VI, *Cotton Production,* pp. 276-442.

Little cotton is produced in this group, less than two per cent of the total crop of the state being raised here. The soil and climate are unfavorable to staple production. The region is characterized by the small white farming element and a self-sufficing economy. So large a proportion of the soil is

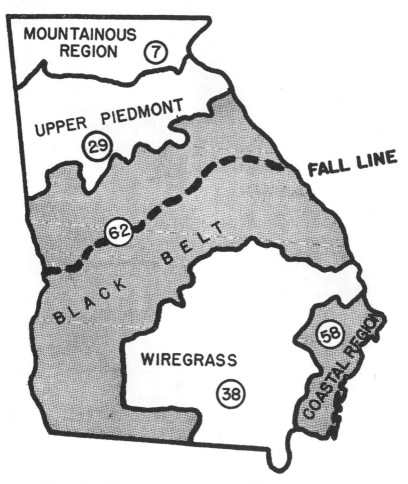

THE FIVE NATURAL REGIONS IN GEORGIA IN 1910

The encircled numbers indicate the percentage of Negroes in the region mountainous and hence unfit for agriculture that the population is relatively sparse and land values low.

The counties of this group, except Rabun and Habersham, were in Cherokee country, acquired from the Indians so recently as 1837. This tract, the last of the Indian lands, was surveyed into lots in 1832 and distributed by a lottery system the same year.[81] Political and legal complications prevented the expulsion of the Cherokees until 1837, but in spite of their presence, and in defiance of law, settlers poured in, attracted by the discovery of gold in the mountains. The soil was unattractive for agricultural purposes, but the gold fever drew thousands of adventurers, many of whom remained after the short-lived boom was over and lands had fallen in price. The forty-acre lots were sold by the original drawers for from ten to twenty dollars, as soon as it was known that the gold was very limited in quantity. The immigrants to this last Georgia frontier were of Scotch-Irish extraction, coming in from Virginia and North Carolina. Many Middle Georgia people were also among the early comers. They were a crude, uneducated people, and in the northeastern counties have remained to the present day almost untouched by the civilizing influences of the lower country. The opening of the state railroad from Atlanta to Chattanooga, in 1851, effected a great transformation in the northwest. The northeast, or Blue Ridge section, remained without railway facilities until the seventies, when the Southern Railway and its branches opened up the country.

During the last few decades, this area has been declining in population. Many mountaineers have migrated to the Wiregrass section, but the principal cause of the loss of population is to be found in the fact that the mountain people are the source of labor supply for the cotton mills.[82]

The negro farmer is an insignificant element in this group,

[81] Smith, G. G., *Story of Georgia and the Georgia People* (Atlanta, 1900), pp. 422-423.
[82] *Reports on Georgia Plantation Districts*, I, p. 3.

95 per cent of all farms being operated by whites. The percentage of farms worked by owners is high but decreasing, due to the fact that many small farmers have sold their unprofitable holdings and migrated to other sections of the state, their small farms tending to be merged into large units. There is practically no cash renting. This prevalence of share tenancy is characteristic of those groups of counties containing white majorities.

THE UPPER PIEDMONT

This group contains all those counties of the Piedmont Plateau south of the mountains whose population in 1910 was predominantly white. This region extends across the state like a belt, two counties deep on the Savannah river and widening to a depth of five counties on the Alabama line. The Piedmont or metamorphic region extends southward to the fall line of the rivers. The surface of the country is rolling and hilly, though rarely so broken as to make agriculture unprofitable. The red hill is characteristic of the section. Red sandy, red clayey, and gray sandy soils are found in every county.[83]

The settlement of the Upper Piedmont began in 1784[84] with the laying off of Franklin county on the Savannah river. All lands east of the Oconee river were distributed under a "Head-Rights" system. Each settler was offered two hundred acres of land as his individual head-right, and fifty acres in addition for each child or slave he brought. Later a limit of one thousand acres per family was set. As the land was good, the region was settled rapidly, the first county, Franklin, having a population of 9,156 whites and 1,041 negroes in 1810, though the county had been greatly reduced in area by parts being laid off into new counties.

---

[83] *Georgia Historical and Industrial,* p. 153.
[84] Watkins, Robert and George, *Digest of the Laws of the State of Georgia* (Philadelphia, 1800), p. 291.

Scotch-Irishmen Establish a Non-Slaveholding Small-Farm Region

The settlers were Scotch-Irish people from the Carolinas. Their fathers had taken part in the great movement of the Scotch-Irish from Pennsylvania down the Shenandoah Valley.[85] They were typical frontiersmen, rough, uncultured, without property, but of a sturdy, independent spirit. They settled down as small farmers, producing practically everything they consumed. With each new cession of Indian lands, these small farmers or their sons pushed westward, until in 1826 the Alabama line was reached. At every stage of their westward march, their numbers were reinforced by the non-slaveholding farmers who were being gradually dispossessed in the Black Belt. This region, being cut up into relatively small farms, worked by white owners, escaped in large measure the exploitative system of agriculture which dominated the Black Belt.[86] The small farmers had not the means to effect the transformation from farmer to planter, after the invention of the cotton gin made large-scale cotton production possible. The planters tended to move in a southwesterly direction, beginning at the Savannah river, thinking the land further north to be infertile, so that few negroes were brought into the Upper Piedmont. The section was distinctly a white one, only 31 per cent of the total population in 1870 being colored. This proportion has declined: in 1910 the blacks were 29 per cent of the whole.

It has been customary to regard southern ante-bellum society as consisting of only two classes besides the slaves, the planter aristocracy and the "poor whites." Here in the Piedmont region of Georgia was a third element, the small farmer, quite as distinct from the mountaineer and "piney-woods cracker" as he was from the planter. He belonged to

[85] Smith, *Story of Georgia,* pp. 152-153.
[86] Brooks, R. P., *Race Relations in the Eastern Piedmont Region of Georgia,* in *Political Science Quarterly,* June, 1911, p. 200. [See pp. 27ff in this volume. *Ed.*]

a middle class, in every way comparable to his contemporaries in the free North and West.[87]

Owners and Share Farmers Dominate

From 1880 to 1910, the number of farms nearly doubled. Owner-operated farms, though increasing in number, relatively declined from 58 to 34 per cent of all farms. Several explanations may be offered for this fact. Small farms, owned by their operators, having been the rule throughout the history of the section, and the land having been practically all taken up prior to 1870, there was not so large an opportunity for the spread of small ownership as was the case in the Black Belt or the Wiregrass.

Another reason why ownership has not been widely extended in this region is that, because of the high type of farming and the good treatment the soil has received at the hands of small white farmers, lands have so appreciated in value that tenant farmers are unable to buy. Nine of the eleven counties in Georgia which in 1910 showed an average land value of from $25 to $50 per acre (the highest values in the state) were in this group. The extent to which the section is developed is indicated by the fact that it is the region of the densest population in the state, and that in twenty-one counties 80 to 100 per cent of the land area is in farms. Between 1900 and 1910 real estate values in Franklin, Jackson, Madison, Walton, and Hart counties (considered as a group) advanced 253 per cent.[88] Cases were reported of tenants having cash to buy land, but being prevented from so doing by the high prices. Share farmers, however, are able to stock rented farms, so that a comparatively high type of renter is to be found in the district. The writer was impressed by the fact that the feeling in this group as to the

[87] Stone, A. H., in *The South in the Building of the Nation*, V, p. 139. The author scouts as absurd the idea that non-slaveholders were an economic cypher in the South. In the upper Piedmont region, 200 by 400 miles in extent, there were a million of these people and only a hundred thousand negroes.

[88] *Reports on Georgia Plantation District*, 1911, Report No. 2, p. 2.

evils of renting is not so pronouncedly hostile as in other
sections. One large planter stated that his renters made as
much profits as the wage earners or croppers, "because they
are a superior class of whites."[89] All of the plantation schedules taken in this group contain statements that the planter
prefers white to negro labor, but the consensus was that the
negroes are of a higher type in this district than in the Black
Belt, an opinion which is accounted for by the fact that
they are numerically a small element in the population, and
have felt the effect of white stimulus and competition.[90]
Many negroes are felt to deserve the position of renters.
Still another reason why renting is not thought to be so
unsatisfactory is that the rent contracts are not the usual
one-year arrangements, but commonly run for a term of
years. Planters say that this makes for good farming. The
contracts are in writing and contain provisions intended to
prevent the exhaustion and deterioration of the soil.[91]

Cropping Predominates

The most significant fact revealed by the ownership statistics is the relative position of the two forms of tenancy.
Comparatively few tenant farms are operated by renters
(cash tenants); the percentage of share tenants (croppers)
has been higher than in any other area of the state. Especially
is this true of negro tenants; 64 per cent of their farms were
held on a share basis in 1910. The explanation of this prevalence of "cropping" is that the majority of Upper Piedmont farmers who employ labor live on their farms. They
are therefore in a position to give effective supervision, and
insist on the share arrangement. Of the white farms, only
14 per cent and of the black farms 25 per cent are in the
hands of independent renters. Some of these renters are of

---

[89] *Plantation Schedules*, 1911, No. 38.
[90] *Ibid.*, Nos. 1, 3, 37, 38; *Reports on Georgia Plantation*, Report No. 2, p. 5;
Brooks, *op. cit.*, pp. 204-7.
[91] *Plantation Schedules*, 1911, No. 3.

a superior type, but it is stated that landlord absenteeism is tending to increase in some of the counties,[92] and as absenteeism and independent renting go together, it is likely that part of the renters of the Upper Piedmont are of the same sort as those of the Black Belt.

Remarkable Growth of Cotton Production in this White Area

In 1860, the Black Belt produced 83 per cent of all the cotton grown in Georgia. Every succeeding decade has witnessed a decrease in the relative importance of this belt: in 1910 it produced only 58 per cent of the entire crop. The Upper Piedmont, on the contrary, produced only 89,000 bales in 1860, or 13 per cent of the total crop. In the fifty years following, while the Black Belt has barely doubled her output, the Piedmont section has increased hers 377 per cent. This development is one of the most noteworthy facts in the post-bellum history of the state, and is attributable to a variety of causes. First in importance is the character of the population, a small white farmer element. The superiority of the white farming was indicated by the Census of 1880, wherein it appeared that the per acre product of the Upper Piedmont was .398 bales, while in the Black Belt the average was .286 bales.[93] This superiority has been maintained. Secondly, the majority of the farmers in ante-bellum days did their own work, having few slaves; hence their operations were less disturbed by the débacle of emancipation, and recovery was quick. In the third place, commercial fertilizers made cotton production much more profitable in this section, as the best cotton lands were further south.[94] The comparative absence of independent negro farmers, the rapid extension of railroads, and the use of superior farming implements, favored the development of the group.[95]

---

[92] *Reports on Georgia Plantation Districts,* Report No. 1, p. 4.
[93] [See the table, compiled from the Census reports, 1880 to 1910, on p. 124 of the original publication of this study. *Ed.*]
[94] Avery, I. W., *History of Georgia, 1850-1881* (New York, 1881), p. 643; Grady, Henry W., in *Harper's Magazine,* October, 1881.
[95] U. S. Department of Agriculture, *Report,* 1876, p. 127.

A study of part of this area, published elsewhere,[96] shows that the influence of a preponderant white population was altogether favorable to the colored farmers, as indicated by their per capita wealth, percentage of landowners, and school facilities. These conclusions are applicable to the entire section, as the available statistics prove.

THE BLACK BELT

The Black Belt of Georgia embraces a variety of physiographic divisions and soils. That part of the Belt which lies north of the fall line of the rivers is a rolling and hilly country of metamorphic soil, as it is a continuation of the Upper Piedmont. Below the fall line a narrow strip of sandhills crosses the state, and then comes a belt of oak, hickory, and long leaf pine uplands, covering about a third of the Black Belt. The remainder of the section is a limesink and Wiregrass region. Below the fall line the country is generally level and the soil gray and sandy, though red hills and a considerable amount of clay lands occur.[97]

From Small Farming to Slavery

The settlement of the Black Belt extended over a century, beginning about the middle of the eighteenth century, on the Savannah River, and pushing westward by regular stages. Successive waves of frontiersmen, small farmers, and cotton planters moved in a westward and southwestward direction until, shortly before the Civil War, the extreme southwestern counties were filled. Immigrants direct from Europe occupied the coast region, but the middle Georgia counties were settled by Americans pushing down from Virginia and the Carolinas. Burke County is believed to have had white inhabitants before Oglethorpe came in 1733, probably Indian traders from the Carolinas.

---

[96] [See pp. 27ff of this volume. *Ed.*]
[97] *Georgia Historical and Industrial*, pp. 156-162.

Three years before the Revolution there was obtained from the Creeks a cession of land from which many counties were carved, such as Wilkes, Elbert, and Lincoln.[98] This land was at once thrown open for settlement under the head-rights system. The early comers were from the same class of people that filled the Upper Piedmont. The first wave of frontiersmen was followed at the close of the Revolution by men in better circumstances, Virginians constituting the most important element.[99] Exhaustion of their tobacco fields was the immediate cause of the migration. The newcomers practiced for a generation a self-sufficing economy: cattle raising, diversified agriculture, and home manufactures. But the invention of the cotton gin in 1793, and the development of the cotton industry in the two decades following, revolutionized the economic life of the Lincoln and Wilkes county farmers. Being men of large ideas, possessing more property than their fellows in the Upper Piedmont, and occupying a soil admirably suited to cotton culture, the Virginian element quickly evolved into large-scale producers of cotton. Gradually the holdings of the less efficient were acquired, cattle ranges were put to the plow, and the small farmer and herdsman moved westward to squat on fresh lands. Exhausting their original holdings, the planters soon pushed on after the frontiersmen and small farmers, bought their clearings and created new plantations. This process involved social differentiation, society becoming highly stratified, with the planter element at the top. Presently the planters controlled the state and wielded a powerful influence in national politics during the ascendency of the cotton South just prior to the sixties.

---

[98]Phillips, U. B., *Georgia and State Rights* (Washington, 1902), p. 39.

[99] Gilmer, G. R., *Georgians*, Introduction, pp. 5-6. These Virginians were not the ordinary pioneer type of settlers, but appear to have been people of some consequence. They transplanted to Georgia the contemporary Virginian civilization and were to some extent a distinct element in the population.

Rapid Rise of the Negro Population as Cotton Becomes King

Up to 1820, the small farmers were the dominant element, outnumbering the planters and their slaves. By 1830, however, negroes outnumbered whites in many counties, and each following decade showed a steady absolute decline of whites and a large increase of negroes, indicating the departure of the small farmer and the increase in the size of slave and land-holdings of the planters. The Indian frontier rapidly receded in the first quarter of the nineteenth century. The frontiers-men were usually on the border waiting for the first signal to move over.[100] The planter was not far behind. Gradually the entire region now known as the Black Belt was settled in this way. By 1860, the plantation regime was established in that section.[101]

The subordination of all other agricultural interests to large-scale, slave-produced cotton entailed the abandonment of the diversified farming of the early period. While many planters produced practically everything necessary to their main-tenance and comfort, yet, on the whole, not enough meat and corn were raised for home consumption, and large quantities of foodstuffs were annually imported from the Middle West. Absence of diversification and rotation of crops quickly exhausted the primary fertility of the soil.

Prevalence of Cash Tenancy (Renting)

The outstanding fact about tenure is that between 1880 and 1910 tenant farms increased 181 per cent, as compared to a small rise of 15 per cent in owner-operated farms. The low character of farming in the area may be inferred from the fact that more than 60 per cent of all Black Belt farms are operated by negroes, of whom only nine in a hundred own the farm they manage. This is the region of tenancy

---

[100] Phillips, U. B., *Plantation and Frontier,* II, pp. 187-193. An excellent con-temporary account of the repeated movings of a small farmer.
[101] Smith, *Story of Georgia,* pp. 323-325, 400-405.

par excellence. Ninety per cent of the negro farmers and nearly 50 per cent of the white farmers are tenants.

The tendency has been for the whites of the Black Belt to leave the farm, the heads of families locating in the county towns, renting their lands to negroes or whites, and often going into merchandising, while the active sons have moved entirely out of the region to take business positions in cities. Many of the poorer whites have entered cotton mills. In this way, the rural parts of the Belt have tended to grow blacker.

Cash tenants are the most numerous class of farmers in this region. This is the most fundamental difference between the farm labor situation here and in the white sections of the state, where the share system is in the ascendency. This fact will bear reiteration. Many landowners moved to the towns; a numerous class of merchant landowners came into existence; these absentee landlords everywhere rented lands. Resident landlords competing with them for laborers, were obliged in many cases to rent lands, or see them lie uncultivated. This movement reached its high-water mark in 1900 when 50 per cent of negro farmers were cash tenants. These renters were practically independent of the planters. The slavery system had not made for conservation of the land, improved methods of agriculture, nor frugality. Slaves, of course, learned little of these matters. When the freedmen became renters under no efficient supervision, in a part of the state where contact with small white farmers with better methods of farming was impossible, they settled down to unintelligent cotton raising, living from hand to mouth, and became the poorest class of farmers to be found in any civilized country.

In the decade 1890 to 1900 cash tenancy grew very rapidly, accompanied by a decline in share farming. Those who favored the position of renter for the negro held that the negroes were freeing themselves from the supervision of the share system, which was described as "slavery under a new name."

This sudden growth of cash tenancy, however, reflected no credit whatever on the negro race, and indicated economic retrogression, not advance. Agriculture reached a very low ebb in the Black Belt in the nineties, when, added to the other trials of the employers of labor, a prolonged period of depression afflicted the cotton South. The immediate effect of this depression (cotton fell below five cents) was to impel more farmers to give up farming and to accelerate the townward movement. Renters were naturally substituted for share hands under these circumstances. Many small farmers lost their holdings in this decade, being sold out by merchant creditors. These new owners rented to negroes and looked to the supply end of the business for their profits. It is true that the negro gained a little more personal freedom by the change, but at the same time he sacrificed his best opportunity for economic advancement. His position as a renter was indeed a hard one. He could not afford to purchase efficient stock, improved implements and high-grade fertilizers; he was either not alive to the agricultural changes going on about him, or, knowing of the new methods, he was unable to introduce them.[102] This extension of renting became so marked that resident planters found it almost impossible to secure laborers. In many cases known to the writer, farmers had to draw on the negro population of the towns, hauling them six or seven miles, to and from the fields every day.

At the close of the period of depression it is interesting to have expert testimony about the effect of this renting. The Commissioner of Agriculture, testifying before the Industrial Commission, stated:

> . . . the tenant system . . . has a tendency to reduce the [average yield] . . . because a great deal is left to the management of the unintelligent negro farm hand, the landlord being interested to only the extent of his rent.[103]

[102] *Reports on Georgia Plantation Districts,* Report No. 8, pp. 3, 4.
[103] *Report of the Industrial Commission,* 1900, X, pp. 379, 907.

To the same effect was the testimony before the Industrial Commission of a Connecticut man who had come to Houston County to engage in the peach industry. In his opinion it was a mistake to suppose the negro to be an inferior laborer. He had never had as good workers in New England. The real difficulty, as he saw it, lay in the circumstance that "there is too little of the owner's direct management."[104]

The result of this sort of farming may be gathered from the statistical tables. Wealth per capita for both whites and blacks is low, as is the value of farm land. The share of the Black Belt in state cotton production has drastically declined between 1860 and 1910, while the yield per acre keeps steadily behind that of the white sections north and south of the Belt.

Revival of Agriculture, 1900-1910

A great change has been coming over the Black Belt in the last decade. The high price of cotton; better methods resulting from the activity of the College of Agriculture of the University of Georgia; the noteworthy improvement in the roads since the convict lease was abolished and the prisoners began to be used on public roads; and the bettering of rural schools have contributed to reawaken the interest of Black Belt landowners in farming. In some counties the tide of white migration to towns has been checked. The result has been a general improvement in rural conditions. This revival of agriculture has had a most significant influence on land tenure in the Black Belt. Between 1900 and 1910 the tendency for renters to increase and share tenants to decrease was stopped, and the bulk of new farms were share tenants' holdings. This means that supervision on the part of the owners was increasing.[105] Planters all over the Belt are alive to this change, and they are unanimous in holding that it means a return to better farming methods.

---

[104] *Ibid.*

[105] *Reports on Georgia Plantation Districts*, no. 8, p. 4; no. 9, p. 3; no. 6, p. 4.

Inquiry on the ground brought out the fact that the resident planters were the first to change the system of tenancy. Many planters intended to displace all renters as rapidly as possible, even though it entailed letting the land lie idle. The feeling is that lands which are increasing in value at so great a rate cannot longer be allowed to remain in inefficient hands.[106]

A Compromise Type of Tenancy

In some counties an interesting compromise is being tried, looking to a combination of the best features of renting and share farming.[107] Possibly the most important objection the average negro has to the share system is that the landlord owns the work animal used by the tenant and refuses to allow indiscriminate use of the animal for riding purposes. Where an animal is available, it is the negro's custom to spend his nights and Sundays riding over the country, attending "revival" meetings, which frequently last months, lodge meetings, and other festivities. This use of work animals cannot be tolerated by the owners, and consequently the cropper feels his social activities curtailed. As a renter, he has possession of a mule to maltreat as he will. The terms of the conventional cropping arrangement are that the landlord shall furnish land, house, mule and its feed, all implements, half the fertilizer, and supply the tenant; the cropper furnishes all the labor, half the fertilizer and receives half the crop after the charges for supplies advanced have been deducted. Under the new arrangement, when the prospective tenant owns his mule and tools, the landlord furnishes the land, house, feed for the mule, and all the fertilizers. This compromise is being rapidly adopted. From the standpoint of the landlord, its advantages are that he can use plenty of commercial manures and can make sure that the work animal receives sufficient food to maintain working efficiency.

---

[106] *Ibid.*, no. 3, p. 3.
[107] *Ibid.*, no. 5, pp. 2, 3; no. 6, p. 4.

Both are important points. The average renter cannot be induced to use a profitable amount of fertilizers, because he is unconvinced of the wisdom of so doing, while his mule frequently breaks down from sheer starvation. The third and most important advantage to the landlord is that he retains the right of supervision of the cropper's work as under the former arrangement.

From the point of view of the tenant, the most important advantage lies in the securing of an animal for riding purposes; if he has no mule, the planter sells him one on long time payments. Furthermore, the tenant escapes the onerous burden of paying for fertilizers, while reaping the profit of the owner's investment in them.

The Capitalist-Merchants

Absentee merchants and landlords have also moved against the irresponsible renter. A curious situation has come about in some of the most important Belt counties. Absentees, seeing that their lands were becoming impoverished under the renting system, have turned over their plantations on long time leases to a class of capitalist-merchants. These merchants have organized the cotton industry on a scale not hitherto practiced in Georgia. One such merchant operates 22,000 acres, half of which he rents from other owners. Except for a scattering handful on the outskirts of the several places, the renters have been dispensed with on this large tract of land, being replaced by croppers and wage hands. The tract is divided into eight or ten plantations, each with a resident manager, who directs all farming operations. In addition to the managers, the merchant employs two "riders," who spend their entire time in the saddle, going over the crops of the tenants and reporting on their condition to the head office in the county town. The merchant operates in this town a large supply business. Reports of the riders are the basis of credit at the store. All tenants are required to buy exclusively from the landlord, and the amount of their credit depends on the condition of their crops. If the crop be neglected, credit is restricted or stopped until the place is put in order.[108]

This is an efficient system from the standpoint of production and soil conservation. It has a tendency, however, to dissuade absentees from dividing and selling their lands, and consequently discourages the growth of small ownership. The counties where this form of organization is practiced are steadily becoming blacker in population. The small farmers from North and Middle Georgia pass over these counties and go into the Wiregrass further south.

All over the Black Belt, and especially in the lower section, the evils attendant upon absentee landlordism are being greatly lessened by a new method of supervision. A few years ago absentees were unable to give any regular attention to their tenants because of the distance between town and plantations and the condition of the country roads, but now with the transformation in the condition of the roads, landowners are buying automobiles. Owners with this quick method of transportation run out daily to their farms, spend the day in the work of supervision, and return to their families at night. Their plantations apparently suffer but little from the fact of their non-residence on them. It would be difficult to find anywhere farms more excellently operated.

Old Plantation Organization Not Extinct

Despite the agrarian revolution of the post-bellum period, the plantation has not by any means totally disappeared. Here and there in every county one meets with highly organized large-scale farms, and the movement that appears underway from cash renting to share farming seems to indicate an extension of the plantation system, since share tenants

---

[108] *Plantation Schedules, 1911,* no. 40. *Reports on Georgia Plantation Districts,* Report no. 4, p. 4.

are rarely found on any other than efficiently supervised plantations.

Such a plantation may be worth describing in some detail. The plantation selected (*Plantation Schedules*, 1911, no. 8) is one of the oldest of the Black Belt counties, and the soil has been cultivated for many years. The present owners are two young men, both of whom live on the place, giving their entire time to the work of supervision. The total acreage is 3,750, of which 2,500 acres are improved. The two residences of the owners, set in a fine oak grove, are modern structures, with every convenience, such as screens, waterworks, and acetylene lights. Back of the residences are four large livestock barns, two tool sheds, a blacksmith shop, a commissary, a gas plant, automobile garage, hothouse, dairy building, and several model chicken houses. There are two artesian wells.

Scattered over the plantation at convenient places are the tenant houses, eighty-six in number. All are comparatively new frame structures, costing on the average $300. No log houses were seen.

The farm equipment includes a large assortment of tools and machinery. Animal stock consists of 80 mules, 5 horses, 1 ox, 8 milch cows, 150 head of hogs, and about 1500 chickens.

The plantation population includes a white overseer, 15 renters, 90 share tenants, and 3 day laborers, all negroes. The renters pay as rental 1,000 pounds of lint cotton for twenty acres, the laborers are paid $12.00 per month and board, the share hands get one-half the crop.

The owner's principal interest is cotton raising, but he produces all the corn and hay used on the place. Rotation is practiced as extensively as practicable in view of the fact that each year the major part of the acreage is devoted to cotton. All the land is broken in the fall with two- and four-horse plows, large quantities of fertilizers are used ($18,000 worth in 1910), and cultivation is frequent.

The products in 1910 were as follows: 1,000 bales of cotton on 1725 acres, 15,000 bushels of corn on 600 acres, 3,900 bushels of oats on 75 acres, 125 tons of pea vines on the same 75 acres.

The owners have no other business and own no land except this plantation. Their entire time is given to supervision, which they believe to be indispensable. All of the 105 laborers are under the direct control of the owners. No distinction is made in this regard between renters and croppers. The acreage of each crop is regulated, every tenant goes to work and "knocks off" at tap of bell, all products are marketed by the owners. Nothing is left to the judgment of the tenant—absolute control is exercised with respect to the use and application of fertilizers, clearing and opening of ditches, time and method of planting, cultivating and harvesting.

Cash advances are made to tenants, ten per cent being charged to all accounts at the end of the year. Tenants buy their supplies where they please; the commissary is kept for their convenience. They are allowed the use of animals for riding purposes, but this privilege is by permission and is regarded as a return for faithful work.

In 1910 every tenant paid his account. Twelve share tenants cleared more than $300 each, after all expenses were paid. One renter cleared $900 on a two-horse farm. He had a large family to help him. All of these profits, the owner said, were squandered. Even the renter whose profits were so large returned at Christmas to borrow a few dollars for the holidays. Tenants throw away their money on buggies, fine harness, guns, clothes. Peddlers have given a great deal of trouble, selling negroes at exorbitant prices cabinet organs, patent medicines, clocks, and other unnecessary articles. The tenants habitually drink, gamble, and carry weapons. Venereal disease and consumption were reported as prevalent.

Effect of White Migration to the Belt

Remarkable changes are going on in the Black Belt counties bordering on the Upper Piedmont. There is a marked tendency towards intensive culture, diversification and rotation, greater attention to tenants, and the result is seen in the increased yield per acre and the enhanced value of farm land.

There appears to be a movement of white small farmers from the Upper Piedmont to the Black Belt, which is a fact of unusual interest. The high type of farming practiced in the northern counties has sent the price of land up so high that small owners are finding it profitable to sell out, move to the Black Belt and buy there two or three acres for the price received for one. Fifty years ago the fathers of these farmers were moving in the other direction, from the high priced Black Belt cotton lands to the cheap and undesirable Upper Piedmont soil. In most of the Black Belt counties one meets with recent comers from North Georgia. Many of them become tenants for a few years.

Some difference of opinion was found with reference to the desirability of the white tenant. Complaint was heard that they have difficulty in learning to grow cotton, that they are inclined to be less tractable than negroes, that they make demands for better housing. One planter-merchant naively confessed that his principal objection to white tenants was that they did not spend their profits so freely at his store as did the negroes.[109] The majority of planters, however, welcome the white tenant; and their demand for better homes is being met by the erection of a superior type of tenant houses.[110] Planters state that they find the white tenant more intelligent and trustworthy, that they save their profits, become landowners, and thus give stability to Black Belt social conditions. In South Georgia, as well as in

---

[109] *Reports on Georgia Plantation Districts,* Report no. 3. p. 6.
[110] *Plantation Schedules,* no. 32.

Oglethorpe County, the negro tenants are said to be improving as workers as a result of white competition.

This emergence of a class of white tenants and small white owners in the Black Belt is fortunate. Thoughtful observers say that the race problem in the Belt is largely the outcome of the negroes' numerical ascendency, and that any movement tending to increase the proportion of whites to blacks can but have a good result.

Bad Conditions Among the Negroes

Throughout the Black Belt the tenant and laboring class of negroes are improvident. Books of employers indicate that the average tenant makes a profit from his farming. It is the exceptional negro, however, who saves anything. In numerous cases, they squander in a month enough cash to supply them the entire following year, thus heedlessly throwing away the opportunity to escape from exorbitant time prices and the position of debtors. As a general thing the surplus melts away without any substantial return. Whiskey, gambling, indulgence in sexual pleasures, purchase of useless articles of luxury, and excursions to distant towns, absorb their profits. Tenants usually spend all of the proceeds of the year's work before Christmas and return to the landlord for small sums to tide them over the holiday season. The writer cannot recall an instance of a planter who had not found it necessary to make such advances. He usually has no option in the matter. Contracts are made yearly and expire with the harvest season. "Christmas money" is commonly advanced on the agreement of the tenant to renew his contract for another year. It is said that the landlord who would refuse to make these advances would very likely be unable to secure tenants.

A school and church are to be found on practically every plantation. Great interest is taken by the negroes in the church, as it is the center of their social life. A lodge or secret society usually meets in the church. The schools are always taught by negroes and are of a uniformly low standard. Attendance is fitful and confined to the late summer and winter months. During the busy season negro children are used in chopping, and later in picking, cotton.

The moral conditions existing among the blacks appear to vary with the proportion they form of the total population. The larger the plantation, the fewer the whites, the greater the distance from civilizing influences, the worse become the conditions. On an immense plantation of sixteen thousand acres, the manager said he had found it impossible to prevent gambling and drinking. The manager also expressed a doubt whether there was a man or woman on the plantation untainted by syphilis. The same conditions were reported elsewhere. Even the best ordered place the writer visited, where the man and his wife periodically collected the men and women separately and talked to them on the subject, doing everything possible to encourage chastity and fidelity, the planter was obliged to confess failure, and to say "the negroes have no conception of the meaning of sexual purity."[111]

Another habit to which the negroes are addicted is that of carrying concealed weapons. Two or three years ago the legislature passed an act requiring that every person before possessing a pistol should secure a license and obtain personal surety that no improper use be made of the weapon. Under cover of this law a Terrell County planter with a constable went the rounds of his tenant houses and collected twenty-eight pistols, which he holds until the tenants comply with the law.

The presence of many mulatto children in the state is popularly supposed to indicate illicit intercourse between white men and negro women. Special inquiry was made on this point. It was frequently pointed out that mulatto men al-

---

[111] *Ibid.*, nos. 8, 10, 24, 25, 28, 31, 33.

most never marry black women, and that the mulatto children are born to mulatto parents. Practically every farmer interviewed during the summer of 1911 was decidedly of the opinion that this relation between white men and negro women had almost entirely ceased. An elderly planter said that the change in sentiment in this regard in the past twenty years amounts to a revolution.[112] Once or twice the opinion was expressed in towns that the evil was still prevalent, but as a rule town people agreed with the planters that a great change had taken place.

The physical surroundings of the negro tenant houses are wretched in the extreme. No pride whatever is usually taken in keeping the home neat and clean and the premises attractive. Occasionally one sees a well-kept garden spot, but as a rule weeds hold sway between house and field. Efforts to interest tenants in truck gardens and poultry are in most cases utter failures. Land is always given for gardens and patches, and often the seed is furnished, but no results are obtained. It would be a comparatively easy matter for tenants to raise much of their foodstuffs, if they had the inclination to do so. Their failure to take advantage of this opportunity is not due to lack of time. Negro tenants invariably take Saturdays off. Every Black Belt town is crowded on that day. It is an astounding fact to relate, but many farmers do a regular business selling their negro tenants cabbages, potatoes, chickens and the like, when the tenant could easily, without any cost whatever except an occasional hour's work, provide himself with every country product.

THE WIREGRASS COUNTRY AND THE COAST COUNTIES

THE WIREGRASS COUNTRY

The division marked out on the map as the Wiregrass occupies the southeastern section of Georgia, except for

---

[112] *Ibid.*, no. 39.

several border counties of the area which have been placed in the Black Belt because they have a majority of negroes. All of the counties included in the Wiregrass group have white majorities.

This group of counties is a part of the coastal plain of Georgia, and hence for the most part the elevation above sea level is not great, ranging from one hundred feet to five hundred on the northern border. The surface of the ground is usually level, though occasionally slightly rolling. It presents to the eye an unrelieved expanse of pine forests, carpeted with wiregrass. The soil is a fine sand, often ten to fifteen inches deep, underlaid with yellow clay. Malarious lakes and swamps abound, and, until artesian wells became common, health conditions were bad.[113]

Though the Wiregrass only recently began to attract a large population, some of the counties were laid out at an early period, such as Montgomery, in 1793; Bulloch, in 1796; and Emanuel, in 1812. The soil was thought to be hopelessly sterile. Indeed, the country was known until a few years ago as "the Pine Barrens." The only settlers who came to this region were those attracted by the fine grazing for cattle. The early population consisted of typical frontiersmen from the Carolinas and various parts of Georgia. After the manner of the frontier, these people lived on the products of their herds, on game, and cornbread. They were ignorant and illiterate. The population was very sparse. In 1820 the county of Irwin had only 411 inhabitants,[114] notwithstanding the fact that it embraced all the land now divided into seven counties. The total population of the twenty counties of the group in 1870 was 84,000, of which 70 per cent was white. At that census the density of the population was five to the square mile; in 1880, the density had advanced to seven; and in 1889 to thirteen per square mile.[115]

[113] *Georgia Historical and Industrial*, p. 162.
[114] Smith, *Story of Georgia*, p. 321. As late as 1866, Mr. Smith rode seventeen miles on a public road through this county without coming to a house.
[115] Harper, R. M., in Savannah *Morning News*, April 16, 1911.

The sparseness of the population was due to the fact that the Wiregrass was outside the path of the cotton planter in ante-bellum days, while the bulk of the small farmers were in the region north of the Black Belt. Few negroes found their way into the Wiregrass until very recent times. With the improvement in health conditions, due principally to artesian water, and with the spread of cotton production made possible by the liberal use of commercial fertilizers, population has grown rapidly, and many negroes have migrated to the region. In 1910 they were 38 per cent of the population.

The Wiregrass is the great yellow pine region of the state. By 1890 the lumber and turpentine industries were attracting capital and people.[116] Farming interests advanced at the same time. In the decade between 1890 and 1900 about one hundred thousand new settlers came to the region. Eight new counties have been laid off in the group since 1900, and many of the towns have had a rapid growth. In 1910 the population of the group was 460,000, more than five times the population of 1870.

Railroads have done much to develop the Wiregrass country. Up to the time of the Civil War no railroads were to be found in this large section of Georgia. The first line to pierce the group was completed in 1867; today there are some fifteen hundred miles of railway in the area.

High Percentage of Share Tenants and Owners

In 1880, the agricultural development of the Wiregrass had only begun. Less than one tenth of all Georgia farms were in that area. Lands were being advertised by the railroads[117] at extremely low prices: in Pierce County at 25 cents per acre, in Clinch from 50 cents to one dollar, in Lowndes from one to five dollars. By 1880 the use of commercial fertilizers had become general and the sandy soils

---

116 *Ibid.*
117 Atlantic & Gulf Railroad, *Guide to Southern Georgia and Florida,* 1877.

began to rise in the estimation of cotton growers. The soil proved to be quite productive, once the proper method of cultivation became known.

The growth in the number of farms was normal up to 1890, but after that time very rapid. Nearly a fifth of all farms in the state are now in this group of counties. The new farmers are said to come principally from the mountain counties of North Georgia.

The percentage of farms operated by owners has declined steadily. It is not difficult to find the explanation of this fact. Lands in South Georgia were distributed in lots of larger size than elsewhere in the state,[118] often running as high as 490 acres, and the individual holdings have always been larger thaan in other parts of Georgia. As long as grazing and lumbering were the principal industries, the tendency was for holdings to remain large, or even to increase in size. Many thousands of acres often got into the hands of a single individual or company.[119] But as soon as the earlier industries began to wane and agriculture to increase in importance, the tenant class emerged. Many former lumbermen and turpentine farmers became agriculturists, not selling to their former laborers, but retaining them as tenants. This process is still going on. A Bulloch county farmer reports his "plantation" as containing 14,000 acres, but has only thirty tenants. Inquiry elicited the information that 11,500 acres of this holding were pine forests. Turpentining and sawmilling are going on in one part of the "plantation," farming in the other.[120] The farming interest increases every year, with the gradual clearing of the land, and eventually the entire tract will be devoted to cotton production. This process involves a large increase in the number of tenants, but no diminution in the number of land owners;

[118] Banks, *op. cit.,* p. 42.

[119] Some of these huge holdings are still intact. In Emanuel County an elderly planter who has lived in the county since the Civil War, owns 30,000 acres. See *Reports on Georgia Plantation Districts, Report* no. 4, p. 7.

[120] *Plantation Schedules,* 1911, no. 11.

the percentage of farms operated by owners, however, becomes progressively smaller with the extension of agriculture. In 1880, tenants were 19 per cent of all farmers, in 1910, 44 per cent, but the absolute number of farms operated by owners increased from 11,000 to 24,000.

Unusual Type of Renters

Two avenues leading to ownership have been open to the small farmer. In the first place, many lumber and turpentine companies, on the decline of these industries, did not care to engage in farming, and consequently threw their holdings on the market at low prices. The small owner of North Georgia, or the successful tenant, could easily acquire a farm in the Wiregrass country, and thousands took advantage of the opportunity. In the second place, peculiar conditions have attracted a superior type of tenants, who have evolved more quickly into owners than is usually the case. A large part of the area of the group is covered with stumps and small pines left by the sawmill. The main problem of the owner is to get the land cleared for cultivation. The general method is to turn over such lands to white tenants rent free for a term of three or four years, on condition that each year a given amount of clearing be done. The whites who take advantage of this opportunity are North Georgians with sufficient capital to stock a farm, but not enough to purchase land. This type of tenant farmer is not only himself a laborer, but is a manager of labor.

In the study of the Upper Piedmont it was shown that there had been since 1870 a striking development of cotton growing. The same development has occurred in the Wiregrass. The causes have been the same, the increasing importance of the small white farmer, and the use of commercial fertilizers on land formerly thought to be unsuited to cotton culture.

Predominance of Whites Improves Condition of Negroes

The preponderance of white farmers seems to have the same fortunate effects on the tenant class that were noted in the case of the Upper Piedmont. Almost every planter visited by the writer in the summer of 1911 reported that his tenants were saving money.[121]

A decided preference for the white tenant was often expressed. A noteworthy instance was that of the Laurens county planter who owned five farms, some of which were at a distance from his residence. Formerly all the farms were worked by negro tenants, but they have recently been displaced by whites. The reason given was that the owner found that, on farms so inaccessible as to prevent constant oversight, whites could be trusted to work steadily, whereas negroes could not be trusted. He stated that the whites were a much better element, saving their money and becoming landowners. From a commercial point of view, the whites were not so profitable (the owner was also a merchant), because they did not spend so freely as did the former black tenants.[122]

Little complaint was heard among Wiregrass farmers of disorder, drunkenness, immorality, or venereal disease among the tenants, white or black.[123] The freedom from these troubles was attributed to the presence of many whites. Only where large numbers of negroes are collected on the plantation, without the presence of whites, was trouble reported.

THE COAST COUNTIES

The coast region of six counties covers an area of about two thousand square miles.[124] It includes "savannas," live oak lands, coast tide swamp lands, and islands.

The savannas occupy most of the area of the six coun-

---

[121] *Reports on Georgia Plantation Districts*, Report no. 4, p. 6.
[122] *Plantation Schedules*, 1911, no. 14.
[123] *Ibid.*, nos. 11, 12, 14, 30.
[124] *Georgia Historical and Industrial*, pp. 165-166.

ties. They are a belt of meadow-like land from ten to fifteen miles in width, less than fifteen feet above tide-water. The western limit of this belt is the wiregrass bluff, ranging from twenty-five to fifty feet above sea level. The savannas are covered with a sparse growth of long-leaf pine and a thick undergrowth of saw-palmetto.

The live-oak lands spread along the coast and the islands. The soil is yellow and mulatto sand. Immense live-oaks, festooned with streamers of gray moss, are the most noteworthy characteristic of the coast region. Some of the live-oak lands are rich, having a blue clay subsoil well adapted to sea-island cotton.

Several of the large rivers of the state, the Savannah, the Ogeechee, the Altamaha, and the St. Mary's, find their way to the ocean through the coast counties. Along the banks of these rivers, ranging from ten to twenty miles, lie the coast tide swamp lands. These swamp lands formerly produced large quantities of rice.

The sea-islands, about five hundred and sixty square miles in total area, form a network along the coast. They are some fifteen feet above sea-level, have a sandy soil, suitable for sea-island cotton and diversified crops, though very little farming is done on them.

Struggle in the Colonial Period Over Slavery

Beginning with the settlement of Savannah in 1733, the coast was occupied during the middle of the eighteenth century by successive colonies of English, Scotch, German, and Swiss immigrants. One important colony of New Englanders settled in what is now Liberty County. These immigrants were scattered about in numerous villages, many of which have wholly disappeared.[125] During the first twenty years of the colony an effort was made to establish something resembling the New England economy of small farms

---

[125] Jones, C. C., *Dead Towns of Georgia* (Savannah, 1878), *passim.*

grouped about villages. Slavery was prohibited, and the area of land each settler might have was strictly limited, with the view of preventing the growth of large estates. From the first, however, the colonists were dissatisfied with the rules of the trustees of the colony.[126] They claimed that the heat and the swampy malarious nature of the country made sustained physical exertion on the part of white men impossible, and that they were unable to compete in the markets of the world with South Carolina, where slavery was allowed. Petition after petition was sent to the trustees, praying that the restriction as to slavery be removed. It was further asserted that fifty acres of land was too small a tract for practical purposes, especially in view of the fact that part of the holding might be swampy and unavailable for agricultural purposes.

After resisting the pressure for twenty years, the trustees finally yielded, and slavery was introduced in 1751. The coast immediately began to develop. The tide of population which had started away from the colony was checked, and many new settlers came. With one exception, the seaboard counties had black majorities by 1790. At the close of the ante-bellum period, the coast was the region of largest slave-holdings in the state. The average was twenty per owner (for the state, the average was eleven), and more than one-fourth of all the owners of one hundred or more slaves were in these six counties.[127]

With the introduction of slavery, social differentiation took place. The poorer element was obliged to leave the richer regions along the river banks. Many drifted into the pine barrens of the coast and into the nearest tier of Wiregrass counties. The upper class developed into the planter type. The social prestige and political power of the coast planter were marked. The poorer folk were wholly illiterate

---

[126] Stevens, W. B., *History of Georgia* (New York, 1847), I, chaps. VIII, IX.
[127] U. S. Census, 1860, *Agriculture*, pp. 226-227.

and sustained themselves with difficulty on the infertile soil of the pine barren lands.[128]

Rice growing was the principal interest of the sea-coast planter. Many of these plantations were very large and extremely productive.[129] The rice planter as a rule lived on his plantation only in winter. As soon as the warm weather approached, he retreated to a more salubrious climate, leaving the plantation in the hands of an overseer.[130] Absenteeism, the absolute power of the overseer, his low moral standards, and the crowding together of many negroes, brought about more unfortunate conditions on the coast than were to be found elsewhere in the state. The coast negroes were said to have been less intelligent and capable than those of the up-country.

Destruction of the Rice Industry After the War

Civil war and emancipation brought ruin to the coast rice planter. The creation of a rice plantation was an arduous and expensive undertaking. The swamp lands had to be reclaimed and then kept up by constant attention to dikes and canals. Reliable labor was absolutely indispensable. The losses of the upcountry planter due to the disorganization of labor were temporary, but the coast planter was obliged to look on in helplessness while his valuable property went to ruin for lack of regular work. Negroes refused to do banking and ditching. Some of the planters attempted to import white labor, but lack of capital to repair the ravages of war and the effects of neglect made it impossible to revive the rice industry on a large scale.[131]

[128] Smith, *Story of Georgia*, pp. 147-148, 149-151.
[129] Olmsted, F. L., *A Journey in the Seaboard Slave States* (New York, 1856), pp. 409-442; Lyell, Sir Charles, *A Second Visit to the United States of North America* (New York, 1849), I, chap. XIX.
[130] Mallard, R. Q., *Plantation Days Before Emancipation* (Richmond, 1892), p. 14.
[131] Leigh, *op. cit.*, pp. 263-264.

Stationary Condition of Farming

Under such circumstances agriculture retrograded and the seaboard has for many years been in a stationary condition. "Agriculture in Glynn County at present amounts almost to nothing. If ever revived, there must be better drainage and other sanitary precautions, and perhaps new immigration."[132]

The negroes took almost complete possession of the coast in 1865, constituting 73 per cent of the total population in 1870. In recent years, however, the white element has been rapidly increasing. One of the counties, Bryan, has a white majority, and for the other six counties, the percentage of blacks has fallen to 59.

The large plantations have disappeared and with them systematized industry. The land has been divided into minute negro-owned farms, and the section has become insignificant in the agriculture of the state.

It seems reasonably clear that on the seaboard the disintegration of plantations differed from that of the other sections of the state, in that here it was a real, not a nominal division. In studying the other groups of counties, the position was taken that the prevalence of the tenant system, especially of the share system, meant that the plantation, in many cases, remained essentially a unit, though the method of collecting data for the census made the tenant's farm appear as a separate holding. On the seacoast, however, the tenant system is a negligible factor, and has been of progressively less importance at each census period. Ownership has advanced with great rapidity, each decade witnessing a considerable transference of tenants and laborers to the status of owners. There is a sharp contrast, therefore, between this and the other groups of counties. Here at each census period owners have been a larger percentage of all

---

[132] *Inquiries I*, Letter from Glynn County.

farmers, while elsewhere the percentage of owners has steadily declined.

The average size of farms operated by owners in 1903 varied, according to Banks,[133] from 50 to 365 acres for whites, and from 13 to 53 acres for negroes. The minute size of the negro farms and the unusual poorness and cheapness of the soil indicate the ease with which negroes have climbed into the class of owners. A few months' work for wages would suffice to obtain the price of such a patch as the census dignifies with the name of "farm." The prevalence of ownership in these counties, 83 per cent of all farms being operated by owners, has not served to better agricultural conditions. The percentage of the land area in farms is lower than in any other section of the state, less than eleven per cent in McIntosh County, and in only two counties does the percentage run as high as the forty to sixty class. The per acre value of farm land is as low as in the mountain counties; in only one county (and that Chatham, containing the city of Savannah) is the average within the ten to twenty-five dollar class. Less cotton was produced in 1910 than in 1870, none being reported at the last census for four of the six counties.

The figures of *per capita* wealth for this area are of little value as an index of the condition of the agricultural classes, because nearly 80 per cent of the total property values consists of personal and real property in Savannah. Though negroes constitute 59 per cent of the population, and though 83 per cent of the negro farmers own the farms they operate, they possess less than 5 per cent of the property in the area.

---

133 Banks, *op. cit.*, pp. 119-121.

3

Howell Cobb and the Crisis of 1850

[1916]

A paper read at the joint meeting of the American Historical Association and the Mississippi Valley Historical Association in Cincinnati, December, 1916. Reprinted from The Mississippi Valley Historical Review, *Vol. IV, No. 3 (December, 1917), pp. 279-298.*

IN THE SECESSION MOVEMENT OF THE FIFTIES, HOWELL COBB of Georgia[1] was one of the small group of southern democrats of distinctly unionist principles. He has received only slight attention in the standard histories, and is remembered principally as an ardent proslavery man and a leading advocate of secession in 1860.[2] His leadership in the final movement for disunion and the part he played in the establishment of the Confederacy have tended to obscure the character of his statesmanship in earlier phases of the struggle over the extension of slavery. Cobb's public career extended over the years 1842 to 1860, a period characterized on the whole by extreme sectionalism. Cobb was always ready with a good word for slavery and was never backward in defending the

---

[1] [Cf. "Howell Cobb" by R. P. Brooks, in the *Dictionary of American Biography.* Ed.].

[2] James F. Rhodes, *History of the United States from the compromise of 1850* (New York, 1906-07), 1:117. "His [Cobb's] devotion to slavery and southern interests was the distinguishing feature of his character." Rhodes quotes with apparent approval Horace Mann's dictum that Cobb "loves slavery, it is his politics, his political economy, and his religion." Theodore C. Smith includes Cobb in a group of extremists "of the Davis and Yancey type." *Parties and slavery, 1850-1859 (The American nation: a history,* vol. 18—New York, 1906), 52.

south from attack; but along with his sectional views he held
an intense national patriotism, seeing no necessary incom-
patibility between them. Indeed, his uncompromising advocacy of unionism, especially in connection with the compromise of 1850, alienated him completely from his party
associates in the South; and the political advancement was
sacrificed solely because of his fight against disunion.

Cobb was not yet twenty-nine years of age when he took
his seat in the twenty-eighth Congress as the representative
of the sixth district of Georgia. Remarkably self-controlled
for so young a man, he never indulged in the outbursts of
sectional rancor so common at the time, but strove rather to
emphasize the national point of view. His speech was free
from offensive and threatening expressions, and his manner
to opponents, even under great provocation, was courteous.
He quickly established himself as a man of strong unionist
feeling and became popular with the like-minded element
in Congress. Furthermore, his skill in debate and familiarity
with parliamentary procedure made him a leader on his
side of the house.

The conflict which culminated in the compromise legislation of 1850 began in the closing days of the twenty-ninth
Congress. Two days before adjournment, in August, 1846,
a bill was introduced carrying an appropriation of $2,000,000
to be used in paying for any territory that might be obtained
from Mexico.[3] On the same day Wilmot introduced his
proviso prohibiting slavery in any such acquisition. This
proviso was incorporated in the bill, the entire southern
delegation, with the exception of two Kentucky whigs,
voting against it. The senate struck out the proviso and
killed the bill; but an ominous situation had developed.

In the same session of the same Congress, another bill
was introduced, carrying this time an appropriation of
$3,000,000, to settle the war with Mexico. The Wilmot pro-

---

[3] *Congressional globe,* 29 congress, 1 session, 1211.

viso was again proposed as an amendment, and in the debate Cobb addressed the house.[4] He made a plea for fairness and liberality in the legislation for the territory won by the exertions of all the people of the United States. He did not recognize any moral aspect of the North's unwillingness to see a further extension of slavery. Both parties to the controversy he regarded as engaged in an effort to further economic and political interests; the right of the people of both sections to participate in the fruits of the victory over Mexico was undeniable; and, as free soil and slavery could not exist in the same place at the same time, Cobb thought a division of the territory the only practical way out of the difficulty. He put the argument for a compromise in the strongest possible light by contending that, if this dispute were peaceably settled, the long contest over the extension of slavery would be ended, since the status of slavery would have been determined in all the land owned or likely to be acquired by the United States. At this stage of the struggle Cobb advocated the extension of the Missouri compromise line, the principle of congressional nonintervention not having as yet become the southern rallying cry.

Some time later Cobb expressed the opinion that had the southern representatives stood together it would have been possible to secure an extension of the Missouri line.[5] Certainly Georgia democrats were for a time favorable to such a settlement, as was indicated by their vote on a resolution introduced in the Georgia senate in November, 1847.[6] But the Calhoun influence was beginning to work against a compromise, and the time passed when the North could be induced to accept the Missouri line, if, indeed, such a course had ever been possible.

Throughout both sessions of the thirtieth Congress, con-

[4] *Ibid.*, 29 congress, 2 session, 360-363.

[5] Cobb to Lamar, June 26, 1850, in Cobb manuscripts.

[6] Glenn to Cobb, December 1, 1847, in "The Correspondence of Robert Toombs, Alexander H. Stephens, and Howell Cobb," edited by Ulrich B. Phillips, in American historical association, *Annual report,* 1911 (Washington, 1913), 2: 89.

vening in March, 1847, interest was centered on various bills for the organization of government in the Mexican cession and in Oregon. The Oregon matter was settled in August, 1848, but all efforts to adjust the question in the other territory were futile. Much angry debating took place, however, and the exciting interchange of views and the fixed determination of the North to exclude slavery from the territories lent strength to the Calhoun following. For some time Calhoun had been urging southerners to abandon party allegiances and act together in defense of their sectional interests. Before a meeting of southern representatives and senators, in January, 1849, he laid a carefully prepared paper known as "The Southern Address."[7] It reviewed the history of the sectional fight over slavery, and showed how the northern states had violated the constitutional guarantees of the institution. The aggressive policy of the North, Calhoun contended, looked ultimately to nothing less than the total destruction of slavery. Only by the united action of all southerners could northern aggression be successfully met.

Unfortunately for Calhoun's plan, the southern whigs would not cooperate in the movement.[8] Having just elected their candidate for the presidency, they naturally desired to minimize sectional discord and to give Taylor's administration a chance of success. Only two whigs signed the "Address," and the movement was thus deprived of a nonpartisan character. The democrats were nearly unanimous in upholding Calhoun, but Howell Cobb and a few others refused to do so. Four of the dissentients combined in a letter to their constituents, explaining their action.[9] The communication was written by Cobb. The main point in the letter, as Cobb explained to Buchanan,[10] was a remonstrance against the formation of a southern sectional party. Calhoun had

[7] *The works of John C. Calhoun* (Cralle ed.,—New York, 1856), 6 : 290-313.
[8] U. B. Phillips, *Life of Robert Toombs* (New York, 1913), 60.
[9] Cobb and others, "To our constituents," February 26, 1849, Cobb manuscripts.
[10] American historical association, *Annual report*, 1911, 2 : 164.

disingenuously sought to convince the people of the South that the northern people had been a unit in opposing southern interests, making no discrimination between northern democrats, whigs, and abolitionists. That this had not been true, Cobb showed by contrasting the attitude of whigs and democrats on the various sectional issues that had arisen. He cited particularly the Wilmot proviso. Many votes had been taken on this measure in the house and senate, "and it yet remains for the first northern Whig to record his vote against it. It has at different times been defeated by both branches of Congress and in every instance by the aid of northern Democratic votes."

The communication then related how at the meeting that adopted the "Address," after the whigs had revealed their attitude, Cobb had tried to get incorporated the true history of abolitionism as it had affected party politics. The majority, however, were committed to giving the "Address" as nonpartisan an aspect as possible, despite the defection of the whigs. Cobb's amendments had, therefore, been rejected, and he and his associates had refused to sign the document. He was at a loss to see, he continues, how a distinctly southern organization could give additional security to southern interests. Such an organization ". . . possessed no charms to lure us from the old association which we had formed in the days of our earliest political recollection with the Democratic party of the Union. We preferred yet to rely upon the combined influence of the Southern and Northern Democrats for the protection of the rights of the South, so long as the same were dependent upon the legislation of our national government. We could not see how our strength was to be increased by diminishing our numbers. If Southern Democrats alone could, by party organization, throw ample barriers around the peculiar interests of the South, we were at a loss to understand how the aid and cooperation of our Northern friends would embarrass our movements or weaken

our defences. So long as we contemplate the continuance of
the Union, so long will we look to the preservation of the
integrity of the Democratic party of the Union, as an element of our greatest strength and security. When the time
shall come, if ever, which God, in his mercy, avert, when
the rights and the interests of the South, under the Constitution, are spurned and disregarded, and we shall cease to
be considered as equals with our northern brethren, we shall
look to other and higher measures of redress than those
which promise to flow from the organization of a Southern
sectional party."

Cobb's attitude toward this southern movement is of considerable importance to the student of his career. He planted
himself squarely in favor of national parties, as the necessary
machinery for handling national questions. His faith in the
national democracy remained with him a cardinal political
tenet, to which he held until the Charleston convention in
1860. In the second place, the episode marks the beginning
of his estrangement from the southern extremists. An effort
was made to compel acquiescence in Calhoun's scheme as
a test of loyalty to the Democratic party and the South.[11] A
north Georgia editor complained that a shower of curses
had descended on him for approving Cobb's position.[12] Public meetings in most of the southern states passed resolutions
endorsing the project of a sectional party. One of the signers
of Cobb's letter, Lumpkin of Georgia, wrote him in March
giving details of such a meeting, in which resolutions were
passed, as Lumpkin put it, "to organize a Southern sectional
party and to disregard either democrat or whig, and to make
the love of negroes and the defence of their rights connected
with them as paramount to every other consideration."[13]

[11] *Ibid.*, 2 : 159. *Augusta* (Georgia) *Chronicle and Sentinel,* July 23, 1849 : "It
is known . . . that for some time past the Southern address has been the standard by which the patriotism of all parties has been judged of by certain politicians. Our Democratic friends have denounced as *traitors,* every man that did
not sign it in Washington, and every one that refuses to worship it in Georgia."
[12] American historical association, *Annual report,* 1911, 2: 157.
[13] American historical association, *Annual report,* 1911, 2 :156.

While losing popularity in Georgia and the South, Cobb gained prestige among the northern democrats as the result of this incident. The leaders of the northern wing of the party were pleased with his fairness in recognizing the value of their services to the South. This feeling was doubtless in part responsible for Cobb's receiving the nomination of the democratic caucus in December, 1849, for the speakership of the thirty-first Congress. The Calhoun element made a determined fight against his nomination,[14] and throughout the three weeks of balloting in the speakership contest, a small group of southern extremists threw away their votes rather than support the man who had opposed Calhoun. Cobb was finally elected on the sixty-third ballot, after a resolution to elect by plurality had been adopted. He took the chair free from pledges of all sorts, having even voted against the plurality rule.[15] He had refused overtures of northern whigs to exchange support for a promise to construct the committees to their satisfaction;[16] and of southern whigs, who sought, it was later said, to obtain from him an agreement to appoint the committees so as to prevent the passage of the Wilmot proviso.[17] In electing Cobb the house had come about as near as possible to satisfying all elements.[18] He was popular with unionists everywhere and it was believed he would be fair in his appointments and in the exercise of his power as speaker.

The Congress over which Cobb was thus chosen to preside was a memorable one. The territorial question, of course, was still uppermost, now complicated by the rapid movement of population to California and the demand for her admission as a free state. Clay in the senate introduced his

---

[14] *Ibid.*, 2 : 177, 178.

[15] *Ibid.*, 2 : 179.

[16] *Ibid.*

[17] *Ibid.*, 2 : 189.

[18] The *Washington Union*, December 27, 1849, quoting the *National Intelligencer*: ". . . had it devolved on the Whig members of the House to select a Speaker from the opposite party, it is quite probable that a majority would have chosen Mr. Cobb."

resolutions in January, 1850.[19] At about the same time the
house took up a presidential message presenting the free soil
constitution of California. Doty, a free soil democrat, introduced on February 28 a resolution instructing the committee
on territories to report a bill for the admission of California.[20] After a motion to table the resolution had been
defeated by a strictly sectional vote, the southerners began
a filibuster. The obstructionists were not opposed to the
admission of California on a constitution of her own choice,[21]
but were determined to force at the same time a satisfactory
settlement of the status of slavery in the rest of the Mexican
cession. Cobb assisted the filibuster by recognizing all who
desired to make obstructive remarks, and after adjournment
arranged a meeting of the leaders on both sides at his house.
The conference resulted in an agreement to bring in bills
for the organization of Utah and New Mexico, in which the
principle of congressional nonintervention should be incorporated.[22] The bills were actually introduced, but never
came to a vote, though their substance was later enacted
into law.

Meanwhile in the senate the select committee of thirteen,
appointed April 18 to consider Clay's resolutions, made a
report recommending the settlement outlined by Clay, and
presenting bills to carry their recommendations into effect.[23]
To the first measure, the Utah bill, an amendment was
offered[24] in these words: "and, when admitted as a state,
the said territory, or any portion of the same, shall be received into the Union, with or without slavery, as their constitution may prescribe at the time of their admission." On
the adoption of this amendment, which meant the acceptance

---

[19] William MacDonald, *Documentary source book of American history, 1606-
1898* (New York, 1908), 384.
[20] *Congressional globe*, 31 congress, 1 session, 375, 376.
[21] Alexander H. Stephens, *A constitutional view of the late war between the
states; its causes, character, conduct and results* (Chicago, 1868-70), 2 : 201-203.
[22] *Ibid.*, 2 : 203, 204.
[23] MacDonald, *Documentary source book of American history, 1606-1898*, 386.
[24] *Congressional globe*, 31 congress, 1 session, 1239.

of the nonintervention principle, depended the success of the compromise measures.[25] It was adopted, and by the middle of September the entire program going to make up the compromise of 1850 had been completed in both senate and house, though not without a bitter fight in the house on the nonintervention features of the territorial bills.[26]

The compromise of 1850 was the result of a sincere effort by the unionists to end a dispute that was impossible of adjustment except by mutual concessions. Extremists in both sections believed that a humiliating surrender had been made to their opponents. The politicians had done their best: it remained to convince the masses of the wisdom of the settlement. The arena of discussion was, therefore, shifted to the states.

In the South the source of the opposition to the compromise had been foreshadowed by the house vote at the critical moment.[27] Southern whigs had been nearly unanimously in favor of the measure, while twenty-nine southern democrats had voted on the other side. Shortly after the passage of the compromise a paper was circulated among the members pledging all who signed it not to support anyone for president, vice-president, senator, representative in Congress or in a state legislature, who was not known to be in favor of the compromise and "opposed to the renewal in any form of agitation upon the subject of slavery." Howell Cobb was the only southern democrat who signed.[28] We have seen that in his speech of February, 1847, Cobb favored the extension of the Missouri line. He had now abandoned that plan and was thoroughly committed to Clay's scheme. As early as June, 1850, he turned his attention to creating senti-

---

[25] Stephens, *Constitutional view of the late war between the states*, 2 : 218, 219.
[26] Phillips, *Life of Robert Toombs*, 85-88.
[27] Stephens, *Constitutional view of the late war between the states*, 2 : 234; *Congressional globe*, 31 congress, 1 session, 1764.
[28] *Augusta Chronicle and Sentinel*, February 20, 1850.

ment in Georgia for the settlement. He urged his kinsman, John B. Lamar, to arrange a unionist meeting at Macon.[29] Lamar agreed to do so. He reported that there was a good deal of sentiment among the democratic masses in favor of the compromise, but that the press was seeking to "browbeat our representatives in Congress into the belief that the people are opposed desperately to the Senate Compromise and if they vote for it their doom is sealed."[30]

Democratic opposition to the compromise was due in large measure to a revival of the demand for the extension of the Missouri line, which after the rapid movement of population to California and the demand for statehood on a free constitution seemed more advantageous than nonintervention.[31] Cobb was convinced that the demand for the Missouri line was insincere. He had said in the letter to Lamar above referred to: "Does it not present a singular spectacle to see the very men who would have ostracized me for advocating the Missouri Compromise line, now making that their *sine qua non*. If they had united with me *at the proper time* we could have obtained that line as the basis of settlement, but Mr. Calhoun said, the South was sick of compromises and demanded *the constitutional principle of non interference*. Well, non interference is tendered and is to be rejected on the ground that the heretofore repudiated Missouri Compromise is preferable. I have no patience with such men. If they believed today that we could settle the question upon

---

[29] Cobb to Lamar, June 26, 1850, Cobb manuscripts.

[30] American historical association, *Annual report*, 1911, 2 : 191.

[31] Benning to Cobb, March 29, 1850, Cobb manuscripts. This letter is an able presentation of the views of the extremists. The Nashville convention, meeting in June, also demanded the Missouri line. The *Augusta Chronicle and Sentinel*, a whig paper, commented editorially June 25, 1850, on the astonishing change about face of the radicals on the Missouri compromise line. "Prior to the Convention we were wont to hear the advocates of the measure [the convention?] denounce the Missouri Compromise as a degrading concession on the part of the South, and yet we find the Convention commending it as the only just measure of compromise to the Southern people." A state meeting in Macon, in August, approved the acts of the Nashville convention, particularly the demand for the Missouri line. See *ibid.*, August 30, 1950.

the terms now proposed, they would reject it and demand something else."

Correspondents confirmed Cobb's belief that the cry for the Missouri line had been raised simply to keep alive the agitation. A. H. Chappell, a middle Georgia unionist and former congressman, wrote Cobb in July urging that he bestir himself to stem the tide setting towards disunion.[32] "The game of the destructives," he said, "is to use the Missouri Compromise principle as a medium of defeating all adjustment and then to make the most of succeeding events, no matter what they may be, to infuriate the South and drive her into measures that must end in disunion."

Responding to this appeal, Cobb prepared an exhaustive statement of his views.[33] The communication is too long for even an adequate résumé. He argued strongly for the several parts of the compromise, and gave particular attention to the California question and the southern agitation for the Missouri line. So far as California was concerned, Cobb saw no tenable ground of opposition. The people of California wanted a free soil constitution, and it was a cherished southern principle that the people should decide this labor question for themselves. "We have the satisfaction of knowing that the constitution which California presents to us has received the sanction and approval of her people. . . . The mere fact that her constitution excludes the institution of slavery constitutes no valid or constitutional objection to her admission as a State. The right of the people to pass upon this and all kindred questions in the organization of their State governments is a principle which needs only to be stated to be admitted and sanctioned." He had disapproved of the irregularities which attended the organiza-

---

[32] American historical association, *Annual report*, 1911, 2: 193, 206. The *Augusta Chronicle and Sentinel*, May 17, 1850: "Is there nothing in all this coalition of Free Soilers and Abolitionists and Ultraists of the South, to mark the purposes and designs of these factions to prevent an adjustment, and thus leave the question open for future agitation?"

[33] American historical association, *Annual report*, 1911, 2: 196 ff.

tion of government in California, but ". . . these objections are not so grave and formidable in their character as to require at my hands the entire rejection of California as a state when the question is prescribed to me as part of a general system of settlement by which peace and quiet is to be restored to my country, torn and distracted by the most angry and alarming dissensions."

As to the rest of the Mexican cession, after a long fight the principle of congressional nonintervention had been wrested from Congress. This settlement he held to be preferable to the extension of the Missouri line, because it threw open the whole of the territory to the slaveholders. Under either plan, he frankly pointed out, the final decision of the labor question would not be a matter of legislation, but would be determined by natural conditions. ". . . but whether recognized by Congress or not, no one proposes to force the institution of slavery into any portion of the territory against the wishes of the people who may emigrate there and inhabit it; so that at last its existence there must depend, as it should, upon the decision of the people of the territories. This fact should be borne in memory to prevent the public mind from falling into the fatal error of supposing that the adoption of the Missouri Compromise line was the absolute establishment of slavery in any portion of that country. Such a result does not necessarily follow upon this, mode of adjustment. Soil, climate and the general adaptation of the country to slave labor, are the great elements that must mould and regulate the institutions of those territories if left free from the operation of Congressional restrictions."

This letter placed Cobb in direct conflict with the current of opinion in his party. Excitement in Georgia was intense. The democratic press all over the state was denouncing the settlement and angrily threatening disunion.[34] For example,

---

[34] *Columbus* (Georgia) *Sentinel*, September 12, 1850. In a similar strain the editor of the *Macon* (Georgia) *Telegraph* wrote on September 17: "It remains to be seen whether the men of the South will, with freemen's hearts, strike for

the *Columbus Sentinel* said: "We have all along contended that the admission of California would fill to overflowing the poisoned cup of degradation which the North has for years been preparing for the South. . . . We now abandon the Union as an engine of infamous oppression. We are for secession, open unqualified secession. Henceforth we are for war upon the government; it has existed but for our ruin, and to the extent of our ability to destroy it, it shall exist no longer."

In February, the legislature of Georgia had adopted a set of resolutions calling for a state convention to consider measures of redress, should Congress force on the South the program which was being urged.[35] The passage of the California bill was taken by the governor as justification for calling the convention, to meet in December. A lively contest ensued between secessionists and unionists for the control of the convention. Toombs, Stephens, and Cobb worked hard to bring out a full unionist vote, and a large majority of conservatives were chosen as delegates.

The convention met and adopted a preamble and set of resolutions known as the "Georgia platform,"[36] which pledged Georgia to the support of the compromise and the union as long as her constitutional rights were respected and the North remained faithful to the provisions of the adjustment of 1850. This action of the state of Georgia was hailed

---

their rights, or with the spirit of slaves and dastards submit to this Congressional quackery, until they are driven from their country like the Poles. If the territory—the land and property of the South, can be taken by a vote of the majority, why not her slaves? The question then which springs to the lips of everyone, is, what are we to do? the mere politician who waits to see the course of the popular breeze before he sets his sails—the time-server and office-seeker, who palters with the great issues of equality and degradation, submission and slavery, despicable at all times is doubly so now. FOR OUR OWN PART, WE ARE FOR SECESSION, FOR RESISTANCE, OPEN, UNQUALIFIED RESISTANCE."

Other newspapers openly advocating secession were the *Columbus Times, Savannah Georgian,* (Augusta) *Constitutionalist.*

[35] H. V. Ames, *State documents on federal relations, 1789-1861* (New York, 1907), 259-261.

[36] Journal of the Georgia Convention of 1850.

with rejoicing by unionists everywhere,[37] and the decision of the state to uphold the compromise contributed much to a general acceptance of the settlement in the South.

Unionists had for the time being laid aside party differences and combined against the disruptive movement; but the whigs contributed far the larger part of the membership of the convention. The radicalism of the day, as has been seen, was in the democratic ranks, and Cobb's exertions had swung to the unionist cause only a minority of his party, coming principally from the two north Georgia districts, one of which he represented in Congress. As the real problem was to secure enough votes from the ranks of the democracy to win the fight, Cobb deserves the largest share of the credit for the success of the movement. Stephens admitted that but for Cobb's efforts the "Georgia platform" would not have been possible.[38] Toombs and Stephens in advocating the compromise in Georgia had not jeopardized their popularity, but Cobb had had to incur the hatred of many erstwhile firm political allies.

The attitude of the Georgia convention had been due rather to conservative restraint in the presence of a situation that looked dangerous for the union than to a thoroughgoing approval of the compromise. Unionist leaders, aware of the widespread dissatisfaction with the settlement, felt it necessary to effect an organization to uphold the decision of the state in accepting the compromise. Accordingly, a "Constitutional union party" was formed in December, 1850.[39] To a unionist rally in Macon in February, 1851,

[37] The *Augusta Chronicle and Sentinel*, January 1, 1851, quotes the *Providence (Rhode Island) Journal* as follows: ". . . and so ends the convention which was called to take the lead in the work of resistance to the federal government. The patriotism of Georgia, manifested in this act, will long be remembered with gratitude by the people of the whole union; and when her orators shall sum up her claims upon the country, this will stand among the most valuable and conspicuous services which she has rendered."

[38] Stephens, *Constitutional view of the late war between the states*, 2: 332.

[39] The *Augusta Chronicle and Sentinel*, December 28, 1850, gives an account of the organization meeting.

Cobb sent a letter in which he expressed the opinion that the danger to the union had not passed.[40] Abolitionists and their allies in the North and secessionists in the South were exerting themselves to keep alive sectional feeling. The friends of the union, he thought, should stand firmly on the compromise and a final adjustment. "The success of this movement," he said, "decides in my honest judgment the fate of the Union."

The constitutional union party enlisted the bulk of the whigs and the more moderate democrats. The extremists also organized, under the name "Southern rights party." Both parties nominated candidates for the governorship in the approaching election. The union party named Cobb; the southern rights party, Charles J. McDonald, already twice governor and a very popular man.

In the stirring and bitter campaign that followed the issues were the same as in the election of delegates to the Georgia convention the year before. Cobb visited every part of the state, maintaining the wisdom of the compromise and combating secession doctrines. The extremists succeeded in making the abstract right of secession the principal issue.[41] This question the union party in convention had sought to avoid.[42] Cobb, however, foresaw the issue and exchanged letters with Toombs on the subject.[43] Stephens also wrote[44] advising Cobb how he thought the matter should be handled. Cobb prepared a communication in August containing an explicit statement of his views.

He denied that at the time of the adoption of the constitution any right of secession was recognized. "When asked to concede the right of a State to secede at pleasure from

[40] American historical association, *Annual report*, 1911, 2: 221, 222.
[41] *Columbus* (Georgia) *Enquirer*: "But according to the views, or pretended views, rather, of our opponents, there is but one thing now that is worth talking about, and that is the abstract right of secession." (Quoted by the *Augusta Chronicle and Sentinel*, July 18, 1851.
[42] Toombs to Cobb, June 9, 1851, Cobb manuscripts.
[43] Toombs to Cobb, June 9, 1851, Cobb manuscripts.
[44] American historical association, *Annual report*, 1911, 2: 237, 238.

the Union, with or without just cause, we are called upon
to admit that the framers of the constitution did that which
was never done by any other people possessed of their good
sense and intelligence—*that is to provide in the very organization of the government for its own dissolution.*"[45] Had
the framers of the constitution intended to leave the per-
petuity of the union to the caprice of each state, it seemed
to Cobb that such a principle would have been clearly
enounced in the document itself instead of leaving it to
"inference and metaphysical deductions of the most complicated character." That a ratification of the constitution
was regarded as irrevocable he showed from the hesitation
of Rhode Island and North Carolina. Had it been a recognized principle that a state need stay in the union only so
long as it pleased, Cobb contended that these two states
would have adopted the constitution immediately with the
intention of withdrawing should the other states refuse to
adopt the amendments they desired. He thought it was
especially absurd to claim that states made from territory
bought by the United States had the right to secede. Our
governmental arrangements are pitiable, Cobb thought, if
the existence of the union is at the disposal of each state:
"By admitting the doctrine of the secessionists we are brought
to the conclusion that our Federal Government . . . is nothing more than a voluntary association, temporary in its character, weak and imbecile in the exercise of its powers, incapable of self-preservation, claiming from its citizens allegiance and demanding annual tribute from their treasure,
and yet destitute of the power of protecting their rights
or preserving their liberties. . . . I do not so understand
our government; I feel that I owe my allegiance to a government possessed of more vitality and strength than that
which is drawn from a voluntary obedience to its laws. I
hold that no government is entitled to any allegiance that

----

[45] *Ibid.,* 2: 251 ff.

does not pass wise and just laws, and does not possess the power to enforce and execute them."

Up to this point Cobb's argument was directed against secession as an abstract right, a measure to be resorted to peaceably at any time that interest or inclination prompted states to such a course. The emphasis is on the conception of secession as a peaceable process; otherwise it is indistinguishable from revolution. The right of revolution Cobb recognized. Such action, however, could not possibly be allowed to go unchallenged and had no constitutional justification. On this point he said: "The right of a State to secede in case of oppression or 'a gross and palpable violation' of her constitutional rights, as derived from the reserved sovereignty of the States, I am prepared to recognize. In such case each State, in the language of the Kentucky and Virginia resolutions of 1798-99, is to be the judge, not only of the 'infractions,' but of the 'mode and measure of redress.' It is the just right of the people to change their form of government when in their opinion it has become tyrannical in a mode not provided for in the constitution, and is therefore revolutionary in its character and depends for its maintenance upon the stout hearts and strong arms of a free people."

Much emphasis was being laid on the question of the use of force to quell a secession movement. Cobb sought apparently to make this aspect of his views as palatable as possible to his opponents and to win over the less extreme of them by advancing the proposition that, theoretically, the exercise of military power would not necessarily follow the secession of a state. Resort to force would come only if such action were compelled by the "rights and interests of the remaining States of the Union." But as a practical proposition, Cobb appeared to think violation of the rights of other states would inevitably follow secession. If he, as governor, were called upon to furnish militia to coerce a seceding state, he would first summon a convention of the people and let them decide between the union and the seceding state or states.

This exposition of his views on the right of secession has been viewed as an effort on Cobb's part to straddle.[46] The judgment is based on his failure to come out unequivocally for the use of force to crush an attempt at secession and on his statement that participation by individuals in such a movement would not, in his opinion, amount to treason to the national government. The position taken in the quotation last above given is also open to objection, as Cobb found constitutional justification for an action which in the next breath he speaks of as a revolutionary right to change the form of government "in a mode not provided for in the Constitution." There was a good deal of complaint during the campaign that he spoke in a different tone at different places; but the communication now being considered was intended to clear up all doubts as to his position and may be taken as final. On the whole, it must be pronounced distinctly nationalist in tone, though not uninfluenced by Cobb's natural tendency to compromise on disputed questions.

The election returns showed that Cobb had been elected by an overwhelming majority. The people of Georgia had spoken emphatically against disunion and secession, and in favor of the finality of the compromise. The secession movement of the fifties was over, for a similar result had been obtained by unionists in other southern states.[47] There remains to be considered the effects of Cobb's stand for the union on his political fortunes.

In organizing the constitutional union party, Toombs[48] and Stephens and some of the democratic leaders[49] hoped to make it the nucleus of a national third party. But Cobb

---

[46] Arthur C. Cole, *The whig party in the south* (Washington, 1913), 204.
[47] Cole, *Whig party in the south*, 188, 189.
[48] American historical association, *Annual report*, 1911, 2:227.
[49] *Ibid.*, 2: 229.

seems never to have favored the idea.[50] The whig party he thought permanently denationalized and incapable of being used any longer as the instrument of fostering unionist feeling or for the protection of the South.[51] The democratic party at large, on the contrary, he believed "sound" on both these points. The wing of the party led by himself in Georgia he regarded as representing the national democratic position; the southern rights wing he considered schismatic. He desired, therefore, to keep up the union organization and throw its strength in national elections to the democratic party, a course to which the principal obstacle was the traditional hostility of whigs and democrats.

The test whether the whig and democratic elements of the union party could be kept together came with the preliminaries to the presidential election of 1852. The southern rights organization, arrogating to itself the sole title to regular democracy, appointed delegates to the Baltimore national convention, to meet in June. The union party held a meeting in April to decide what action should be taken about delegates.[52] The democratic wing desired to be represented, but the whigs refused to agree. The convention adjourned without taking action, but after the meeting the democrats got together and appointed delegates. The whigs had acted at the behest of Toombs and Stephens, who opposed acting with the democratic party. They desired to hold aloof from both national organizations and throw the strength of the unionists to the party that embraced the compromise and named a compromise candidate.[53] After the nomination of Pierce on a compromise platform, there seemed no reason why the whig leaders should hesitate to support the democratic ticket. Indeed, soon after the adjournment of the democratic convention, Toombs wrote Cobb: "You and your

---

[50] *Ibid.*, 2 : 221, 275.
[51] *Ibid.*, 2 : 311.
[52] *Augusta Chronicle and Sentinel*, April 28, 1852. Proceedings of the convention.
[53] Stephens to Cobb, January 26, 1852, Cobb manuscripts.

friends are fully and thoroughly in line. The resolutions of the Baltimore Convention on the Compromise are full, clear and explicit. No honest Compromise man can object to them, and the candidate, Genl. Pierce I doubt not from what I can learn of him is a fair, great and upright and honest man without the least objection on the slavery issue."[54] Stephens also was reported[55] as entirely satisfied with the platform and the candidate. The nomination of Scott by the whigs should apparently have clinched the argument, as Scott was known to entertain anti-compromise views and had been used to prevent the nomination of a compromise man.[56] Despite the favorable outlook, Toombs and Stephens after a period of vacillation backed down and brought out a third ticket, headed by Webster. They could not endure the idea of affiliating with the democratic party which was being "reorganized" by what they regarded as an infamous coalition of southern fire-eaters and northern free soilers.

Notwithstanding the defection of Toombs and Stephens, Cobb and other union democrats made an effort to keep the party together. A convention was held in July, a majority of those attending being democrats. When the democrats tried to force through a resolution favoring Pierce and King, the whigs bolted, and the party was disrupted. The democratic wing then put up a Pierce and King ticket. Shortly after the convention the executive committee issued a statement formally dissolving the union party, the principal reason for the abandonment of the organization being stated as "the rallying of the Whigs on a third candidate endangering the success of Pierce and King."[57] The reference was to the Webster ticket.

---

[54] Toombs to Cobb, June 10, 1852, Cobb manuscripts.

[55] American historical association, *Annual report*, 1911, 2 : 300. Also Stephens to Cobb, January 26, 1852, in Cobb manuscripts.

[56] American historical association, *Annual report*, 1911, 2 : 311; Stephens to the *Augusta Chronicle and Sentinel*, June 28, 1852.

[57] American historical association, *Annual report*, 1911, 2 : 316. The announcement, called "Address of the executive committee to the constitutional union party of Georgia," is in the Cobb manuscripts.

While these events were happening, indeed, ever since the disruption of the union party had been threatened by the business of sending delegates to Baltimore, an effort had been afoot to bring together the two wings of the democratic party. Influential democrats of the union party urged this compromise.[58] Cobb advocated a reunion in an open letter.[59] His reasons for favoring a reunion were that the union party of Georgia had been formed for the sole purpose of committing Georgia to the compromise measures of 1850; it had succeeded in its effort and fulfilled its mission; the opponents of the compromise had embraced it and the issue was a dead one, both national parties in convention having adopted compromise platforms. There was, therefore, no reason for the continuance of an organization cut off from affiliation with the national parties, and it was desirable that the two wings of the democracy should forget past differences and work together for the Pierce and King ticket. Several leaders of the other wing were also eager to effect a reconciliation,[60] and for a time it seemed likely that democratic harmony would be restored.[61] A democratic rally was held in Atlanta in September for the purpose of patching up a truce; but it turned out that a large majority of the southern rights leaders were utterly opposed to reconciliation. It had been hoped that at this Atlanta meeting the two Pierce and King tickets in the field (one that of the southern rights democrats, the other representing the democratic wing of the union party) might be fused, with a fair representation to each faction. The southern rights men, however, refused to make any concessions to the unionist minority.[62] The leaders of the union democrats thereupon

---

[58] American historical association, *Annual report,* 1911, 2: 280.
[59] *Ibid.,* 2: 311; Cobb to Thomas Morris, March 7, 1853, *Augusta Chronicle and Sentinel,* April 11, 1853.
[60] American historical association, *Annual report,* 1911, 2: 318, 319.
[61] *Ibid.,* 2: 318.
[62] *Augusta Chronicle and Sentinel,* September 25, 1852, copy of editorial from the *Marietta Union.*

took down their ticket, against the wishes and advice of Cobb.[63] This withdrawal was bitterly resented by a portion of the union democratic press and soon thereafter a new Pierce and King ticket was put out.[64] In the election this ticket polled about 6,000 votes, the southern rights ticket receiving 39,000.

The opposition of the southern rights leaders to reconciliation was due largely to their determination to crush Cobb.[65] Numerous correspondents agree on this point.[66] Forced to support a platform and candidate hateful to them, the extremists vindictively desired to punish Cobb for his part in the situation and for what they regarded as his apostasy to the South. He had met them on their own ground, boldly challenged their favorite dogmas of state sovereignty and secession and had worsted them in the conflict. Now, through the failure of the third party movement, due to the action of Toombs and Stephens, the advantage lay with the former minority on the issues of 1850-1851; and this minority, the majority of the old democratic party of Georgia, used their power in every way possible to hurt Cobb. Every effort was made to win back the rank and file of the union democrats, but Cobb was expressly excluded. In this hue and cry after Cobb, the southern rights leaders were ably assisted by the entire democratic press of Georgia. Even some of the union democratic press was full of bitterness against him, as he was held responsible for the withdrawal of the union Pierce and King ticket.

[63] *Ibid.*, April 6, 1853, Hull to the editor of the *Constitutionalist*.

[64] *Augusta Chronicle and Sentinel,* October 2, 1852. Hopkins Holsey, editor of the *Southern Banner* (Athens), regarded as Cobb's personal organ, was one of the leaders in this movement, and was named as an elector on the new Pierce ticket.

[65] *Augusta Chronicle and Sentinel,* September 18, 1852, quotes the *Savannah Republican*: "The object of the Southern Rights Party is apparent. The leaders have determined to crush Howell Cobb. That is the source of all the difficulty. If he were to die tomorrow, the ticket would be reorganized and everything done to re-unite the party. For his Excellency, they have no terms but such as the executioner gives his victim."

[66] American historical association, *Annual report,* 1911, 2: 271, 307, 308; Fannin to Cobb, April 11, 1852, Cobb manuscripts.

These developments left Cobb politically stranded so far as Georgia politics were concerned. He was forsaken by the whigs and the overwhelming majority of his own party. His position was made clear in 1854 when the legislature was called upon to select a senator to succeed Dawson, the whig incumbent and a candidate for reelection.[67] In the numerous ballotings Cobb's highest vote was thirty-four. The small group of unionists was finally forced to witness the election of one of the most radical of the secessionist group, Alfred Iverson, of Columbus.

Defeated in the senatorial contest, Cobb was returned by his old district, strongly unionist in feeling, to the thirty-fourth Congress and resumed his seat in 1855. He never recovered his popularity with the Georgia democracy. In 1860 the party refused to put his name before the Charleston convention for the presidency;[68] and even at the Montgomery convention of the seceding states, the undying resentment of the southern extremists prevented consideration of his name for the first place in the new government.[69] In embracing the cause of the union in the fifties, Cobb paid the price of political proscription in his native state. No expression of regret has been found anywhere in his writings for having followed the course he elected to pursue. His name deserves an honorable place among the unionist statesmen of the ante bellum period, despite the fact that the sudden and unlooked for revival of sectionalism after 1854 forced him to follow the fortunes of his people.

[67] *Savannah Republican*, January 20, 1854.
[68] Phillips, *Life of Robert Toombs*, 188, 189.
[69] Stephens, *Constitutional view of the late war between the states*, 2 : 331.

4

Conscription in the Confederate States of America, 1862-1865
[1916]

Reprinted from the Military Historian and Economist (*Harvard University Press*), *Vol. I, No. 4, (October, 1916), pp. 419-442.*

IN THE FIRST YEAR OF THE CIVIL WAR, THE ARMIES OF THE Confederate States were composed wholly of volunteers. Facilities for manufacturing were in the rudimentary stage, skilled labor was far from abundant, and consequently great difficulty was experienced in providing munitions, while the Federal blockade prevented their free importation from abroad. It was found, therefore, that volunteering supplied as large a force as could be equipped.[1] No special pressure was felt, as the early engagements were favorable to the Southern cause. But in the spring of 1862 the reinforced and improved Union armies won a number of important victories: the superior numbers of the North were being rapidly recruited, the initial enthusiasm of the South was beginning to wane. The first call for troops had asked for volunteers for twelve months' service. Great difficulty was being encountered in inducing the volunteers for a year to reenlist for three years, and it was feared that the army would melt away when the period of enlistment of the great majority of the soldiers expired in April, 1862. As the end of their term of service approached, we are told that the volunteers grew restive, disci-

---

[1] Jefferson Davis, *Rise and Fall of the Confederate Government*, vol. I, pp. 505-506.

pline relaxed, and it was apparent to the Secretary of War that the army was "passing through successive stages of disorganization to dissolution."[2]

I

Under the circumstances President Davis, in a message to Congress on the 28th of March, 1862, recommended the inauguration of a system of conscription, and Congress, on the 16th of April, 1862,[3] enacted the first legislation on this subject, imposing the obligation of military service for three years on all white males between eighteen and thirty-five years of age who were not legally exempt. The act directed all men of conscript age already in the army whose term of enlistment would expire "before the end of the war," to be kept in service for three years from the date of their original enlistment. All persons subject to conscription and not in service were given a short period of grace in which they might volunteer.

President Davis states[4] that the effect of the new method of raising armies was at once apparent in the increased strength and efficiency of the army. Many victories were won in the summer of 1862, but a sharp check to the triumphant career of Lee's army came at Antietam, on the 17th of September. This defeat was the signal for an extension of the conscript age to forty-five, by Act of the 27th of September.[5] At first President Davis called out only those between thirty-five and forty; but in July, 1863, after Vicksburg and Gettysburg, the act went into full operation.[6]

After the middle of 1863, the end of the Confederacy was only a matter of time. The Northern armies steadily

[2] War of the Rebellion Official Records, Series IV, vol. II, pp. 42-43. (The initial letters O. R. will hereafter be used to indicate this source.)

[3] Public and Private Laws of the Confederate States of America, 1862-1864, pp. 29-32 (J. M. Matthews, editor).

[4] 58th Congress, 2nd sess. Senate Documents, vol. 27. *Journal of the Confederate Senate*, p. 15.

[5] Public and Private Laws of the C. S. A., 1862-1864. pp. 61-62.

[6] O. R. Series IV, vol. II, p. 635.

penetrated the South from west to east, and in the fall of
that year the Federal victory at Missionary Ridge compelled
Bragg to raise the siege of Chattanooga. This important event,
coupled with the diminishing strength of the Southern forces
through desertion, explains the next extension of conscription. In accordance with recommendations in the presidential
message[7] of the 8th of December, 1863, the Confederate
Congress on the 17th of February, 1864, passed a new measure,[8] extending the age limit to include all between seventeen and fifty years of age. The act provided that all persons
between seventeen and eighteen and between forty-five
and fifty might volunteer before conscription and constitute a Reserve for state defense and detail duty; but failing
to volunteer they were to be enrolled and sent to the field.
Another act[9] of the same date authorized the conscription of
free negroes and slaves for such auxiliary services. Free negroes between the ages of eighteen and fifty were made liable
for service in various capacities enumerated in the act, such as
work upon fortifications, in shops, manufacturing munitions,
and in hospitals. Free negroes so used were to be clothed,
fed and paid eleven dollars per month. The Secretary of War
was authorized to hire from owners 20,000 slaves for duty
similar to that required for free negroes. If unable to hire
them, the government was empowered to impress slaves,
liability being assumed in the event of death or loss.

The final step in the extension of compulsory service was
taken, after much argument, on the 13th of March, 1865, when
Congress authorized the conscription of slaves for field service.[10] There was considerable opposition to this measure,
but both President Davis and General Lee advocated it.[11]
The law permitted the enrollment of not more than twenty-

---

[7] Messages and Papers of the Confederacy, vol. I, pp. 370-371. (J. D. Rich-
ardson, editor).
[8] Public and Private Laws of the C. S. A., 1862-1864, pp. 211-215.
[9] Public and Private Laws of the C. S. A., 1862-1864, pp. 235-236.
[10] O. R. Series IV, vol. III. pp. 1161-1162.
[11] Davis, *op. cit.*, vol. I, pp. 518-519; O. R. Series IV, vol. III, pp. 1012-1013.

five per cent of the slaves between the ages of eighteen and forty-five in any state; the status of the slave was in no way to be affected by his conscription, except on the consent of the owner and the state; no slave was to be accepted or recruited except with his own consent and the approval of his master. No evidence has been found of any slaves having actually been sent to the front. The end of the Confederacy was at hand, and by the time the preliminary steps had been taken peace came.

II

The conscription acts called into service all persons of designated ages "who are not exempt by law." The matter of exemption is, therefore, a material part of the conscription system, and it was a subject productive of endless perplexities. On the 21st of April, 1862, five days after the enactment of the first conscription legislation, an exemption act[12] was passed. It declared exempt from enrollment the following principal classes: (1) the physically and mentally unfit; (2) Confederate officials and the higher state officials; (3) mail carriers, telegraph operators, and employees of common carriers; (4) ministers of the gospel, members of college faculties, teachers having as many as twenty pupils; (5) workers in employments essential to the production of munitions, such as iron mines, furnaces, foundries and operatives in cotton and woolen factories.

Immediately on the publication of the exemption act agitation commenced looking to the extension of its scope. The most serious complaint was directed at the failure of Congress to exempt overseers of plantations.[13] Physicians demanded exemption; the Governors of certain states were insistent that all state officials, high and low, be excused from service; exemption was asked for students in theological seminaries and military schools. This pressure resulted in the

---

[12] Public and Private Laws of the C. S. A., 1862-1864, pp. 51-52.
[13] O. R. Series IV, vol. II, pp. 401-402 ; Series IV, vol. I, pp. 1084-1106.

passage of a new act on the 11th of October, 1862.[14] The minutely detailed character of the act was doubtless due to the desire of Congress to settle questions of interpretation that had arisen in connection with the very brief original act. Among the new classes of exempts were: (1) editors of newspapers; (2) postmasters; (3) members of religious societies opposed to service, such as the Quakers. These conscientious objectors were required to furnish substitutes or pay $500 into the public treasury; (4) all physicians; (5) government contractors and their employees; (6) persons engaged exclusively in stock raising were granted one exempt for every 500 head of cattle, one for every 250 head of horses or mules, and one for every 250 head of sheep; (7) one owner or overseer on each plantation of twenty negroes, on which there was no white male adult not liable for military duty.

A second amendatory act[15] was passed on the 1st of May, 1863, apparently intended to stop abuse of the provision exempting overseers. The act required that plantation owners make affidavit that they had been unable to secure as overseers persons not liable to military service, and, furthermore, a payment of $500 per annum was exacted for every overseer exempted. But great pressure was brought to bear on the Conscription Bureau not to enforce this provision, "in view of the great demand for provisions and their scarcity, and of the fact that many persons have made their arrangements for cultivating their farms upon the conditions of the law of the 11th of October, 1862." It was, therefore, decided by the War Department to enroll overseers and temporarily "detail" them for service on plantations.[16]

Another important exemption was made in this act of the 1st of May. Neither of the former acts had met the wishes of the recalcitrant governors of North Carolina and Georgia in the matter of exempting state officials and officers of the

---

[14] Public and Private Laws of the C. S. A., 1862-1864, pp. 77-79.
[15] Public and Private Laws of the C. S. A., 1862-1864, pp. 158-159.
[16] O. R. Series IV, vol. II, p. 582.

state militia. The government at this point surrendered, the new act excusing from service "all state officers whom the Governor of any state may claim to have exempted for the due administration of the government and the laws thereof; but this exemption shall not continue in any state after the adjournment of the next regular session of its legislature, unless such legislation shall by law exempt them from military duty in the provisional army of the Confederate States." This appeal to the people through the legislatures was unsuccessful. In both states the legislatures stood by the Governors.

Another method of escaping service was provided in the original conscription act, section 9 of which extended to conscripts the right to offer substitutes. Such substitutes had to be of the class not liable to conscription and were required to produce certificates of physical soundness; unnaturalized foreigners could not be offered as substitutes, nor could youths under eighteen. Of all classes of soldiers the substitutes were found most troublesome. They deserted in such numbers that the War Department was forced to lay down the rule that if a substitute became lost to the service through any other reason than casualty of war, the principal should immediately become liable for enrollment.[17] Any one claiming exemption because of having provided a substitute was required to exhibit to the conscription officer seeking to enroll him a discharge by the commanding officer of the regiment or command to which the conscript had belonged, or an exemption signed by the Commandant of Conscripts.[18] A good deal of fraud and collusion was practiced in this connection;[19] unscrupulous persons representing themselves to be officers in distant commands drove a thriving business in selling to prospective conscripts discharges on the pretence of having furnished substitutes. It became necessary to employ a detective to ferret out professional substitute agents.[20]

---

[17] O. R. Series IV, vol. II, p. 648.
[18] *Ibid.*, p. 168.
[19] *Ibid.*, p. 808.
[20] *Ibid.*, pp. 582-583.

The problems connected with exemption grew more formidable with every passing month, especially after the middle of 1863. In his report to the President, dated the 20th of November, 1863, the Secretary of War discussed the subject in great detail.[21] He recommended the lessening of the number of details by employing free negroes and slaves where they might be used; the repeal of the exemption acts and the passage of a new measure enrolling every able-bodied man within the ages then prescribed, and then detailing such individuals of the professional and mechanical classes as the best interests of the country seemed to dictate, instead of exempting whole classes; and the absolute prohibition of substitution. On this last point his observations are interesting:

"The law allowing substitutes has proved a means for depleting the Army, while it has done more than any single measure to excite discontent and impatience under service among the soldiers. The persons received as substitutes have proved, for the most part, wholly unreliable; have in many cases, only entered to desert, and often elsewhere again to make sale of themselves with a view to like shameful evasion; while the fact that the wealthy could thus indirectly purchase liberation from the toils and dangers necessary for the defense of the very means that gave them the privilege, and of the country itself, naturally produced among the less fortunate and poorer classes repining and discontent."

This report contains the statement that there were at that time no less than 50,000 principals escaping service through substitution.

President Davis was in entire agreement with Mr. Seddon on this subject, and, in a message to Congress of the 7th of December, 1863,[22] repeated the recommendations of his Secretary of War. Congress shortly thereafter enacted legislation, in December, 1863, and January and February, 1864, disallow-

---

[21] *Ibid.*, pp. 996-998.
[22] Messages and Papers of the Confederacy, vol. I, pp. 370-371.

ing further substitutions and declaring all principals liable for service.[23] The "Rebel War Clerk" Jones notes in his Diary[24] on the 2nd of January that "The speculators and extortioners who hired substitutes are in consternation—some flying the country since the passage of the bill putting them in the army, and the army is delighted with the measure. The petition from so many generals in the field intimidated Congress, and it is believed that the Western army would have melted away in thirty days, if no response had been accorded to its demands by government."

A final modification in the exemption law may be noted at this point. The Act of the 1st of May had required the payment of $500 for every overseer exempted. Confederate money had become practically worthless. Congress, therefore, passed a law on the 17th of February, 1864,[25] requiring the execution by the owner of a plantation of a bond to deliver to the Confederate government one hundred pounds of bacon, or its equivalent, for every slave on the plantation for the direction of which the owners or an overseer was exempted; and that he sell his marketable surplus of grain and provisions to the government or to families of soldiers at prices fixed by the impressment acts. Towards the close of the war landowners in ever increasing numbers seem to have taken advantage of this provision. "Nearly every landed proprietor has given bond to furnish meal, etc., to obtain exemption," says Jones,[26] who was continually harping on the idea that the rich and the slaveholding farmers were shirking service, leaving the fighting to the poorer classes.

The Superintendent of Conscription, in a report[27] of February, 1865, gives a statistical display of all classes of exempts. The total number is slated as 67,054 for the states east of the Mississippi and East Louisiana. This number includes

---

[23] Public and Private Laws of the C. S. A., 1862-1864, pp. 172, 211.
[24] J. B. Jones, *A Rebel War Clerk's Diary*, vol. II, p. 123.
[25] Public and Private Laws of the C. S. A., 1862-1864, vol. II, pp. 213-215.
[26] Jones, *op. cit.*, vol. II, pp. 271, 272.
[27] O. R. Series IV, vol. III, pp. 1101-1110.

18,785 officials certified by governors as necessary for the maintenance of state governments, of whom 13,818 were exempted in Georgia and North Carolina, an indication of the hostility of the governors of those states to conscription. The statement includes no exempts for the Trans-Mississippi states, over which the Bureau of Conscription never exercised authority; and it may be that there is an understatement of the number east of the river. The Bureau had great difficulty in getting reports from subordinate enrolling officers. Professor Schwab estimates the number east of the Mississippi at 100,000, on what authority it is not stated. General Lee, in a letter to President Davis, in September, 1864, states on the authority of General J. L. Kemper, Commander of the Virginia State Reserves, that there were no less than 400,000 exempts in that state alone.[28]

III

The administration of the conscription system was at first under the direct control of the Adjutant and Inspector General's office, a bureau of the War Department. In each state an officer not below the rank of Major was detailed to superintend the work of enrollment.[29] Camps were established in each state for the preliminary instruction of recruits. It was sought to cooperate with state governments by having the actual work of enrolling conscripts performed by officers of the state militia; but in cases where the state governments refused to cooperate, Confederate army officers were to be detailed for the work. A set of instructions issued by the War Department in a General Order[30] of the 3rd of November, 1862, conferred on the officers controlling conscription in the several states the title of "Commandant of Conscripts;" and required the detailing of a commissioned officer for the direction of the work in each Congressional district, and a

---

[28] D. S. Freeman (ed), *Lee's Dispatches to Davis,* p. 298.
[29] O. R. Series IV, vol. I, pp. 1097-1100.
[30] *Ibid.,* Series IV, vol. II, pp. 160-168. General Order No. 82.

non-commissioned officer or private in each county, town, or parish. This order contains two other clauses of importance. First, the administration of conscription west of the Mississippi River was put under the control of the General commanding the Trans-Mississippi Department. The subsequently established Bureau of Conscription operated only east of the river. The records of the Bureau make only casual reference to conscription in the Trans-Mississippi Department, and this paper makes no attempt to treat the subject in that part of the Confederacy. Secondly, enrollments were authorized for particular organizations already in service, and commanding generals of departments or armies in the field were allowed to detail officers for that purpose. There was thus instituted a dual system of conscription, which resulted in much confusion and conflict.

Administrative detail in connection with the work of conscription became so onerous that, in December, 1862, a special Bureau of Conscription[31] was established, as a sub-bureau in the Adjutant and Inspector General's Department. Brigadier General G. J. Rains was made "Superintendent of Conscription," being superseded after five months' service by Brigadier General C. W. Field. In July, 1863, Colonel (later Brigadier General) J. S. Preston became Superintendent, and retained the office until it was abolished early in 1865. The Rebel War Clerk repeatedly states,[32] however, that the real directing force in the Bureau was Assistant Secretary of War, J. A. Campbell, a former justice of the Supreme Court of the United States. He describes Preston as a sinecure-holding aristocrat, inefficient from indolence and ill health. General Preston's administration was characterized throughout by quarrels with the commanding officers in the field over the method of conscription. In one of his first communications[33] to the Secretary of War he stated that the most serious diffi-

[31] *Ibid.*, p. 266. General Order No. 112. Dec. 30, 1862; *Ibid.*, p. 286.
[32] Jones, *op. cit.*, vol. II, pp. 398, 428, 442.
[33] O. R. Series IV, vol. II, pp. 723-726.

culty being encountered in the administration of conscription was the interference with the operations of the Bureau
by officers detailed from the armies to recruit for their individual commands, under the terms of the General Order
above mentioned. General Preston maintained that the whole
system of raising conscript levies was designed by Congress
as a civil process, and throughout his term of office he constantly reiterated his conviction that it was a mistake to allow
the purely military authorities to participate in the work or
to interfere with the operations of the Bureau. His idea was
that the enforcement of a system of compulsory military
service made necessary a careful consideration of many other
problems in addition to the primary one of enrolling recruits.
The industrial organization, he insisted, was quite as important as the military organization; but when conscription was
enforced by military authority, the army officers lost sight
of every consideration except the single one of finding soldiers, and when they were given discretionary power in
passing on questions of detail and exemption it was inevitable
that the public interest should suffer. He believed that the
civil arm of the government was entirely adequate for the
work, attributing the partial failure of the Bureau to a variety of adverse conditions, such as the opposition of state
authorities, the large territory to be covered, the small number of enrolling officers provided, but "above all, the interference, authorized and unauthorized, of military authorities."
He was firm in the conviction that the civil authorities should
have absolute control of the work of providing the armies
and maintaining them, and that the military authorities should
be confined to the task of making the best use of the means
provided them for the purpose of fighting the enemy. In a
letter to Hon. Porcher Miles,[34] a member of Congress, General Preston gave his views in full:

"The true issue is, whether the law of Congress is that con-

[34] *Ibid.,* Series IV, vol. III, pp. 883-886.

scription is to be determined by purely military authority and administered by military force, and on principles of mere military regulation, or whether it is a law covering and protecting civil and personal rights, and at the same time, providing that the wants of the government are to be supplied by a process which, after adjudication, may be enforced by military power. . . . The predominant and pervading principle, inferable from every clause (of the law), is that Congress intended to make a law which would keep as distinct as (under the circumstances of the country) could by possibility be achieved the creation and maintenance of the armies from their organization and movement. . . . But war was not confined to merely the military business to organize, discipline, and movement. War embraces the legislative action and the civil process necessary to the creation of armies; it embraces the Treasury, the Department of Justice, the civil and social institutions, the industries and productions, the support and protection of the people."

The commanding generals, on the other hand, claimed that the red tape established by the Bureau, the interminable appeals allowed from the decisions of subordinate enrolling officers, and the minute attention given to claims for exemption, made the service at times worse than useless. This conflict between the civil and military arms of the service had already become serious before General Preston assumed office. General Joseph E. Johnston, commanding the Department embracing Tennessee, Alabama and Mississippi, had been so persistent in his charges of inefficiency that, in January, 1863, the Bureau had been divested of control of conscription in General Johnston's department and a thoroughgoing system of military conscription had been instituted under the administration of Brigadier General Pillow.[85] General Preston described Pillow's work as a "reign of terror."

The position of the army officer was expressed in the

---

[85] O. R. Series I, vol. XX, pt. 2, pp. 498-499 ; Series IV, vol. II, p. 1020.

following forceful manner by the Adjutant and Inspector General,[36] who was strongly in favor of a change in the method of administering conscription:

"The Bureau has been so far removed from its agents as to lose its control over them. The Bureau, in attempting to investigate and adjudicate cases of every description, coming up from all the cis-Mississippi States, is seeking to accomplish what can only be done with intolerable delay, uncertainty, and confusion. When the cases are gotten into this routine it seems to be the hardest of all possible things to get the men into the Army, for while the cases are dragging their slow length along, the applicants (for exemption) often change their residence or occupation, or somehow their States, or appear to be buried beneath the accumulated office matter. Let no one be surprised that cases should be found pending from six to twelve months, or that the records of conscription should show in a single district twenty-odd hundred conscripts reported and less than one-tenth of the number sent to the Army after the lapse of many months, or that dispassionate judges, well acquainted with the working of the system, should aver that it has kept more men out of the armies than would have sufficed to close the war. Such a system of conscription can only be likened to Milton's Serbonian bog, where armies whole have sunk."

Space is lacking for a further consideration of this subject. Suffice it to say that the views of the army officers finally prevailed, and by an act[37] of the 7th of March, 1865, the Bureau of Conscription was abolished and the Generals of Reserves[38] in the several states were given complete charge of the enforcement of conscription, exemptions and details; the Generals to report direct to the War Department. General

---

[36] *Ibid.*, Series IV, vol. III, pp. 861-862.

[37] *Ibid.*, pp. 1176-1177.

[38] The "General of Reserves" was an office created by the Act of Feb. 17, 1864, establishing a State Reserve to consist of the new classes of conscripts called into service by that act, namely those between 17 and 18 and 45 and 50.

Preston was thus legislated out of a job, and the civil administration of conscription came to an end.

IV

A people so imbued with particularist principles as were the ante-bellum Southerners naturally resented the centralization to which the Confederate government was forced by the exigencies of war. Every extension or proposed extension of the federal authority met with determined opposition from ultra state-rights politicians, unwilling, even in a struggle for independence, to lay aside their cherished conceptions of state sovereignty. Regarding the war as at bottom a clash between two irreconcilable constitutional theories, the state rights people did not propose to endure from a new government evils which had driven them from the old. At various times the President and the governors of most of the states came into conflict over questions growing out of the policy of compulsory service administered by the central government, such as the interference of state courts in releasing conscripts on writs of *habeas corpus;* disagreements as to the necessity of suspending conscription in certain districts; the attempted enrollment of officials of the states and offices of the state militia. To economize space, the subject of state opposition will be confined to North Carolina and Georgia, whose governors proved most troublesome.

Governor Vance, of North Carolina, was especially insistent in the matter of securing exemption for all civil officials of the state. He protested against the enrollment of any state officials whose services he felt were necessary to the due administration of the state government,[39] and maintained that the state authorities, not the Confederate, must be the judges of this necessity. He regarded justices of the peace, constables and the police of towns, among others, as classes whom it was essential to excuse from service.

---

[39] O. R. Series IV, vol. II, pp. 464-466.

To meet this situation and a similar one in Georgia, the revised exemption act[40] of the 1st of May, 1863, was passed, exempting all state officials whom the governor of any state might certify as necessary for the administration of state government. Shortly thereafter the Supreme Court of North Carolina declared,[41] in a test case, that all officers and agents provided by the Constitution of the state or the laws made in pursuance thereof were exempt from conscription, without regard to any act of Congress. The legislature also indicated its approval of the governor's position. He therefore insisted on certifying every office holder and officer of militia, no matter how insignificant the place held might be. In response to a request from the Confederate Senate, the War Department in November, 1864, reported[42] that the total number of persons exempted on the certificates of governors was 18,843, of whom 14,675 were in North Carolina. By the end of the war, however, North Carolina had yielded her primacy in this connection to Georgia.

Governor Brown, of Georgia, was even more insistent than Governor Vance in his determination to prevent what he considered the military despotism sought to be established by President Davis. Six days after the passage of the first conscription act, he protested against it. "The conscription act," he wrote to President Davis,[43] "gives the President the power to enroll the entire militia of the States between eighteen and thirty-five, and takes from the States their constitutional right to appoint the officers and to train the militia. While the act does not leave to the states the appointment of a single officer to command the militia employed in the service of the Confederate States under its provisions, it places it in the power of the President to take a major-general of the militia of a state, if he is not thirty-five years of age, and place him

[40] *Supra,* p. 422.
[41] O. R. Series IV, vol. III, p. 755.
[42] *Ibid.,* p. 851.
[43] *Ibid.,* Series IV, vol I, pp. 1082-1085. Also in Chandler, *Confederate Records of the State of Georgia,* vol. III.

in the ranks of the C. S. Army under the command of a
third lieutenant appointed by the President, and to treat
him as a deserter if he refuses to obey the call and submit to the command of the subaltern placed over him. . . .
This act not only disorganizes the military power of all the
states, but consolidates almost the entire military power of
the States in the Confederate Executive with the appointment of the officers of the militia, and enables him at pleasure
to cripple or destroy the civil government of each State by
arresting and carrying into the Confederate service the officers charged by the State Constitution with the administration of the State government."

A long correspondence ensued, in which Brown contested
the constitutionality of conscription, rehearsing the usual
strict construction doctrines,[44] Davis countering with implied powers.[45] The Constitution, the President contended,
gives Congress the power "To raise and support armies." It
also contains a clause "To make all laws which shall be necessary and proper for carrying into execution the foregoing
powers." Conscription in the opinion of Congress is necessary
and proper: hence it is constitutional.

Doubt as to the constitutionality of the law was settled by
the opinion of the Attorney General of the Confederate
States, and by decisions favorable to the government in the
Confederate District Court (in the absence of a Supreme
Court), and by the decisions of the Supreme Courts of Georgia, Alabama, Virginia, and Texas.[46] Governor Brown then
yielded the point, and no evidence has been found to sustain
Professor Schwab's statement that Brown after these decisions "refused to permit it (conscription) to be carried out
in Georgia, defying the Confederate authorities."[47] It is true
that, in November, 1862, he notified the enrolling officer

---

[44] *Ibid.*, Series IV, vol. I, pp. 1116-1120.
[45] *Ibid.*, pp. 1133-1114.
[46] Schwab, *Confederate States of America*, p. 195.
[47] *Ibid.*, p. 200.

that he would not permit conscription under the recent act extending the age limit to forty-five,[48] but as a matter of fact he did not actually interfere, though he did protect state officers and officers of state militia from enrollment, and declined to render any assistance in carrying the law into effect.

After the unanimous decision of the Supreme Court of Georgia against him in the matter of constitutionality, Governor Brown created much trouble over the question of the enrollment of state officers. Under the exemption act of the 1st of May, 1863, he had the legislature pass a resolution[49] to the effect that all state officers were necessary to the proper administration of state affairs. In this connection the governor became involved in an acrimonous correspondence with Major General Howell Cobb, commanding the State Reserves, General Cobb accusing the governor of making a false certificate as to the necessity of certain classes of officials for the maintenance of civil government.[50] Mutual recriminations flew back and forth, neither party to the controversy disdaining the liberal use of the *argumentum ad hominem*. This correspondence, while it is highly diverting to the reader, had only the effect of making it impossible for the governor to recede from his position.

Several prominent Georgians endorsed Brown's constitutional views on the subject of conscription, among them Alexander H. Stephens,[51] his brother, Linton Stephens,[52] and Robert Toombs.[53] To offset the powerful influence of these men, Senator Benjamin H. Hill made an address before the legislature of Georgia,[54] on the 11th of December, 1862, in which he upheld the constitutionality of conscription and the necessity for compulsion. The effect of Governor Brown's

---

[48] O. R. Series IV, vol. II, p. 170.

[49] *Ibid.*, Series IV, vol. III, p. 345.

[50] *Ibid.*, Series IV, vol. III, p. 419.

[51] U. B. Phillips, (ed). *Toombs, Stephens and Cobb Correspondence*, pp. 597-8. Also H. Cleveland, Stephens, p. 765.

[52] J. D. Waddell, *Life of Linton Stephens*, p. 246.

[53] U. B. Phillips, *Life of Robert Toombs*, p. 248.

[54] B. H. Hill, Jr., *Life of Benjamin H. Hill*, pp. 252, seq.

course was to impede conscription in Georgia and to make the enforcement of the law very difficult. As the Commandant of Conscripts in the state wrote: [55]

"The Executive of the State and his officials and partisans, aided by a few prominent and influential public men in the State, have persistently labored to oppose the execution of these laws and to create public opinion not only hostile to their execution, but commendatory of their evasion. The class of men now liable to conscription, and who have hitherto been kept out of the service, cannot be reached under the present system. Instead of finding their security condemned as dishonorable, they find it approved, if not connived at, by some whose positions ought to be a warrant of a different course of conduct."

V

It was to have been expected that the element of the population who were unwilling to volunteer for service would go to any length to avoid compulsion. Family physicians discovered physical disabilities among their clients to such an alarming extent that it became necessary to set up medical examining boards of non-resident physicians; minor state offices suddenly acquired a desirability theretofore unknown;[56] it was charged that people made a rush into industrial employments which afforded exemption. Some fifty thousand persons secured temporary immunity by buying substitutes. But the total number who evaded service by taking advantage of legal avenues of escape was small in comparison with the number of deserters and those who escaped by flying on the approach of enrolling officers and hiding out in swamps and mountains.

In the fall of 1862 Commandants of Conscripts in the several states began to report trouble in the enforcement of the law. In Alabama an enrolling officer was killed while attempt-

---

[55] O. R. Series IV, vol. III, p. 1049.
[56] *Ibid.*, p. 346.

ing to enforce the act. "The consequence is," reported the Commandant,[57] "that the impunity with which enrolling officers can be defied has emboldened opposition, until now the evil has increased to such magnitude as to threaten the loss to the Government of a large share of the advantages that might result from a vigorous enforcement of the conscription. . . . I am subjected to the daily mortification of receiving reports from enrolling officers of inability to execute the law without being able to afford them any assistance."

In December of that year the Governor of Alabama reported[58] to the War Department that an armed mob in Randolph County had compelled the jailer to surrender the keys and had liberated captured deserters.

The contiguous mountain sections of North and South Carolina, Tennessee, and Georgia were from the first an area in which it was particularly difficult to enforce conscription. The people of this region were small non-slaveholding farmers, strongly imbued with the Unionist spirit. To political disaffection was added suffering on account of the absence of a large part of the men, the breadwinners. In the winter of 1862-63 the State Senators and Representatives of the Tenth District of North Carolina, in a memorial[59] addressed to President Davis, requested the suspension of conscription in that section, and made so convincing a plea that the request was granted. This western part of the state, it was alleged, had already sent to the army by volunteering and conscription a number almost equal to the voting population, and if the remaining men of conscript age were called out, nothing short of starvation would result to helpless women and children. "Most of the cases of desertion among the soldiers from this section have been produced," states the memorial "by the suffering of their families and

[57] *Ibid.*, Series IV, vol. II, p. 207.
[58] *Ibid.*, p. 258.
[59] *Ibid.*, p. 247.

parents at home." This condition of affairs seems to have been typical of all the mountainous regions.

Evasion and desertion became more prevalent in 1863. The Superintendent of Conscription informed the Secretary of War that in every state of the Atlantic Coast deserters and evaders were banding together under arms to resist arrest.[60] Enrolling officers were being shot and communities terrorized. General Pillow, in charge of conscription in Alabama, wrote[61] in July that there were from 8,000 to 10,000 deserters in the mountains of that state, many of whom had deserted the second, third, or even fourth time. In another communication General Pillow says that these deserters were so well armed and organized and were so numerous as to hold the citizen population in terror. "They rob, burn, and murder the unarmed and defenseless population of the country with impunity." The disposition was said to be prevalent among the people of Alabama to afford shelter and protection to deserters.

Similar reports of numerous deserters congregating in northern and central Mississippi were made in 1863 by the Commandant of Conscripts.[62] In North Carolina, also, conscripts, renegades, and "Tories" were terrorizing the countryside, breaking into "smokehouses," killing cattle, sheep and hogs.[63] In this state, deserters were reported to be armed and brigaded, and to have raised the United States flag.[64] Governor Vance in September issued a proclamation, reciting the fact that a number of meetings had been held in various parts of the state in which threats of combined resistance to the government were made. Jones notes in September that in one of the northern counties of Georgia the deserters and Tories had defeated the Home Guard sent against them; that disaffection was growing in Tennessee,

[60] *Ibid.*, p. 607.
[61] *Ibid.*, pp. 680-681.
[62] *Ibid.*, pp. 681-682.
[63] *Ibid.*, pp. 732; 733-734.
[64] Jones, *op. cit.*, vol. II, p. 42.

North Carolina, Mississippi, and Georgia. "All our armies seem to be melting away by desertion faster than they are enlarged by conscription."[65]

General Lee wrote[66] in August to President Davis that desertions were so numerous from the Army of Northern Virginia that, in his opinion: "Nothing will remedy this great evil which so much endangers our cause except the rigid enforcement of the death penalty in future in cases of conviction." Judge Campbell, Assistant Secretary of War, thought at this time that: "The condition of things in the mountain districts of North Carolina, South Carolina, Georgia and Alabama menaces the existence of the Confederacy as fatally as either of the armies of the United States."[67]

Conditions grew worse in 1864 and 1865. Reports from Commandants of Conscripts and other officials were similar to those already quoted except that resistance was now more determined, as the gangs of deserters had grown larger and the means of apprehending them less powerful. The most intelligent and best organized resistance to conscription in the last year of the Confederacy came to light in Virginia.[68] A secret society was organized with signs and passwords, to give aid to the enemy and shield members from conscription. The members were obligated to encourage desertion and to pass or harbor all deserters, escaped prisoners and spies. The stronghold of this traitorous society was in southwest Virginia, and consisted, of course, of people of the poorer sort, though some men of position were implicated. At the time the activities of the society were brought to the notice of the government by detectives, a movement was on foot looking to the formation of a new state of Southwest Virginia and secession from the mother state. A prominent lawyer, Mr. N. F. Bocock, was sent to investigate the situation. He reported that the evidence was conclusive, but that it would

[65] *Ibid.*, pp. 34-35.
[66] Freeman (ed), *op cit.*, p. 122.
[67] O. R. Series IV, vol. II, p. 786.
[68] O. R. Series IV, vol. III, pp. 802-846.

be impossible to secure convictions. On his recommendation President Davis suspended the writ of *habeas corpus* in that region.[69]

No more difficult problem confronted the Confederate government than the matter of desertion and evasion. The arrest of deserters was a function of the Bureau of Conscription. As long as desertion was confined to isolated cases, it was a simple matter for the enrolling officers to arrest the fugitives and return them to the ranks; but as the practice of fleeing from the army became more general and as deserters began to congregate in inaccessible places, under arms and thoroughly organized, it was easy for the renegades to drive off the enrolling officers, and the Commandants of Conscripts had no adequate force to handle the situation. The reports from which quotations have been given were principally taken from communications sent by enrolling officers, demanding assistance. The problem began to demand the serious attention of the government in the summer of 1862, when a General Order[70] was issued, containing the first of a series of remedial measures. Employees of railroad companies were authorized and requested to examine the furloughs of soldiers traveling by rail and to arrest deserters. A reward of thirty dollars was offered for each deserter delivered to an officer or fifteen dollars for each one jailed. In the following January, Congress passed an act[71] charging sheriffs of counties with the duty of returning deserters and fixing a penalty for their failure to do so. Sheriffs were authorized to summon the *posse comitatus* to assist them if necessary. In April, 1863, another act was passed,[72] imposing a penalty for desertion, the minimum being one year's confinement in the penitentiary, the maximum, death. President Davis, in August, 1863, tried the experiment of granting

[69] *Ibid.*, pp. 819-820.
[70] *Ibid.*, Series IV, vol. II, p. 14.
[71] *Ibid.*, pp. 763-765.
[72] *Ibid.*, p. 496.

amnesty to all deserters who would return to the colors within twenty days.[73] Finally, on the 15th of February, 1864, Congress authorized[74] the suspension of the writ of *habeas corpus* where the situation with regard to desertion made it advisable.

None of these expedients was successful. The only remedy was a strong military force to support the Commandants of Conscripts, but the depleted condition of the armies made details for this purpose out of the question. The only period when any considerable success was obtained in returning deserters was during the year when General Pillow was directing conscription in Tennessee, Alabama, and Mississippi. He organized about twenty companies of conscripts, nonconscripts and exempts, attacked the deserters in their strongholds, and captured and returned to the army from 6,000 to 8,000 deserters.[75]

The futility of all efforts to cure desertion was revealed in a communication[76] of Superintendent Preston, dated the 3rd of March, 1865, in which he recommended that the entire civil machinery of the states be brought to bear on the problem, that special courts be established for the trial of deserters, and that a special force to include the State Reserves be used for the capture of deserters. The formidable character of the problem may best be judged from the words of the Superintendent:

"I assume that the matter of returning deserters to the Army is one of the greatest and most pressing necessities now upon the country, the importance of which no terms can exaggerate. That there are over 100,000 deserters scattered over the Confederacy; that so common is the crime it has, in popular estimation, lost the stigma which justly pertains to it, and therefore the criminals are everywhere shielded by

---

[73] *Ibid.*, p. 687.
[74] Public and Private Laws of the C. S. A., 1862-1864, pp. 187-189.
[75] O. R. Series IV, vol. II, pp. 805, 819-820 ; 963.
[76] *Ibid.*, Series IV, vol. III, pp. 1119-1120.

their families and by the sympathies of many communities. They form the numerical majority in many localities."

VI

The essential facts in connection with the system of compulsory military service in the Confederacy have now been given. Whether the results of conscription may be regarded as having been worth the exertion, internal dissension, and opposition it aroused is doubtful. Tested by the result in terms of numbers conscripted, the showing of the Conscription Bureau was not impressive. In the final report[77] of Superintendent Preston, purporting to summarize the activities of the Bureau from the beginning of February, 1865, the total number of men sent to the armies by the Bureau is given as 81,993. This report does not, however, include any men sent from the states of Texas or Arkansas, and only 81 from Louisiana; nor does it include any conscripts sent from Alabama, Mississippi, or West Tennessee in 1863, in which year the control of the service in those states was withdrawn from the Bureau. The figures, therefore, are a patent and serious understatement of the facts. During the period covered by the report, 72,292 men volunteered, under clauses of the conscription acts leaving the way open for volunteering for a limited time. General Preston claims, with some justice, that these volunteers were such in name only, since they had volunteered practically under compulsion in order to escape the odium of being conscripted; and maintains that they should be credited to conscription. Of course the Superintendent's contention will not hold in the case of young boys coming of military age during the war. At any rate, the volunteers added to the conscripts make a total of 154,000. This is a small percentage of the total number of soldiers in the Confederate armies. Just what the total was is a matter of controversy. Colonel Livermore's estimate fixed the number at 1,082,119, while a leading Southern authority, Colonel R. C. Wood, maintains that

600,000 would cover all levies. Accepting the latter estimate as affording the most favorable possible showing for conscription (a procedure which more than makes up for the manifest inaccuracy in the Superintendent's report of the number of conscripts), conscription appears to have put into the army not more than twenty-five per cent of the total. But it is unfair to credit conscription with having augmented the armies even to that extent, because the conscripted classes were confessedly almost worthless as fighting material, and no doubt the 100,000 deserters admitted by General Preston to be at large were principally conscripts. Compulsory service was, furthermore, a weakening force in that it brought conflicts with the states, which led to half-hearted support in some instances and did much to make service in the army unpopular. Another untoward result may be laid to the door of the system as organized; the very lax laws of exemption provided an easy and more or less honorable avenue of evasion, thereby keeping out of the armies thousands who might otherwise have been forced by public opinion to volunteer.

It was perhaps unavoidable that a new government, hard pressed by a superior foe, with no time for working out a sound system of compulsory service that would utilize to the best advantage the strength of the Confederate States, should have committed serious errors; and it is difficult to avoid the conclusion that compulsion was, as administered, a failure. There is, however, against this view one consideration of first importance. The Confederacy might have collapsed in the spring of 1862 but for the resort to conscription. The twelve months for which the overwhelming majority of the soldiers had volunteered was about to expire, reenlistment was progressing slowly, and the reason why the first conscription act came when it did, in April, 1862, was to catch the men whose term of service had nearly ended. It cannot be doubted that the most important service conscription rendered was to keep in the armies the men of conscript age already there—a fact which must always be kept in mind by one who would justly estimate the value of conscription in Confederate military history.

PART TWO

GEORGIA GOVERNMENT AND FINANCES

5

Legislative Representation
in Georgia
[1925]

An address delivered in 1925 before the annual convention of the Georgia League of Women Voters in Atlanta.

THE SUBJECT ON WHICH I AM ASKED TO ADDRESS YOU tonight does not lend itself well to quotations from the English poets, nor to brilliant sallies of wit and humor. Few matters are so dreary as discussions of constitutional reform. Yet on someone must fall the task of keeping before the public those problems of fundamental importance which condition our social progress; and you, as a body of serious-minded women, organized to prepare yourselves the better to exercise the franchise, may be assumed to have come here expecting the worst in the way of entertainment. At any rate, I must shift to your President at least a share of the blame for the sadness of the occasion, for she suggested the topic for discussion.

Those of us who think at all about the status of affairs in Georgia may be divided into two sharply contrasted groups. One group thinks largely in terms of the past—of the glorious part Georgia has played in the nation's history, of Georgia's great statesmen and military heroes. They are continually prattling about things in which Georgia is first; their favorite saying is, "It's great to be a Georgian."

The other group, while yielding nothing in love for Georgia or in respect for her great traditions, and while admitting that remarkable progress along many lines has been made during the past few decades, looks outside of Georgia and sees that in comparison with other states, many of them not nearly so favored by nature, Georgia has woefully failed to keep the pace. The list of matters in which Georgia is last would probably be quite as impressive as the list of her firsts, should one take the trouble to itemize them. But I shall take time to mention only one, the matter of higher education. No informed person will dispute the statement that in proportion to her means Georgia ranks in this respect absolutely last. The physical equipment and the maintenance funds of the University are a reproach to our state. The finger of scorn is constantly being pointed at Georgia for her backwardness in this and many other matters.

Now I desire to place myself squarely in the second group. Not that I would shout out Georgia's shortcomings from the hilltops of Maine or California, or write anything for outside publication that reflects on Georgia; but here among ourselves I feel that no truly patriotic Georgian should blind himself to the patent truth. I have little patience with unthinking, undiscriminating optimism. We will never improve ourselves by self-praise or boasting. We might as well admit that we are a backward state, face the facts bravely and make a searching inquiry into the causes of the situation.

I have pondered this subject a great deal in an effort to put my finger on the trouble. I have listened with impatience and incredulity to people who tell me that we can make no great progress in Georgia because our masses are an inferior people with no abiding concern for the higher things of life; that our leaders are incapable, spineless and self-seeking; that our wealthier citizens have taken a determined stand against tax reform, are able to block reform measures, and that, lacking money, our institutions must languish. I question all such ideas. I believe the people of Georgia are the same sort of p.. le as are to be found in North Carolina, South

Carolina, Virginia, Kentucky and Texas, states that are leaving us far behind in all matters of social progress. The citizens of these states have no better heritage than have we, no finer traditions of public service, no greater wealth or intelligence. What then is the explanation of our situation?

To my mind the answer is to be found, at least in part, in the threatened breakdown of representative government in Georgia. I feel that the Legislature does not truly reflect the will of the people. Let me illustrate. The last three Governors of Georgia, Dorsey, Hardwick and Walker, advocated in their campaigns tax reform as the most urgent need of the state. The people elected them to office. They appointed able Commissions to make a study of the tax problem. These Commissions made reports which could have revolutionized our finances. Their recommendations were scientific, sound, and practical. The Legislature, in a half dozen or more regular sessions and one special session, has utterly failed to put through the important changes in the tax laws proposed in the Governors' recommendations or the reports of the Tax Commissions, though I believe the intelligent people of Georgia ardently desire reform. Why is this so? I may be wrong, but I am convinced that at least a part of the trouble is to be found in the fact that the legislature is not so constituted as to register accurately the will of the majority.

Our legislature is defective in two main particulars—first, it has entirely too many members; and, secondly, the seats in the General Assembly are distributed in such a way as to enable a minority of the people to elect a majority of the members. Let us consider these two problems in detail.

I

No one could have spent hours in the gallery of the House, as I have, without being impressed by the great difficulty the House experiences in carrying on its work by reason of the great number of members. The place is disorderly beyond belief. The utmost efforts of the Speaker rarely suffice to quiet the clamor long enough for one to hear distinctly what is going on. The Speaker is always under the greatest strain in keeping down the tumult of voices and in preventing members from wandering about and engaging in conversation while the session is in progress. Passing over to the Senate, one appears to enter a new world, so calm and unruffled are the proceedings. The contrast is impressive. With no difference whatever in personnel, the Senate performs its functions with a fraction of the noise, delay and excitement which result from the unwieldy size of the House.

The preposterously large membership of the lower chamber entails interminable delay in expediting business. Every member has of course the right to be heard, and the days are frequently spent in endless repetition of similar views. If the ayes and nays are demanded when a measure is put upon its passage, an extraordinary amount of time is consumed in calling the roll, each one of the members being entitled to a few minutes in which to explain his vote. Should a filibuster be inaugurated, the constant calling of ayes and nays on motions eats up the hours.

A further disadvantage in a large membership is that the standing committees are huge. Every member must have committee assignments and there is great pressure on the Speaker for membership on the important committees. A meeting of the Ways and Means Committee or of the Appropriations Committee may bring together a group as large as the entire legislative assembly should be. Sometimes it is hard to get a quorum and sometimes there are so many present with views to express that it is difficult for the Committees to report out bills.

Of more fundamental importance than any of these considerations is the fact that in so large a mass of members (a majority of whom perhaps sit for only one session and never return) leadership is slow in developing. Since we do not have a two-party system with a natural cleavage running between the "ins" and the "outs," the membership tends to fall into groups or blocs, each with its separate, primary interests. The House sometimes resembles a number of rather distinct flocks without shepherds. There are always in the House men of real political ability, but it is difficult for them to get into stride in so large and inert a mass of members. Many members freely admit the truth of these statements. We have always in Georgia suffered from too large a House. As far back as 1833 the Legislature passed a resolution calling upon the Governor to summon a constitutional convention for the express and sole purpose of reducing the size of the Legislature, but nothing came of it.

Georgia's House of Representatives numbers 207 members. The average for all the states is 125. If we exclude Connecticut, Massachusetts, New Hampshire and Vermont where the representative situation is even worse than in Georgia, the national average is 102, or less than half the Georgia number. Texas with nearly twice our population manages to do famously on 142 members; New York, with four times our population, has only 150 members; of the Southern states in Georgia's class with respect to area and population, Alabama has 106 members, Kentucky 100, and Virginia 100.

The Georgia Senate is not unwieldy in size, being limited to 50 members. Probably 30 members would be adequate.[1] The Senate, however, is defective in the distribution of seats, as will appear later. The bi-cameral system is supposed to be a check on hasty legislation. Our Georgia practice often leads to lengthy disputes between the two houses and the holding up of necessary legislation. However, this is an academic question since the bi-cameral system is here to stay. A more practical suggestion is that the terms of the Senators should be four years, as was the situation before the consti-

---

[1] [The 1945 Constitution raised the number of Senators from 50 to 54. *Ed.*].

tution of 1877 was adopted; moreover, half of the Senators should be elected bi-annually, so as to give some continuity to the body. At present, the Senate is elected for two years only. Since the Legislature meets bi-annually, the Senators serve for the one term only. They are then ineligible for re-election for several years. The consequence is that every Senate is an entirely new body. In practice, however, this situation is not so bad as it seems, since experienced members are constantly passing from one house to the other. (You will understand that there are several counties, usually three, in a senatorial district. The counties rotate in nominating the Senators. This system automatically retires the Senator at the end of his term. He then frequently stands for the House in his county, holds his seat until his county's turn to elect the Senator comes around again, and then runs for the Senate.)[2]

II

The second major defect in our Legislature is that the seats are distributed on a wrong principle, in that membership is based on geographic lines rather than on population. In the lower house of our national Congress, as you know, representation is entirely based on population. This is the only fair basis for distributing the seats, any other method being highly undemocratic.

Our Georgia system of basing representation on political units (counties) rather than on population is of English origin. For centuries the House of Commons was composed of two members for each county and two from each borough or town. This system disregarded the size and relative importance of the counties and towns. Miserable little hovels

---

[2] [This rotation rule is not contained in the Constitution but is a rule of the State Democratic Party. "The primary election is thereby confined to the county whose turn it is to nominate a Senator to the district. This rule cannot be waived without the consent of the Democratic executive committee of each county in the district." A. B. Saye, *A Constitutional History of Georgia* (Athens: University of Georgia Press, 1948), p. 401, n. 10. *Ed.*].

with a handful of voters, and some with none at all, had representation in Parliament, while the great industrial cities which had sprung up since the Industrial Revolution had none. This iniquitous system made social progress almost impossible. The system was abolished by the reform of 1832, and the effects were immediate.

When the American colonies threw off their allegiance to Great Britain and established state governments, they naturally adopted the then current British practice. In the South, representation has always been based on the county unit idea. At the present time it prevails in all Southern states except Kentucky, Texas, and Virginia, as it indeed prevails in some form or another in one third of all the states of the Union. Now it must be clearly understood that wherever representation is based on the county as a unit, misrepresentation is unavoidable, for some counties will grow faster than others and the larger counties will suffer in the distribution of seats. The system will tend to approximate the English conditions before 1832.

In Georgia, county unit representation works worse than in most other states because of our preposterously large number of counties. Texas, with 245 counties, is the only state which has more counties than Georgia, and you do not need to be reminded that Texas is more than four times as large in area. For many years practically every Legislature has created new counties and every new county has added members to the Legislature. The result is an unmanageable House of Representatives.

Moreover, we must not lose sight of the fact that we are in a democratic country. The democratic theory is that one man's vote is worth as much as that of any other man, millionaire or pauper, scientist or moron, saint or sinner: each man, we hold, is entitled to his vote. We boast of this political equality. Yet in apportioning the seats in the House, we largely ignore the principle of equality. We say in effect that the 5,000 people in Rabun County shall have the same representation as the 10,700 in the adjoining county of Habersham; that the 3,200 in Echols shall be entitled to one third as many representatives as the 232,000 in Fulton. The present constitution makes a concession, though an entirely inadequate one, by giving three representatives to each of the eight most populous counties, and two to each of the thirty next in size. This arrangement, though an improvement, falls far short of justice.

I have tabulated the population of the thirty-eight counties which are granted extra representation. Their total in 1920 happened to be almost exactly one half of that of the entire state. This one half of the people elected 84 members, the other half 123 members, or 50 per cent more.

This does not, however, give a sufficiently arresting picture of the situation, because a grave inequality in representation exists among the 38 preferred counties. Muscogee, with a population of 44,195, has three members, the same as Fulton with 232,000; Laurens, with 39,000, is represented by three members, whereas Bibb County, almost adjacent, has three members for its 71,000. Fulton is especially badly treated. With 8 per cent of the population, she should be entitled to 16 members instead of 3.

All this inequality emphasizes the unfairness of representation on a county unit basis. Some states have gotten away from this evil by creating representative districts consisting of groups of counties on the same lines as our Georgia Senate districts. A large number of states definitely fix the number of seats in the legislative body, House and Senate. The Senate is often a fixed proportion of the House, usually one half or one third. If new counties are created in these states, such counties are added to the already existing representative districts, no additional members of the House being authorized.

The existence of a large city in a state does of course present a problem. The people outside the city do not want the legislature dominated by the metropolis; nor is the city disposed to be patient under the control of the rural sections. States differ widely in the degree to which they today recognize the claims of the larger city. In several states efforts have been made, more or less successfully, to give fair representation to populous counties or cities. But the fact remains that representation without adequate reference to population is clearly out of harmony with our ideas of democracy and popular government. If the representative assembly does not actually represent the people, it provides no reflection of their will, and the vote of the progressive people in the cities is liable to be thwarted by the entrenched interests of over-represented small counties.

III

I think that Georgia should reform its system of representation. This can only be done by a constitutional convention. The Constitution requires membership in such a convention to be based on population, not on the county unit system. Only through a convention of delegates so chosen would there be any chance of fairly treating the large counties. Such a convention might reduce the House to 100 seats. The counties should be grouped together into 100 districts each comprising about one per cent of the state population, which districts should be reorganized after each decennial census so as to preserve their essential equality. (Of course a large county like Fulton would comprise several districts determined by ward lines). The Senate districts should remain approximately what they are in number, but the counties should be regrouped so as to contain about twice as many people as the House districts.[3]

[3] [According to the Constitution of 1877, a constitutional convention could only be called by a two-thirds vote of the total membership of both houses; as a result, several attempts to call such a convention prior to 1945 failed. The Constitution of 1945 was the work of a Commission for revision headed by the Governor, which "gave Georgia the distinction of being the first State in the

While I regard the reconstitution of the Legislature as the most important task of a constitutional convention, there are many other tasks which it should undertake. First among them is the matter of taxation. The hands of the Legislature are quite effectively tied by clauses in the constitution which limit taxation to the ad valorem system with the five mill maximum and restrict the power of the Legislature to increase the debt of the state.[4] It should be remembered that the Constitution of 1877 was made just at the close of the Reconstruction era. For a time in that period our Southern legislatures had been controlled by carpetbaggers, scalawags, and negroes who indulged in an orgy of spending public money. Woodrow Wilson once described the situation as "a carnival of crime under the form of law." The legislatures issued state bonds for railway projects and stole the proceeds with no railroads built; the credit of the states was pledged to various road-building schemes; the State of Georgia was saddled with a liability of thirty million dollars on the endorsement of railway securities; large sums were voted for the most senseless and extravagant purposes. It was only natural that an outraged people, after getting control over their own affairs and with the memory of these days still fresh, should have gone to extremes in tying the hands of the Legislature. While we therefore can easily understand the influences at work and sympathize with the feeling of the men of that day, we have to admit now that their work was so thoroughly done as to hurt the progress of Georgia most seriously. Robert Toombs, the leading spirit of the constitutional convention, spoke the truth when he said "the convention had locked the doors of the Treasury and given the key to the people." We

Union to adopt a constitution proposed by a commission rather than a constitutional convention." (Saye, *Constitutional History of Georgia*, p. 397). It is not surprising that "fully ninety per cent of the provisions of the Constitution of 1945 were taken from the amended Constitution of 1877" (*ibid.*), including all the provisions for legislative representation. *Ed.*].

[4][The Constitution of 1945 left these limitations unchanged, though it liberalized the provisions with regard to counties and municipalities. *Ed.*].

must reform our Legislature so as to make it truly representative, and then give it a large measure of freedom of taxation[5] if Georgia is to emerge from her present plight.

---

[5] [The constitutional limitations applied (and apply) only to *ad valorem* property taxes. The freedom of the legislature to open up new sources of taxation was never limited, and the great development of Georgia public finances (toward which Dr. Brooks did much spade work) took place through the introduction of new types of taxes, as was indeed the case throughout the nation. *Ed.*].

6

Georgia Tax Reform

[1935-1952]

[*The following selections from Dr. R. P. Brooks' copious writings on matters of Georgia public finance recall the twenty years of struggle for a reform of the revenue system that began during the Great Depression and eventually led to the emergence of a sound financial structure. The excerpts are arranged by subject matter and are preceded by a retrospective survey prepared by Dr. Brooks for this volume. Ed.*]

[1952] LOOKING BACK: A SURVEY

WITH THE ADOPTION OF A GENERAL SALES TAX IN 1951, THE great transformation of Georgia's revenue system that began in the 1930's has been almost completed. Economic forces which changed both the agricultural and the industrial structure have been the main factor in this transformation, as I have shown in my monograph *The Financial History of Georgia, 1732-1950.* Another factor was the reform movement, widely supported by the most active and progressive civic organizations and citizens in the state, to which I have tried to contribute over the years by discussing urgent matters of taxation in speeches, in the daily papers, and in special publications and reports.[1] The following summary gives a list of the tax problems that have arisen in my time, together with my attitudes, and the actions taken so far.

---

[1]It was Professor J. H. T. McPherson, the leading authority on Georgia public finance at the time, who first directed my attention to the need for tax reform in the state.

1. *The State Income Tax.* It was adopted in 1929 but radically improved in 1931. I always favored the income tax since it tends to distribute the tax burden according to ability to pay. I favored linking the state income tax with the Federal income tax to combat tax evasion and to improve the method of collection.

2. *Property Tax Limitation.* In 1935 a constitutional amendment to place a 15-mill overall limit on the property tax rates imposed by the state, municipalities, and counties was before the people. It would have ruined the financial support of the cities and counties of Georgia, as it had already done in Ohio. I made many speeches on the subject. This was one of the hardest fights of my life. The amendment was defeated.

3. *Allocations.* This is the practice of setting apart certain revenues for specific objectives. The time came when upward of 60 per cent of all state revenue was thus allocated. In other words, the General Assembly had largely abdicated its control over expenditures. The services enjoying allocations were always in clover while the others, including education, were constantly in dire need. This matter I discussed in many speeches, in a series of articles in *The Atlanta Georgian* in 1934, and especially in *Georgia State Taxes*, written for the Citizens' Fact Finding Movement in 1938, and again in 1939 in the pamphlet *Georgia Faces a Financial Crisis.* The new state Constitution of 1945 prohibits further allocations.

4. *Classification of Intangibles.* Intangibles should be taxed, but at low rates. It was therefore proposed that property should be classified for purposes of taxation. I advocated this change over a long period of time. A constitutional amendment permitting classification was adopted in 1937.

5. *Abandonment of the State Levy on Property.* For many years I advocated reform in the assessment procedures in connection with the taxation of property—procedures which

caused gross inequalities, aided tax evasion, and deprived the state of control over assessment practices. But I always disapproved of abandoning the state levy altogether because it would manifestly benefit big tax payers, such as out-of-state insurance companies, which own immense areas in Georgia. The Governor has recently reduced the state levy from 5 mills to a small fraction of one mill, which is tantamount to abandoning it altogether.

6. *Nuisance Taxes.* I have been in favor of abolishing the licensing system because it yielded very little, cost a good deal to administer, and was a nuisance to the taxpayer. These nuisance taxes were abolished by the General Assembly in 1951.

7. *The Homestead Amendment.* I was opposed to the amendment which exempted homesteads from all ad valorem taxes to the value of $2,000, with power to the General Assembly to reduce the exemption to $1,250. The amendment was adopted in 1937 and it ruined the tax base of many counties.

8. *Tax Exemptions to New Industries.* I opposed granting such exemptions. These are prohibited by the new state constitution of 1945.

9. *State Liquor Monopoly.* I advocated a state monopoly of the liquor business in 1946 and I still favor it as a better way of controlling the liquor traffic.

10. *General Sales Tax.* For many years I fought the general sales tax on the ground of its regressivity. However, when the state expenditures increased so enormously after the war, there seemed no other way to raise the money needed, and in the light of the fact that the low income groups received great benefits from the enlarged expenditures (in the form of improved educational facilities, pensions, etc.) I changed my attitude. In 1946 and 1949 I came out for the tax, which was adopted by the General Assembly in 1951.

11. *The Poll Tax.* I advocated abandonment of the poll tax. The General Assembly abolished it in 1945.

In summary, the above survey indicates that the recent reforms have given Georgia a fairly well balanced system of taxation, one that will probably endure for many years. Two major defects remain to be cured, both of an administrative character. In the first place, the state government has throughout the history of the state failed to provide adequate machinery for a scientific assessment of the property tax, to the end that the burden of this tax might be more equitably distributed among the counties and the individual citizens. This problem has become of minor importance to the state government, now that we have abandoned the property tax for state purposes. The other matter yet to be handled, and one of far greater importance, is the establishment of state supervision of local finance operations, involving annual reports and state auditing. These two open problems are discussed at length in my monographs *The Georgia Property Tax* (1950) and *State Supervision of Local Fiscal Affairs in Georgia* (1948). Suffice it to say that the tax reform movement should carry the fight for better balanced and better administered taxes to the county and local level where the main work still remains to be done.

[1935] THE CALL FOR REFORM[1]

I feel that we are taking as much as we should from the people in the way of taxes, but the burden is most inequitably distributed, and in other respects our system of taxation also leaves much to be desired. We levy too heavy a burden on real property without any regard to the income it yields to the owner, this merely because such property cannot be concealed. We fail to tax equitably intangible forms of property such as stocks, bonds, and mortgages. We allow

---

[1] From an unpublished address, delivered in Atlanta, Georgia, March 18, 1935, before the Business Women's club.

thousands with sizable money incomes to escape our income tax; the rates of our income tax are too low and the exemptions too high; we have no inheritance tax; we permit the counties and towns to tax property as they please and require no reports or audits of their activities; our system is such that there are gross inequalities in educational and other services among the counties of the state; we support an army of unnecessary officials because of our absurdly high number of counties. We permit our principal source of revenue to be monopolized by one interest, the highways, whereas it should be used principally for general purposes. The whole system is just about as bad as it can be and the people are naturally restive under it. Surely in Georgia a healthier sense of economic and social security would result from a drastic recasting of our entire tax program. The Georgia system of taxes has been built up or rather has grown up almost wholly without reference to the only scientific criterion of taxation, namely, ability to pay.

[1935] THE PROPERTY TAX AMENDMENT

The Issue[2]

The time has come when the owners of real property in Georgia are in rebellion and are agitating for a constitutional amendment to impose a severe and rigid limitation upon the municipalities and counties as well as the state, by providing for an overall or blanket property tax rate of 15 mills, five for county purposes, five for municipal purposes, and five specifically for schools.

I should say first of all that I am in entire sympathy with those who would break down the general property tax and bring about a better distribution of the tax burden. There is little question, I think, of the justice or reasonableness of the attitude of the advocates of limitation. My opposition

---

[2] From a speech before the Albany, Georgia Rotary Club on April 9, 1936. Condensed.

Georgia Tax Reform

to the amendment arises from the belief that so drastic a cutting of the rate will bring about a calamitous decrease in revenue and that there are no satisfactory substitutes available in Georgia. If our state were anything more than a poor agricultural community; if it had great cities with flourishing manufacturing enterprises producing a large volume of taxable wealth; if it had boundless natural resources in oil and other minerals; if it were a populous state with a relatively high per capita income, I would favor the amendment. But Georgia has none of these resources in any important degree. There is no chance that I can see of replacing the anticipated revenue losses, and the only result I forsee is a serious reduction of our already small expenditures for socially necessary functions.

Clearly the state would be forced to impose a general sales tax, if the amendment were adopted. But a sales tax is such an unfair substitute for the property tax that it should not be adopted. In order to prevent the imposition of a sales tax you should vote against the constitutional amendment.

Critique[3]

A prominent member of the last General Assembly has told me that the pending constitutional amendment calling for a 15-mill limit on property taxes was suddenly sprung on the House as a Conference Committee Report; that this proposed amendment was never referred to a committee; and hence that there were no public hearings on the subject. The amendment was presented one morning and after three hours consideration obtained a favorable vote in the afternoon of the same day. This member of the legislature also says that the amendment was suggested to the Governor [the Hon. Eugene Talmadge] as a way to head off the $5,000 property tax exemption measure being pushed by the Speaker of the House, and that the Governor eagerly embraced the

[3] From a paper read before the City Officials of Atlanta, Georgia, June 19, 1936. Condensed.

proposition the moment it was suggested. My informant also alleged that the plan was hatched up by real estate operators and corporation lawyers in Atlanta as a practical way of getting through the legislature the 5-mill limitation on intangibles, defeated a year or so ago, by tying up that device with the always popular notion of reducing the taxes on tangible property.

Thus without adequate consideration or debate or public hearings, without any investigation of the effects of this revolutionary action, there was thrust before the people of Georgia one of the most momentous proposals in our financial history. The proponents of the amendment have of course a very strong plea to make to the people, especially during a depression, when everybody feels the burden of taxation and is eager for relief. If you tell any ordinary citizen that this measure will reduce his taxes, he is not likely to listen patiently to any discussion of the long-term effects; and this is particularly true of real property owners because real property does in fact bear a very large share of the tax burden in such states as this, where there is little else to tax. So it looked for a while as if the amendment would ride through without any difficulty, and it would have done so but for the efforts of a few people who began to do some figuring about the results of the limitation movement. The leadership of the opposition has been provided by local government officials and the educational interests of the state.

The first thing they did was to estimate the probable loss of revenue. They came up with an estimate of about $17,-000,000, which is a minimum since the present value of property is low. When prosperity returns, property taxes will yield more, so that the loss will be much greater.

The next line of investigation was to look into the matter of substitute taxes, which the limitation people have flatly refused to consider. They know of course that any definite substitute tax they might propose would arouse some powerful groups, and they hope to beguile the voters into approving the amendment, making the while vague and unctious statements about the wisdom of the legislature and the profound and scientific study being undertaken by the Governor's commission. My own studies have convinced me that there is no reasonable substitute tax or combination of taxes that would fully replace the loss and that we shall be forced, if the amendment be approved, to lower our already deplorable standards in all social concerns.

Let us turn to the benefits of limitation, as claimed by its advocates:

1. The total tax burden will be reduced by the economies that limitation will force upon the government.

2. The tax base will be broadened by adopting substitute taxes that will not rest directly upon property.

3. Tax limitation, by lessening the taxes on land and improvements, will encourage small home-ownership and the development of small farms.

4. Limitation will result in shifting the tax function largely to the state, since the new taxes to be imposed can be best administered by the state government.

As to the first of these claims, I do not know of any case in the United States where limitation has resulted in a decreasing tax burden through government economies. Where the total tax levy has declined, the depression and not limitation has been the decisive factor.

The second claim, that limitation results in shifting of the tax burden, has in a measure been realized elsewhere, but in what a way! In every case limitation has resulted in the immediate imposition of a sales tax. What a sorry spectacle is it to see such wealthy states as Illinois, Ohio, and Michigan shift the major part of the tax burden to the shoulders of people least able to pay taxes, namely the poor, who have to spend by far the major part of their meager income on commodities that are taxed! Some of these states have shamefully declined to put any of the tax burden on the rich. Imagine a state like Michigan with its tremendous output of automobiles, its hundreds of millionaires, having no state income tax, while every one of the thousands of workers in the automobile plants is paying the sales tax in order that the well-to-do may enjoy a remission of taxes on property.

The third argument of the limiters is that lower real estate taxes would encourage small home and farm ownership. If there had been any real desire to encourage small-owned property, the way to do that would have been to exempt small property altogether. Of all the claims put forward for limitation this is both the most attractive and the one least likely to be realized.

The fourth and last major claim of the limiters is that the substitute taxes would produce a unified and centralized administration of the tax machinery. This claim, I think, is well founded. If we want centralized bureaucratic control, that is a good way to get it.

Over and beyond these considerations, experience with limitation has developed some other interesting though undesirable results. One of the most important of these is that the principal benefits of tax limitation accrue to those citizens who least need help, namely large property owners and absentee owners. Another point is the unwisdom of imposing a uniform rate of taxation on all government units of the same kind—15 mills on all cities and towns, and 10 mills on all rural areas. It would be just as sensible to require all men to wear the same size shoes. Some of the Georgia counties do not want as much as 15 mills, others need two or three times as much.

But what seems to me the most important fact emerging from the experiences elsewhere is the unquestionable truth that tax limitation is a deadly contrivance for the cities which are forced to bear the cost of financing the social services of the state. It is somewhat amusing to reflect that the active propagandists of limitation have almost always been city people, and that they are now finding limitations acting like a boomerang: higher income taxes and a general sales tax must be adopted to make up for the revenue loss, and these two taxes bear most heavily on the city dweller.

[1939] THE EVIL OF ALLOCATIONS[4]

Georgia faces a major crisis in state financial affairs. The threatened collapse of our financial structure is attributable to the efforts of the General Assembly under the leadership of Governor Rivers to meet popular demands for highly desirable improvements in, and extension of, the public services. The taxation changes designed to produce the necessary additional funds unfortunately proved inadequate, and it is therefore of prime importance that the situation be carefully analyzed and that possible solutions be suggested. The main problem lies in the system of "allocations." In the following discussion, this system will be explained and alternative courses of action will be examined.

The annual budget is divided into two parts. One of them is called the *fixed sum* part, in which a definite sum of money is appropriated to a given service. The other part, called the *allocated sum* part, makes appropriations to those services to which all the revenue from specified sources has been permanently and exclusively allocated. The "appropriations" are therefore mere estimates of the probable yield of these sources of revenue; the General Assembly has no control in that matter. Thus the services coming under the allocations part receive all that the allocated sources will yield; the others must share what is left, namely the revenue which goes into the General Fund. What happens if the General Fund is not sufficient to meet the fixed appropriations made in the budget? According to a provision adopted in 1937,

[4] From *Georgia Faces a Financial Crisis,* Institute for the Study of Georgia Problems, Pamphlet No. 1 (Bulletin of the University of Georgia, Vol. 39, No. 2b, January, 1939). The material used has been condensed and in part rewritten.

all services receiving fixed sums must in this case take *pro rata* cuts, except for the judicial and legislative branches of the government and the public debt service, which receive all that has been appropriated to them.

This provision of *pro rata* cuts, known as the "grandfather clause," is an excellent device to forestall deficits. But it works grievous injustice to those services which receive "fixed sum" appropriations. Foremost among such services are those upon which the social and cultural progress of the state depends: elementary education, welfare, the funds for the aged and the blind, for dependent children, and for the University System. To give an example of how the "grandfather clause" works in practice, we may compare last year's payments to the fund for old age pensions with those made to the Highway Fund. Old age pensions were provided for in the budget by an appropriation of 3.15 million dollars. Under the "grandfather clause" half a million dollars was deducted from that in the budget, and the actual payment made was 1.87 million dollars, or only 60 per cent of the original appropriation. The Highway Fund, on the other hand, received all the income from highway revenue, correctly estimated at 13.5 million dollars, plus three additional millions carried over from the preceding year.

This is a grievous situation. While many vital services are forced to emasculate their budget, others go blithely ahead spending their allocated sums, totally unaffected by arbitrary reductions under the grandfather clause.

It should be borne in mind that the sources of revenue permanently allocated to certain services are the most dependable sources of income. People will drive automobiles and use tobacco with little regard to changes in the business cycle, whereas those sources of revenue that go into the General Fund are peculiarly subject to changes in economic conditions. This is especially true of the most important of these sources, the income tax, the receipts from which dwindle away during depressions. The same thing occurs with property taxes, which also go into the General Fund.

Is there a way out? No one will welcome new taxes, yet something must be done, since Governor Rivers' program of progressive legislation, endorsed by the voters who re-elected him, is already failing. Several alternative courses offer themselves.

First. *Uproot the system of allocations.* Any service that can count upon receiving the revenue from specified sources will automatically expand its operations so as to utilize all the money in sight. An intelligent view of Georgia's fiscal position demands that every dollar collected from the people go into the Treasury; that every spending agency be required to submit and defend detailed plans for its operation; and that all the anticipated revenue be distributed according to the relative needs of the services. It will, of course, be objected that such a procedure would end the present practice of devoting nearly half of the total state revenue to roads. But it is no answer to insist that, since the money expended on highways comes from taxes on gasoline and from motor licenses, it ought all to be used for road improvement. Gasoline taxes are just like all other taxes. When the state takes nearly 20 million dollars from the pockets of the people in the form of these taxes and licenses, it lessens by that much the ability of the citizens to pay other taxes.

Second. *Continue the present system of allocations and increase the tax burden.* We have already tapped nearly every possible source of revenue except a general sales tax. There is no arguing away the fact that a sales tax is regressive, since the poor are forced to spend a far greater part of their incomes upon taxed commodities that those who have large incomes. But under present Georgia conditions, one might be willing to embrace a faulty method of financing when the alternative is the partial abandonment of a program of improvement in general social conditions.

Third. *Abandon or curtail some of the progressive measures upon which we have embarked during the past two years,* taking the position that the people of Georgia are already bearing as severe a tax burden as they can stand. This alternative, which amounts to a confession of failure, raises the question: Are we Georgians overtaxed? A previous investigation undertaken by this writer for the Georgia Citizens' Fact Finding Movement showed that Georgians are only mildly taxed in comparison with the people of other states. Georgians could pay a much larger amount of taxes than they do and still surrender a much smaller per capita in taxes than the U. S. average. If a sales tax should yield 10 million dollars, the per capita increase would be only about $3.50 and the per capita tax burden would still be only 62 per cent of the national average.

[1936] AGAINST A GENERAL SALES TAX[5]

The only fair criterion in taxation is ability to pay. All citizens ought to be forced to contribute to the expense of government, not in proportion to their need or their helplessness or the benefits they receive from government, but solely according to their ability to pay. The graduated income tax is the best of all taxes because the citizen does not have to pay anything under it unless he makes a net income above a minimum level, and because the exaction increases as his net income increases. It is therefore entirely fair and not very burdensome if the rates are kept within bounds. A sales tax on the contrary is the worst of all taxes because the poorer the citizen is, the harder the tax bears on him. This is easy to demonstrate.

The smaller the income of a man, the greater the proportion

---

* From a speech before the Rotary Club of Albany, Georgia, April 9, 1936. Condensed.

of it he has to spend on the necessities of life. On the average, 35 per cent of the income of persons having less than $1,000 per year goes for food. This proportion falls sharply as income rises. It follows, therefore, that a sales tax on food is no burden whatever to a man with a large income, but that it may be disastrous to one with a very small income. What is true of food is true of other expenditures for the necessities of life, though to a smaller degree. If the income is under $1,000, over 60 per cent of it goes for goods and services usually subject to the sales tax. If the income is $10,000 a year, only 30 per cent of expenditures pay the sales tax. Moreover, consider the matter of savings. A man with an income less than $1,250 is not able to save anything, on the average. If his income is between $1,250 and $1,450, he saves, on the average, 2.8 per cent of it. It will be apparent, therefore, that a three per cent sales tax would wipe out half of his savings, since in this income class it would affect some 58 per cent of his expenditures. Since persons with incomes under $1,250 are not able to save a cent, a sales tax would reduce their expenditures and would hurt business that much. It so chances that the average family in Georgia has now an income of $1,250 per year. You can, therefore, imagine what a calamity a sales tax would be.

[1949] THE CASE FOR A GENERAL SALES TAX IN GEORGIA[6]

It is no pleasure to point out that in the last fifteen years during which many other states have revitalized their state institutions by adopting sales taxes, we in Georgia have stubbornly refused to take the only step that can possibly save our financial life. We have seen our schools lag behind those in other states, school buildings falling into disrepair, and thousands of teachers leaving the state because of the low

[6] From: "Georgia Should Have a General Sales Tax," Memorandum dated August 27, 1949, prepared for the use of the state administration. Condensed.

salaries in Georgia. Our state colleges are in like condition. They are crowded beyond endurance, their physical plant being totally unable to care for the great enrollments, and hardly a week passes without public notice of some faculty member of the University System resigning to accept a more lucrative position elsewhere. Our public welfare institutions have become a disgrace to the state—especially the one at Milledgeville. Our roads are rapidly disintegrating, as all drivers of automobiles know. An aroused public opinion demands that this situation be ended and that Georgia be enabled to take her rightful place among her sister states.

Faced by a financial crisis, the administration recently called a special session of the General Assembly and pushed through increases in the rates on already heavily overtaxed commodities and of the corporation income tax. These palliatives will not solve the problem. Nothing will, in fact, except a general sales tax.

The principal objection to sales taxes comes from the lower income groups, particularly organized labor, who dislike the tax because of its regressive nature. There is no denying the contention that sales taxes bear most heavily on the low income groups, but that fact becomes unimportant in Georgia for the following reasons:

1. If we had no personal income tax, it would be grossly unfair to impose a general sales tax. But here in Georgia we have had an income tax for many years and it is distinctly a class tax, since only four per cent of the citizens pay it. It is therefore reasonable to have a sales tax which affects the lower income group; and, of course, the higher income groups pay it too.

2. The homestead and personal property exemptions adopted in 1937 have provided a tremendous tax relief for persons in the lower income group.

3. It may be said in general that the majority of the people in Georgia contribute nothing in direct taxes to the support

of government. They are exempt from the income tax; they own no property and hence pay no property tax; they are not even required to pay a poll tax. The only contribution they make results from special taxes on gasoline, liquor, and tobacco, and the nuisance taxes, these latter being levied primarily by the Federal government. It is therefore fair that the masses of the people should be called upon to help pay some of the costs of government.

The second group that opposes the sales tax are the merchants. Their opposition is based on three grounds:

1. It is an expensive nuisance to collect the tax, keep the records of it, and remit the proceeds to the state. This objection can be met in large measure by allowing the merchants to retain a small fraction of their collections as reimbursement for their costs and labor.

2. The merchants claim that purchasing power is reduced by the amount of tax collected. There is no validity in this contention. The money collected is paid back to citizens of all sorts who in turn spend the money for commodities, so that the total of consumers' expenditure is little affected.

3. Borderline cities lose business if the contiguous states have no sales tax. This is a valid contention. But the spreading adoption of sales taxes by the states will in time lessen this tax avoidance by citizens of border line areas. The adoption of the "use" tax, requiring commodities brought into the state from non-sales tax states to pay the equivalent of the sales tax, can cure such avoidance to some extent.

On the other hand, merchants sometimes profit by the sales tax in cases where it is "pyramided." This occurs when the tax has been paid on the manufacturing and wholesale level and the retailer applies his usual mark-up, so that the consumer will ultimately pay more in increased prices than the government receives. The merchants receive the difference, and, so to speak, make a profit on the tax.

To sum up, the advantages of a sales tax in Georgia are:

1. It is very productive and would yield more than $30,-
000,000 in revenue.

2. Its burden is negligible. It would exact only about $10
per capita from the citizens. The 1948 per capita income of
Georgia was $971.

3. It would force contributions to the cost of government
from these elements of the citizenry that presently pay little
or nothing. This applies with special force to the colored
population.

4. It would produce revenue from the great number of
tourists now passing through Georgia who cannot be reached
in any other way.

5. It would revitalize the public services of Georgia, notably education at all levels, and the institutions for the care
of dependent classes.

PART THREE

IN DEFENSE OF THE SOUTH

7

Economic and Social Aspects
of Slavery
[1913]

Reprinted with minor omissions from R. P. Brooks, History of Georgia (*Ch. 18, pp. 221-236*).

THE WORLD IS COMING TO UNDERSTAND NOW MUCH BETTER than formerly the true condition of the Southern slaves. During the two decades preceding the Civil War, when the feelings of men were wrought up to a high tension, it could hardly be expected that justice would be done the slaveholder. Northern people came into contact with only the most unfortunate aspects of slavery, such as the arrest of runaway slaves and their forcible return to bondage, and the unpleasant incidents connected with the slave trade. Incidents of cruelty to slaves were not heard of as exceptions to the rule of good treatment, but as representing the general attitude of owners. Such a book as "Uncle Tom's Cabin" created a powerful public opinion against slavery. Southern slave owners resented being constantly denounced as morally deficient. Many of them would have gladly escaped the responsibility of caring for the slaves, but were convinced that the negroes would be in a worse condition as freedmen. An instance of this type of slaveholder was the Reverend J. O. Andrew, of Georgia. In 1812 he was elected a bishop in the Methodist church, which at that time had not been divided into northern and southern branches. Bishop Andrew owned no slaves when elected and never bought one in his life, but his wife inherited a number of negroes and in this way the bishop became a slaveowner. In 1844 the matter of his possessing slaves was brought before the general conference of his church and he was asked to resign his position because he would not give up the slaves. Answering the charge brought against him, Bishop Andrews said: "Strange as it may seem to you, brethren, I am a slaveholder for conscience' sake. I have no doubt that my wife would, without a moment's hesitation, consent to the manumission of those slaves, if I thought proper to ask it. But how am I to free them? Some of them are too old to work and are an expense to me, and some are little children. Where shall I send them? But perhaps I shall be permitted to keep these helpless ones. Many of them would not go. I believe the providence of God has thrown these creatures into my hands and holds me responsible for their proper treatment." These words fairly represent the attitude of the vast majority of slaveowners in Georgia. Every one knew that there were masters who abused their slaves, but such owners were held in contempt by the gentlemen of the South.

RECORDS OF GEORGIA FAMILIES

The plantation records and letters of Georgia families afford abundant evidence of the great care and consideration exercised by slaveholders for their servants. Specific rules were laid down about the punishment of slaves. For instance, one planter prohibited his overseer from inflicting punishment until twenty-four hours after the offense; another did not have a driver, but held the overseer responsible for the work. A driver was a sort of gang-boss, set over a group of slaves to see that they performed their tasks. He was a negro of more than common mental capacity. Other rules regulated the hours of work, required the overseers to inspect the clothes, shoes and blankets of the negroes to keep them comfortably clad; work in the rain was prohibited, and provision was made for numerous holidays. Several times a year the owner directed the overseer to kill beef for the negroes. The general policy was to keep them happy and contented. They usually had the right of appeal to the master, an important matter, since it afforded a check on arbitrary treatment at the hands of the overseer. It was even charged that some overseers allowed the negroes to leave their work undone in order to avoid complaints to the owner.

COAST AND UPLAND

The coast or rice plantations were low, marshy and malarious. Few owners had the courage to live on their places during the hot season. The overseer was necessarily an important person, and the rules above mentioned were in nearly every case those of coast plantations. In this way planters sought to avoid the dangers almost inseparable from absenteeism. Overseers as a class were uneducated, unrefined and irresponsible. Management of negroes was their stock in trade, and, of course, their temptation would be to make as great profits as possible. In the upcountry, slaves were fewer per owner and the planters normally lived on their places, in close contact with the laborers. As a consequence, conditions were better in the cotton planting districts. On the other hand the most conscientious efforts for the betterment of slaves were sometimes found on the coast, as in the case of the Association for the Religious Instruction of the Negroes, in Liberty County, Georgia. The Reverend C. C. Jones, father of the historian of that name, spent his life in missionary work among the coast negroes.

PUBLIC SENTIMENT

The treatment accorded slaves depended in large measure on the character of the individual slaveholder. If he were so ignorant and brutal as not to know his own interests, he might maltreat his slaves, thus reducing their efficiency as workers. Public sentiment was strongly against a slaveholder who abused his servants, and the consensus of opinion among modern scientific students of history is that on the whole slaves were well treated. Their hours of labor were not as long as those of free laborers in the North, their food was quite sufficient to keep them in prime condition, their clothes and housing as adequate as those of any other laboring people, taking into account the difference in climate. At the time negro slaves were introduced into America in the early 17th century, there was little moral sentiment against slavery, either North or South. As time went on the civilized world came to regard slavery as a relic of barbarism that ought not to be tolerated any longer. Many Southerners sympathized with this view and emancipated their slaves; but to the vast majority of Southerners wholesale emancipation seemed to be unthinkable. The ante-bellum planters found the slaves already at hand; they were convinced that negroes were unfitted for freedom and could be made a source of social advantage only by being taken care of by white men. It was all very well to talk of the blessing of freedom, but Southerners could only hear with misgivings any suggestion of freeing masses of ignorant slaves; and they deeply resented constant attacks from the outside directed against their own moral character. On the whole slaveholders were as religious, moral, high-minded a race of men as ever lived. They felt slaveholding as a great responsibility and did everything they could for the slaves that was consonant with their conception of public safety.

SLAVEHOLDING AND NON-SLAVEHOLDING FAMILIES

The total white population of Georgia in 1860 was 591,-550, or about 118,000 families. Of these families 41,084 were slaveholders, leaving the overwhelming majority, about 77,000, in the non-slave-holding class. But not all the slaveholders were farmers: 6,713 possessed only one slave each; 4,355 two each; 3,482 three each. These owners of a few slaves were usually residents of towns and kept their slaves as household servants. About twenty slaves was the number that could be most profitably managed by one overseer; and we may take the possession of that number as the minimum that would place the farmer in the planter class. Of such slaveholders there were in Georgia 6,363 in 1860. The massing of the bulk of the slaves in so few hands indicates the system of agriculture that dominated the state in ante-bellum times, namely the plantation.

THE COTTON PLANTATION

Cotton growing was admirably suited to slave labor. Cotton can be produced almost anywhere in the state. It occupies the labor practically all the year, thus enabling the planter to avoid supporting his laborers over long periods of inactivity. Again, cotton raising is a rather simple process, lending itself readily to routine work, the only sort of exertion slaves were capable of. Moreover, each laborer could cultivate a much smaller area growing cotton than if he were raising corn or other cereals, and hence the laborers could easily be massed together under the eye of the overseer. It was more economical to conduct operations on a large scale, because expert supervision was absolutely necessary, and, as overseers were expensive, it paid to have each overseer control a large number of slaves. These facts taken together explain the existence of the plantation system.

The profits to be made from cotton raising during times of high prices were attractive, and the low character of the labor made diversified farming impracticable, so that planters gradually left off trying to produce anything but cotton. It was a "one crop" system. There were some wise planters who produced nearly everything they used, but the majority did not, and all during the ante-bellum period Georgia was a heavy buyer of Western corn, wheat and forage.

SLOW GROWTH OF MANUFACTURES

Another unfortunate result of the domination of "King Cotton" was that the increased demand for slaves sent prices soaring. The African slave trade was abolished in 1808, so that the planters had to depend upon natural increase for slaves. Competition for laborers became very keen. In 1800 a prime field hand was worth, in Georgia, $300.00. By 1860 the price had advanced to $1,800.00. At the same time the constant tendency was for the price of cotton to fall. In 1800 it brought 24c; in 1830, 17c; in 1850, 12.3c; in 1860, 11c. Hence the planter who would keep up his accustomed standard of life had to be always increasing his acreage and his force of slaves in order to obtain the same income. The result was that every available dollar went into cotton lands and negroes, and little was left for investment in manufacturing and other industries. On this point a traveller, F. L. Olmsted, remarked that in Georgia, where "there is more life, enterprise, skill and industry than in any of the old slave commonwealths"; where the natural resources for manufacturing were fine; where "land rent, water power, timber, fuel and raw material for cotton manufacturing are all much cheaper" than in New England, there was a total lack of any diversity of labor, due to the absorption of capital in slaves and cotton lands. Promoters found it impossible to sell shares in proposed manufacturing enterprises, because all the spare cash went the traditional way. It is not to be inferred that there were no manufacturing enterprises in the South. Cotton mills were in operation before the war in Athens, Eatonton, Sparta, Columbus and in other towns. But in comparison with the industries of the northern states these establishments were insignificant in size and number. The South did not take a leading part in the great economic revolution which, during the first half of the 19th century, transformed England, France, Germany and the northern United States from agricultural to manufacturing communities.

Low Character of the Labor

Of the slavery system in general, it may be said that slave labor cost the South more than free labor would have cost, had it been available. Negroes were lazy, inefficient, and unintelligent. A noted traveller, Sir Charles Lyell, was interested in Louisiana to find that it took three negroes to cut and bind two cords of wood in a day, whereas in New York one white man prepared three cords daily. He was also told that where negro and white laborers were worked together the negro was required to do only two-thirds as much work as a white laborer. Another reason why slave labor was so expensive was that the negro, like all stupid and ignorant people, was stubbornly opposed to new ideas. It was found impossible to introduce improved methods of tillage. At the time when the northern and western farmer were using the drill, the horse-hoe, the reaper, and was threshing by machinery, the bulk of work on Southern plantations was done with an ordinary hoe. Planters tried to use labor-saving machinery, but the negroes invariably either broke the tools or were careful to waste time so that the net result would be in favor of the old methods.

Support of Idle Slaves

Under a free system, when one desires certain work done, a laborer is hired for that particular job or for a given length of time, and the employer pays for actual services rendered. Under slavery, it was not always possible to keep the laborers at work, but they had nevertheless to be maintained while idle. This point was stressed by a Northern preacher, Nehemiah Adams, who, during a visit to the South, observed that the kindness of owners prevented them from disposing of superfluous negroes. Susan Dabney Smedes, in the *Memorials of a Southern Planter*, says that on her father's plantation the work of the women and children and of some of the men amounted to so little that he made little effort to utilize it.

"It was very laborious to find easy work for a large body of inefficient and lazy people, and at Burleigh the struggle was given up in many cases. The different departments would have been more easily and better managed if there had been fewer to work." Another element of cost was the expense attached to rearing the slave children to the age where they could be used, and the support of superannuated slaves.

EFFECT ON THE SOIL

The one-crop system and the absence of fertilizers were unfortunate for the land. Rotation of crops was not practiced and little effort was made to conserve the soil. When the areas under cultivation at any given moment became less productive by reason of the methods of tillage, the planters pushed on westward with their slaves, bought the holdings of small farmers, cut down the trees, used the virgin soil, and presently abandoned the country to the mercy of the washing rains. The state of Georgia is now, through her teachers of agriculture, trying to overcome the effects of this disastrous system of farming. Rotation, diversification and the use of fertilizers, cattle raising, dairy farming and like industries are revolutionizing the state.

EFFECT ON SOCIETY

As has already been said, the majority of Georgia families owned no slaves. The large-scale planters were a small percentage of Georgia farmers. Below them in the social scale was a class of smaller slave owners who are said to have been unprosperous. The third element in society was the independent, non-slaveholding farmer. Among this element of the population, constituting the great majority, there were striking variations in conditions. It is not true, as has usually been said, that all non-slaveholders were a destitute class. It is certain that in the constant westward march of the planter in search of new lands, the independent farmer was dispossessed. Constantly on the move, he found it difficult to develop a secure, satisfactory agricultural system. Many men of this class took positions as overseers on the plantations and in time saved money to buy slaves and become planters. Another part of the independent farmer class got out of the path of the planter and established a strong and sound section of small farms, worked intensively and carefully. The counties in the northeast section of the state, for instance, afforded homes for many thousands of these men, who were, as a rule, thrifty and saving. Yet another element of the small farmer class, discouraged by the continual encroachments of the planter, lacking industry and initiative to develop their own small farms, unwilling to work for wages in competition with slave labor, drifted into the pine barrens, waste places and mountains, and there led miserable lives. They were entirely cut off from contact with the planter class and all it represented. They knew nothing of the great movements in the world about them. The color of their skin raised them above the negro, their pride of blood and the degradation of labor in a slave régime made it impossible for them to be hired to do work. They accumulated nothing, rarely acquired even the rudiments of learning, and were utterly disregarded by the other elements of society. Even the slaves themselves on large plantations held these people in contempt.

The negroes came at the bottom of the ladder. In many respects they received more benefit from slavery than any other class. Coming to America as savages, members of a race which had never contributed anything to civilization, the enforced labor of two hundred years taught a considerable proportion of them habits of industry. No primitive people ever got their upward start under such happy auspices as did the American negroes. That many thousands of them are now prosperous landowners, that tens of thousands are being trained in schools for lives of usefulness, while still others have gone forth into every sort of industrial work, are facts which can only be understood by reference to the training of slavery.

SOCIAL LIFE

There were many very attractive features in the lives of the upper class of Southern ante-bellum society. Though the planters had always hanging over them the problem of managing a difficult system; though the mistresses of the homes spent lives of service, tending the sick, making clothes for the slaves and listening to their real and imaginary complaints—the slave was simply a child—yet the sense of large responsibility produced a race of men whose superiors in masterful qualities have never existed. With wealth and leisure, the sons of the planters went North and to Europe for their education, and, on returning home, naturally entered politics and the law. So great was their political capacity that the planters and lawyers controlled the national government for many years previous to the Civil War.

A cultured, refined race of men, many of whom are still with us, the Southern planters threw open their doors to men of their own class. Hospitality was the universal practice. "Nowhere in the world," says F. L. Olmsted, writing from the Georgia-Carolina coast, "could a man with a sound body and a quiet conscience, live more pleasantly, at least as a guest, it seems to me, than here where I am." By living in long and intimate contact with the lower race, the white men of the South learned the black man's character; he valued the essential fidelity of the slave, and is not too greatly exasperated at the present-day negro's shiftlessness and aversion to work. This insight into the nature of the negro gives the southern man a vantage ground of great importance in studying the race problems resulting from the Civil War.

SUMMARY

While it is a well substantiated fact that the slaves were on the whole well treated, when we look at slavery from the point of view of the economic welfare of the South, the picture is less cheerful. The absorption of practically all the available capital in the purchase of land and slaves prevented the development of manufacturing, and, in fact, of any except agricultural industry. Further, wholesale cotton planting with inefficient negro labor resulted in a too rapid exploitation of the land. Another unfortunate effect was the too great stratification of society; opportunity was not sufficiently equal, and though a race of masterful and capable men was produced by the Southern system, the position of the poorer people was not as good as it is now.

8

On Lynching

[1916]

The following letter, reprinted with omission of the first paragraph, was published in the October 5, 1916, issue of The Nation (pp. 321-322) in reply to an article by Herbert L. Stewart. For the author's present views see his 1952 postscript.

To the Editor of The Nation:

SIR: THE ARTICLE BY MR. HERBERT L. STEWART IN YOUR issue of August 24, entitled "The Casuistry of Lynch Law," seriously misrepresents the Southern attitude towards lynching. Mr. Stewart ignores the fact that the press of the South for many years has been as outspoken as the press of the North on this subject. He is unaware of the fact that there is practically complete unanimity among all educated persons, not merely in deploring, but in openly denouncing, lynching. Editors, preachers, lawyers, teachers, indeed all the professional classes, and all business men of consequence are as sincerely outraged when a lynching occurs as are the people of the North. I know of no educated persons in the South who condone lynching. Far from having grasped the truth, Mr. Stewart would leave the country with the idea that a sort of philosophical system has been developed among us to justify mob violence. To his mind lynching is a cold-blooded matter of policy to keep the negro down. Any one relying solely on Mr. Stewart would expect to find in our

state universities chairs of comparative lynchology, sustained
by Legislatures quick to respond to public needs, for the
purpose of working out new modes of torture; the material
for laboratory experimentation supplied by the county chain
gangs, and mayhap, extension lecturers carrying the gospel
of new methods to a grateful people in remote rural communities, where the uncultivated imagination of the citizenry has never been able to hit upon anything more original than hanging.

Mr. Stewart falls into another error when he states that
Southerners pretend "that the prevention of rape is the
sole purpose of lynching." This statement amounts to a libel
on the intelligence of Southern people. We know and admit
that rape is rarely the cause of lynching. We have long since
progressed beyond the original excuse. Lynching may occur
on any occasion in which a negro attacks the honor, life,
property, or pride of a white person. Still, Mr. Stewart must
set up his man of straw, so that he may valiantly beat him
down by reciting facts familiar to everybody.

Another lament raised by Mr. Stewart is that Southerners
are resentful of criticism in connection with lynching. The
impatience of the Southerner (and I speak here as throughout this letter of the educated portion of the population)
arises in part from the fact that he is tired of mere denunciation and abuse. He is well acquainted with outside views on
the subject; he is prepared to admit that the criticisms are
generally justified by the facts; but it irritates him to see
his section's shortcoming held up in constant reiteration to
the scorn of the world. The common man of the type that
engages in lynching is wholly unconscious of utterances in
the *Nation*, or any other high-grade organ of opinion. He
has never even heard of the *Nation*. The clarion tones of that
doughty champion of national righteousness fall on the ears
of only the suffering few who need no call to repentance.
And to this minority, the intellectual leaders of the South,

such diatribes as those of Mr. Stewart seem to get nowhere.
They never contain any suggestions that will help us. We
would like our Northern brethren to tell us how to stop
lynching. We would like to know what you would do about
it if you were citizens of the South. Thoughtless critics,
emanating heat rather than light, seem strangely unaware
of the magnitude of the race problem, and give us insufficient credit for our efforts to cure the social ailments resulting from the situation. This brings me to a second cause
of resentment of outside criticism.

Writers of the sort here under discussion quite frequently
appear to think that every negro charged with rape is lynched.
The truth, of course, is far otherwise. Thousands of crimes
are committed every year by negroes against the life and
property of the whites. In more than 99 per cent of the
cases the law takes its regular course, and the public at large
hears nothing of the matter. The presence of thousands of
negroes in the chain gangs and the frequent legal executions
testify to the truth of this statement. At intervals gusts of
popular passion sweep over communities visited by crime, and
a lynching occurs. The educated South then bows her head
in shame, and the press raises a chorus of protest. No excuse
is attempted. But I should like to register this opinion as a
man born and reared in the heart of the black belt: when I
consider the social conditions in that region, I wonder that
instances of mob violence are so few, and praise Allah that
we are a people who generally manage to restrain our bar-
barous impulses.

Yet another explanation of Southern resentment of criticism is to be found in this circumstance. The informed
among us, while not disposed to make excuses for lynching
or for any other of the ills from which we suffer, illiteracy,
child labor, general backwardness in progressive legislation,
or what not, yet feel that the count is not entirely against
the South. Crimes attendant upon commercialized vice, the

crime of white slavery, crimes resulting from industrial disputes, crimes committed by organized gangs of thugs and assassins, such *mala in se* as the shameful exploitation of unskilled labor, sweatshop industry, the dominance of municipal government by the organized forces of evil—all the maladjustments, in short, characteristic of a highly developed, densely settled, industrial society—are ills from which the South has largely escaped, simply because our section has ..ot as yet developed conditions favorable to them. These cancerous running sores on the body politic, any one of which is as serious as the Southern crime of lynching, sometimes seem to us in the South not to receive in responsible Northern newspapers and periodicals anything like the emphasis that is given to our peculiar form of social malady; and we cannot help wondering if the Northern record on lynching would be any better than is ours were the conditions reversed. When I read the report of the Chicago Vice Commission one day and on the next an intemperate attack on the South in the *Tribune;* when I read William Dean Howell's description of slum life in New York, in "Experiences and Impressions," and then such an article as Mr. Stewart's, I am accustomed to marvel at my kind. With what wonderful facility do men see the mote in their neighbor's eye despite the hindrance of the beam in their own!

But enough of the *tu quoque* argument. Like Mr. Stewart's article, it gets nowhere. Is it possible wholly to eradicate lynching? What are we doing to stop the evil? Personally, I fear I shall not live to see the day when there will be no mob violence in the South. But to what instance can the historian point in which two dissimilar races in close proximity have got along with less friction than the whites and blacks in the South? After a thousand years the Anglo-Saxons and Celts of the United Kingdom have not yet worked out a satisfactory adjustment of their differences; the English are reported to bear very hardly on the natives of

South Africa; the negroes are fortunate in not being Jews in Russia or Armenians in Turkey; the treatment accorded the Indians by the American people as a whole is a shameful chapter in our history. I have even seen published advice from negro leaders warning their fellows not to migrate to the Northern states on the ground that racial hostility there is so great that opportunity to work is denied. No, so long as the negro is with us there will be race friction, and, no doubt, for a long time outbreaks of violence. We hope even in Georgia, however, to reduce the crime, and several expedients have been adopted.

First among these is our educational policy. Georgia is committed to the education of her masses, white and black. We believe that ultimately education is the only solution of the question, though our confidence in the beneficent effects of education has been somewhat shaken by the recrudescence of barbarism among the warring peoples of Europe. Georgia appropriates nearly $3,000,000 annually for common schools, more than half of the total revenue, and, though our schools are still poor, due to the failure of communities to supplement the state fund by local taxation, we hope in time to elevate the masses a few inches, and perhaps inculcate a better attitude towards the enforcement of law. The last Legislature enacted a compulsory education law, an inadequate law, it is true, but the principle is established, and amendment should not prove difficult.

Secondly, we have destroyed the saloon. State-wide prohibition of all forms of alcoholic drink would not have been adopted but for the connection between negro criminality and drink.

In the third place, the Legislature this year gave consideration to a proposal to empower the Governor to remove from office any sheriff in whose jurisdiction a lynching occurs. This bill, after its passage by the Senate, was killed by the House, though urgently demanded by the enlightened sentiment of the state. Its failure simply reflects the inability of the best thought of the state to control the suffrages of the masses, a situation to which the people of the North are not strangers.

The eradication of lynching is not a matter of a few years. It is a malady the causes of which lie deep in human nature. Of one thing, however, the world should be assured: all the forces of enlightenment in the South are banded together to the end that the stigma shall ultimately be removed from our midst.[1]

R. P. BROOKS

Athens, Ga., August 29, 1916.

P.S. While wading through the formidable mass of my writings for material to be used in this volume, Dr. Sebba came across this letter about lynching written thirty-five years ago to *The Nation*. I yielded somewhat reluctantly to his wish to include the letter. My reasons for this attitude were that the missive was written in an angry mood and contains statements that I would not now make, such as the allegation that a lynching might occur whenever a Negro "attacked the honor, life, property, or pride of a white person." Again, in the fourth paragraph the reader might infer that most of the crimes of Negroes are committed against white persons, whereas they commonly enough result from quarrels among themselves. Furthermore, I do not adequately indicate that Negroes are far from enjoying equal treatment in the courts. Happily, the chain-gang is gone and lynching

---

[1] [In a note to this letter, the Editors of *The Nation* agreed "with most of Professor Brooks' contentions" but took exception to his last sentence. Referring to a recent lynching in Waco, Texas, they said: "Not a single teacher, or preacher, or newspaper, or public official has spoken out against the mob which publicly burned a convicted negro there. We have yet . . . to see a single sign that . . . anybody has banded together there to remove the stigma of that atrocious crime. It is precisely because the 'forces of enlightenment' are so little vocal in the South that there is so little headway against lynching. The conviction of a few lynchers in Waco and their punishment would do more to stop the evil than anything we can readily think of." The note ends with a wish for more severe criticism of lynchings wherever they may occur, "both North and South." *Ed.*].

is no longer a serious problem. Racial strife in the South now takes the form of resisting the admission of Negro youths to white colleges and schools. When one reflects upon the present rampant nationalism, with its overtones of racial and religious animosity, one must regretfully conclude that the brotherhood of man is still a long way off.

February 21, 1952   R. P. B.

9

Georgia Goes Marching On

[1926]

An article written at the request of the editors of Forum
*in reply to Thomas Boyd's article in the July, 1926, issue
of that magazine. Condensed from* Forum, *Vol. 76, No. 5,
(November, 1926), pp. 748-755.*

MY BELIEF IS THAT CULTURAL PROGRESS MUST AWAIT
economic progress, that a high state of civilization cannot
be reached without widespread popular education, and that
the character of the educational institutions provided by a
people depends on their economic status. A poverty-stricken
people will inevitably be ignorant and backward. Ignorance
accounts for low political ideals, religious intolerance, anti-
scientific agitation, Kluxism, lynching; it explains the fact
that Georgians are not a reading people, that we are a poor
field for the publishers, that our libraries are few and inadequate. These social defects cannot be eradicated by ridi-
cule and denunciation. Education seems the only remedy.
But it takes money to provide educational machinery, and
until an economic surplus has been built up, funds for this
purpose will not be available.

Only within recent years has Georgia found herself able
to finance educational facilities of a relatively high order.
For three decades after the Civil War the people of Georgia
were engrossed in bringing order out of chaos. During those
years they were in no humor for things of the spirit. They

became indifferent to higher education, to literature, to keeping politics clean. The best minds turned their thought to business instead of public affairs, which had in better days been their chief interest. Farming was almost the sole economic activity. Capital had been largely destroyed; the productive capacity of the land had been impaired by years of neglect; labor was demoralized; cash and credit were alike unavailable. The farmers were dependent upon cotton. This one-crop economy handicapped the state to an almost incredible extent.

During the past two or three decades, however, Georgia has been passing through an agricultural and industrial revolution in every way comparable to that experienced by England and the northern states of the Union in earlier times. This era of change got under way in Georgia about the year 1900. At that time the bulk of the wealth annually produced was agricultural, and cotton made up seventy-five per cent of the value of all crops. In 1923, however, cotton accounted for only one-third of the total farm output, which by that time had grown three-fold. Millions of dollars were being annually poured into the state by such new products as tobacco, peanuts, pecans, melons, and fruit. Great strides had been made in all forms of diversified farming. In other words, we have had an agricultural revolution.

The changes in agriculture tell only part of the story. During this century the amount invested in manufacturing has increased from 80 to 450 million dollars. Bank deposits and railway mileage have grown rapidly; millions are being annually expended on improving the highways; in the development of hydroelectric power only one southern state has outstripped Georgia. These facts indicate an industrial revolution. Georgia is fast becoming a manufacturing state of importance.

Have any cultural dividends been realized from this better utilization of the state's economic resources? I believe I am on firm ground when I venture an affirmative answer. With the people enjoying an annual income of more than seven hundred millions it would be strange indeed if there were not a revival of interest in social betterment and a higher standard of culture. Private fortunes are accumulating and the general well-being is improving. Georgians now have some leisure, some relief from the grind of bread-winning, without which there can be little cultured existence. Thousands of them are annually visiting other parts of this country and Europe, and they are bringing back what our most eminent clerical reactionary has called the "pernicious leaven of liberalism"; in ever increasing numbers our young people are resorting to northern educational centers for postgraduate work in the arts and sciences. Returning home, they are modifying the traditional attitudes towards ethical and religious questions and are contributing much towards industrial and educational progress. Educated young men are taking more interest in politics than formerly. More than fifty alumni of the University were members of the last General Assembly and almost uniformly they were to be found on the side of liberal and progressive legislation. A few wealthy citizens are coming to look upon their fortunes as a public trust and are beginning to give more liberally to education. The State as a political unit is also finding itself able to invest more in education. When compared with other states, Georgia seems to be doing little for public education; when the comparison is with her own past, however, the matter takes on another aspect. Increased property values are producing larger revenues, and nearly all the increment goes into educational channels.

The progress of the University and of other higher educational institutions was for many years retarded by the lack of sufficient secondary schools of high grade. Twenty years ago the University took that matter in hand and began to build up the high schools. A system of standardization and inspection was established, schools which met the standard being permitted to certify their graduates into the freshman class of the University. When this system was inaugurated in 1904, there were seven public and four private high schools that met the requirements; these schools enrolled 3,556 pupils, and the University received by certification forty-three students. At present the accredited schools number 309, with an enrollment of 43,512 and 9,380 graduates this year and the University now receives annually about 500 freshmen by certification. Is this not an educational revolution?

Not all high school graduates who go to college enter the University. Other state-supported institutions and the denominational and private colleges are finding their facilities taxed to the utmost to accommodate the swelling throng of applicants. Hundreds, even thousands, of students are being denied admission to Georgia colleges every year because there is no room for them. There is no more distressing problem today in the state than that of accommodating the great influx of new students. Church support provides the denominational colleges with buildings and increased teaching forces; the private institutions are finding it profitable to increase their investment in equipment; but the state institutions, which should be pointing the way to the others, are woefully lagging behind in the race. Responsibility for this situation rests with the people, who thus far have been unwilling to make the necessary changes in the tax system to produce the required revenue.

Two inexorable conditions work mightily against our cultural progress. One of these is that Georgia has within her borders more Negroes than any other state—a higher percentage of the total than any other state excepting South Carolina and Mississippi. We can never as a state wholly overcome this obstacle. Georgia's low rank in all cultural statistics is due largely to the great proportion of Negroes among us. The other retarding condition is the fact that

Georgia is predominantly a rural state. The cultural advancement of the world has always been principally due to city influences. Whereas half the population of the United States is urban, only one-fourth in Georgia is so classed. Rural conservatism and rural standards must for many years impede our progress. This is said in no disparagement of country people. I know their virtues and their strength as well as their unreceptivity to new ideas. Most of my own immediate kin are country people.

Despite these obstacles Georgia is making real progress in the education of the masses. At the bottom of the ladder the result is seen in the decline since 1900 of white illiteracy from 12 to 5.5 per cent, and of Negro illiteracy from 52 to 29 per cent. It should be remembered that in 1870 the Negroes were practically one hundred per cent illiterate. (Incidentally, the widespread idea that Georgia ranks last in literacy should be corrected. In total illiteracy five states, four of them southern, are in worse condition; and in white illiteracy eight states, all southern but one, fall below Georgia.) At the top of the ladder our educated people are showing greater interest in purifying state politics and in the encouragement of art and music. Earnest work is being done by groups of men and women in bettering interracial relations. The women are rapidly organizing for participation in politics, and their influence is on the side of cultural progress. The growth of a more liberal spirit is evidenced by such matters as the creation of training schools for wayward boys and girls; the establishment of juvenile courts; the passage of a child labor law which experts regard as one of the best in the country; the enactment of the compulsory education law, the workmen's compensation act, and the vital statistics act; the establishment of a State Board of Health and of a State Board of Public Welfare with wide powers of supervision; and the current activities of the Children's Code Commission.

Other signs of progress are not wanting. Mr. Boyd says

that the Ku Klux Klan has Georgia within its grasp. The fact is that the Klan is hardly taken seriously anywhere in Georgia. On September 8 the Democratic primary, equivalent to election, occurred. The Klan candidate for Governor received less than seven per cent of the votes cast and carried only seven of the one hundred and sixty-one counties. The Klan specifically centered its fire on Judge Hines of the Supreme Court, who had angered the brotherhood by a speech made during the summer. Not only was Judge Hines re-nominated, but he received four votes to his opponent's one. Indeed, in all the major contests the Klansmen and those reputed to be Klan sympathizers appear to have been overwhelmingly defeated.

Georgia once enjoyed unenviable primacy as a lynching state; she has now almost eradicated that stigma. During the last days of August we had our first lynching of this year, the victim being a white man charged with the murder of a woman. Last year there was only one lynching. The officers of the counties are taking a very different stand in this matter from that of a few years ago, a reflection, of course, of changing public opinion.

I may finally mention the fact that the Legislature has in two separate sessions emphatically declined to follow the lead of Tennessee and other states in outlawing the teaching of evolution. A permanent victory, we hope and believe, has been won.

We in Georgia would take some comfort from the generous recognition on the part of Northern people that not all of us are political mountebanks, religious zealots, Fundamentalists, heresy hunters, haters of science, baiters of Jews and Catholics, and persecutors of Negroes. These elements of the population are unfortunately numerous everywhere: the problem of eradicating the canker spots in American life is not sectional but national. An occasional sojourner from the North among us finds something to commend, as witness the words of Carl Van Doren after his visit to Georgia last year:

"I encountered liberality towards new ideas, keenness on the part of the students for learning, and a delightful lack of that standardization of type which is to be found in the North and East and which is so deadly to anything creative or thoughtful. . . . Education in Georgia is forging ahead. The youth of the state is keen-minded, and the University is one of the most enlightened schools in the country with great possibilities of reaching the top in the world of learning, if it is not hampered by politics and lack of funds."

PART FOUR

THE UNIVERSITY OF GEORGIA

10

The University of Georgia: 150 Years of Service
[1951]

In 1951 the University of Georgia celebrated its Sesquicentennial. Dean Brooks, the only active faculty member connected with the institution since its Centennial in 1901, delivered one of the major addresses and prepared a study of the developments he had witnessed. These two papers, together with an address in honor of President Harmon W. Caldwell (1948), form the basis of this chronicle.

THE UNIVERSITY OF GEORGIA RECEIVED ITS CHARTER IN 1785. The State of Georgia had just weathered the Revolutionary War, which, in this commonwealth, had been a devastating civil war that left us economically and politically prostrated. The state could do no more than give the proposed institution its blessing, plus an endowment of 40,000 acres of land, at that time worth very little. Sixteen years passed before a modest beginning was made in 1801. Just how many students registered that year is not known. Two years later President Meigs reported that thirty or thirty-five students were on the campus, twelve of them seniors. At that time neither Harvard nor Yale had ever enrolled more than two hundred students.

FINANCIAL FOUNDATIONS

In the long period between 1801 and 1901 surprisingly little progress was made in student enrollment, size of faculty, physical equipment, or annual income. In the centennial year 1901, 328 students were enrolled, the largest number

[233]

up to that year. The faculty numbered eighteen members, and the total income of the University was $66,000.

The significant fact about this meager income was that the state appropriated nothing at all for regular maintenance and support. Two-thirds of the total came from the Federal government. In 1862 the Congress had set aside 30,000 acres of public lands for each representative and senator of every state for the establishment of Land Grant Colleges. After the Civil War Georgia's share was given to the University and the Governor sold it for $243,000. The money was invested in Georgia bonds and yielded, in 1901, $16,954. Furthermore, the Congress had in 1890 appropriated $25,000 annually to each one of the Land Grant Colleges. From the Federal government, therefore, the University received about $42,500, a very large fraction of the total income of $66,000. Meanwhile, the land given to the University in 1785 had been sold for $150,000 in notes, which the state took over, recognizing ever since as a constitutional debt an annual payment of $8,000 interest. The remainder of the $66,000 came from interest on a number of funds established from time to time and from tuition and matriculation fees. This last item was $2,655. Since 328 students were registered, it appears that the annual per capita charge to the students was $8.00.[1] The principal cost of the University was professors' salaries, an item which consumed $37,000. The faculty numbered eighteen; so the average salary was $2,000.[2]

THE UNIVERSITY IN 1901

Such was the University of Georgia after a hundred years of existence. It was a very small liberal arts college, the

---

[1] [The General Catalogue of the University for 1901 lists a matriculation fee of $10.00, a library fee of $5.00, and laboratory fees for students of chemistry or biology ranging from $2.50 to $15.00 per year. "No tuition fee is charged in either Franklin College or the State College." Ed.]

[2] [According to the Chancellor's report to the Board of Regents for 1951, the average professors' salary that year was $3,980, or about $1,390 in dollars of 1901 purchasing power. Thus the real salary of the average professor fell about one third during these fifty years. Ed.].

only other functioning organization on the campus being the law school. Its curriculum was like that of all other institutions of the era, confined to the classical and modern languages, mathematics, history and elementary sciences. In the centennial year, eighteen students received their A.B. or B.S. degrees. The law school, surprisingly enough, turned out sixty-nine graduates.

Alumni returning to the University after many years are always impressed by the tremendous changes in the appearance of the campus. When I entered the University in the fall of 1901, the campus consisted of the area bounded on the north by Broad Street, east by Jackson Street, and west by Lumpkin Street. Just how far southward the land owned by the University extended no one now seems to be sure, but the total acreage was 37. Crowded into this restricted compass were the twelve old buildings with which the students in the earlier part of the last half century were familar—Old College, New College, and Candler Hall (all dormitories), the Library (this old structure and a smaller one adjacent to it, Ivy Building, housing the Law School, were later connected by a portico and became Academic Building, no doubt the most expendable structure on the campus), the Chapel, Moore College, Terrell Hall, Demosthenian and Phi Kappa Halls, and several homes of professors, including Chancellor House. This former residence of the Chancellors stood on the southern boundary of the University's property. The building has recently been demolished and on its site the great new Little Memorial Library is rising.

FIFTY YEARS OF GROWTH

It is a noteworthy fact, it seems to me, that a still active member of the faculty should have witnessed the extension of the campus from some thirty-seven to the present 4,241 acres and the construction of upward of two hundred buildings, including sixty-six major ones. The trivial capital investment of 1901 has now reached the impressive figure of twelve million dollars. Above all I have witnessed the transformation of the institution from a small liberal arts college to the present complex University with its eleven distinct and separate colleges or schools. It is true that in 1901 we also had the State College of Agriculture and Mechanical Arts, but it was invisible except in the catalogue. The federal funds assigned to its support were used for the scientific departments in Franklin College. The broadening of the curriculum, which now includes practically every conceivable field of study, and the automatic acceptance of high school graduates without entrance examinations have attracted large numbers of students and made great increases in the teaching and administrative staff necessary. The greatest enrollment we have had in my time were the 7,000 students of 1948; the faculty then numbered 468.

Whether the University is doing a better job of turning out graduates equipped to function as leaders in our democratic society is another matter. When one calls the roll of the men who made Georgia in the nineteenth century, a very striking number of them were graduates of the tiny liberal arts college or the law school—statesmen, military leaders, writers, editors, educators, business executives. But I must resist the tendency of old men to glorify the past and to deplore present-day tendencies. Professor Bocock, one of the really great scholars who have graced our campus, got much interested fifty years ago in the archaeological work going on in the Near East. He remarked in class one day that the clay tablet believed by the archaeologists to represent the oldest known writing bore these words: "Things are not now as they were in the good old days."

UNDER SEVEN FLAGS

When President Harmon C. Caldwell left the University at the end of 1948 to become Chancellor of the University

System, I was drafted to deliver the farewell address at a dinner in his honor, not because the Committee thought I would shed much sweetness and light upon the occasion, but because they knew I would be brief and to the point. And there is no doubt that I can say all I know about any subject in about twenty minutes.

From one angle, at least, I was perhaps not the worst possible choice, for I had been rather closely associated with the five heads the University has had between 1901 and 1948. Since then, two more men have come into office, so that in my fifty years at the University I have served under seven flags. I should like to appraise these leaders by reviewing the setting in which they acted and the problems they faced.

WALTER B. HILL, '70, CHANCELLOR (1899-1905)

Mr. Hill, a graduate of the class of 1870, was the first alumnus to serve as head of the University and the first, I believe, who was not a minister of the gospel. For three years I had the privilege of close association with him as his secretary. He seemed to me then to have all of the elements of true greatness of character, and I still think him the ablest of our heads. He was somewhat cold and austere, with no great sense of humor, and extraordinarily careful in his attention to details. More than any other Chancellor he educated public sentiment in Georgia to a deeper conception of what a state university might mean to the commonwealth, if it were encouraged and adequately supported. It was a great misfortune that his lifespan was so short.

Realizing that progress depended on a decisive increase in income, Chancellor Hill rallied the alumni around him and inaugurated a movement which within three years produced enough money to begin the construction of the building now known as War Memorial Hall. He enlisted the interest of that great Georgian, George Foster Peabody, who donated $50,000 for a new library and gave funds to increase the land holdings of the University. But his greatest achievement, no doubt, consisted in having the University put on the regular appropriation bill by the state legislature, the initial grant in 1901 being the handsome sum of $27,000.[3]

Mr. Hill was also responsible for the first energetic steps to expand the small liberal arts school into a real university. He led the opposition to the strong movement to remove the Agricultural and Mechanical College (which existed in name only) from Athens. Instead, the General Assembly was induced to appropriate $100,000 with which to create a real State College of Agriculture, to be part of the University. Moreover, a School of Pharmacy was established under his administration, and the nucleus of the present College of Education was provided for when a new chair of Philosophy and Education was created. Chancellor Hill also initiated the movement to establish the high school accrediting system. At the close of his period of service the student body reached the 400 mark for the first time; the faculty numbered thirty-four members.

David C. Barrow, '74, Chancellor (1906-1925)

Chancellor Hill died in 1905 and was succeeded by Dean David C. Barrow, perhaps the most generally beloved of our past Chancellors. He held office over a longer period than any other head except President Church (1829-1859). Kindly, gentle, generous, forbearing, Chancellor Barrow carried into effect the plans of Chancellor Hill, his lifelong friend. Under him the new State College of Agriculture came into being; Conner Hall and many other buildings were erected on South Campus. In addition, Chancellor Barrow's administration saw the establishment of the School of Forestry

---

[3] I undertook to trace through the succeeding administrations the growth of the income of the University. Many difficult problems arose and forced me to abandon the idea. Suffice it to say that with the increase in enrollment and of tuition fees, and the enlarged appropriations, the income of the University for the fiscal year 1950-51 was $4,786,960, of which the State government gave $2,257,800. These figures include the amounts provided for Agricultural Extension, $435,000, General Extension, $44,300, and for Griffin and Tifton Experiment Stations, $352,500.

(1906), the Graduate School (1910), the Peabody College of Education (1911), the College of Business Administration (1912), and the Henry W. Grady School of Journalism (1915). While the School of Home Economics was not formally established until 1933, work of that character was offered as early as 1918 in the Division of Home Economics of the College of Agriculture. It may therefore be said that organizationally the University as now constituted reached its present full development in the period of Chancellor Barrow's service. Since his day only one new school has been added, the School of Veterinary Medicine (1946), and older members of the community will remember that such a school, established in 1918, had operated until 1933. The present school is therefore a re-establishment rather than something new.

The establishment of all these new schools meant, of course, that a far greater variety of services was offered than in the earlier years. The pure and applied sciences were better supported, the social sciences were expanded in personnel and equipment, the task of training teachers for Georgia schools necessitated a great development in psychological and educational subjects. As the offerings of the institution were broadened, far larger numbers of students were attracted. In the last year of Chancellor Barrow's administration (1925) the enrollment was 1,633, while the faculty membership was 100. Naturally this development cost money for new buildings and equipment and for salaries.

Other developments of importance occurred. The doors of the institution were thrown open to women in 1918; by 1925, more than 300 women were registered. The Barrow administration survived the strain of the First World War and did valiant service to the nation in furnishing officers to the army and navy. With the coming of the War the student body naturally declined, but in 1920 it reached 1,000 for the first time. Immediately after the War ended the

Alumni Society was reactivated; the publication of the *Alumni Record* was begun,[4] and a War Memorial Campaign was organized. A million dollars in pledges resulted, and from the money thus obtained War Memorial Hall was finished; the Commerce-Journalism Building and Milledge Hall were built. The beautiful dedicatory inscription around the rotunda of Memorial Hall was composed by "Uncle Dave," as Chancellor Barrow was affectionately known. This inscription reads: "In loyal love we set apart this house, a memorial to those lovers of peace who took arms, left home and dear ones and gave life that all men might be free." Through the activities of the Alumni Society large additions were made to the land holdings of the University.

CHARLES M. SNELLING, CHANCELLOR OF THE UNIVERSITY (1926-1931), CHANCELLOR OF THE UNIVERSITY SYSTEM (1932-1933)

In 1926 "Uncle Dave" was succeeded by Colonel Charles M. Snelling who, like his predecessor, had been Professor of Mathematics and Dean of Franklin College for many years. Colonel Snelling was a delightful person. His home was the scene of many social events long to be remembered (no one could beat him carving a turkey); his courtly manners and his keen sense of humor endeared him to his colleagues.

Colonel Snelling's administration bore the brunt of the Great Depression that began in 1929. In a single year the State's appropriation to the University dropped from $235,-000 to $154,000. This development cancelled the progress made under Snelling in the way of finances, student enrollment and physical equipment. The money was simply not available. In 1930 the total tax receipts of the State were only thirty million dollars and there were twenty-six so-called insti-

---

[4] [Dean Brooks was responsible for this innovation and served as editor of the *Georgia Alumni Record* for four years. Mr. Harry Hodgson, '93, was chairman of the War Memorial organization and Dean Brooks was the executive secretary. *Ed.*].

tutions of higher learning to be supported, to say nothing of primary and secondary schools and of many other services. Yet, despite the financial catastrophe that had befallen the State and its University, several developments of first importance occurred during Colonel Snelling's administration, none more far-reaching than the passage by the General Assembly of the Reorganization Act of 1931.

This measure profoundly changed the organization of higher education in the state. The twenty-six Boards of Trustees were dispensed with, ten institutions were discontinued, and the remaining sixteen were placed under the control of a single Board of Regents. The office of Chancellor was created as the executive head of the University System, and the title of the head of the University and the other units in the System was changed to President. On January 1, 1932, the Regents made Colonel Snelling the first Chancellor of the University System. A year and a half later he retired, having reached the age of seventy. As his successor the Regents named Mr. Philip Weltner, '07, now President of Oglethorpe University, an able and progressive Atlanta lawyer, who, together with Colonel Snelling and Dean S. V. Sanford, had been the driving force behind this legislation. Mr. Weltner resigned from the Chancellorship two years later, on June 30, 1935.

Within the University itself, Colonel Snelling created the Department of Music, which has grown into an important asset of the University. In 1927 he inaugurated the Institute of Public Affairs, which for ten years played a major part in the intellectual and social life of Athens. Large numbers of eminent statesmen, publicists, scientists, economists, and educators graced the platforms of the University.[5] Among the existing schools, the Law School was thoroughly reorganized and alumni and friends gave it a handsome new

---

[5] [Dean Brooks was Director of this organization during the whole of its existence. *Ed.*].

building. Mr. Hughes Spalding, 'oo, was the leader in the drive to provide the new Law School Building, which was named for the late Harold Hirsch, 'oo. Both of these men have rendered distinguised service to their alma mater.

During Colonel Snelling's administration as first Chancellor of the University System the State Teachers College (in Athens) was merged with the University. Moreover, the State College of Agriculture was tied closer to the University through the abolishment of its Board of Trustees and through changing the title of its head from President to Dean.

At the end of Colonel Snelling's term of office in the University, the enrollment was 2,855, and the faculty numbered 170.

STEADMAN V. SANFORD, PRESIDENT (1932-1935), CHANCELLOR (1935-1945)

In 1932, when Colonel Snelling was elevated to the Chancellorship, the Regents named Dr. Steadman V. Sanford, Dean of the University, as his successor to the Presidency of the University, an office he held for three years. In 1935 he was promoted to Chancellor of the University System after Mr. Weltner had resigned.

President Sanford, one of the most colorful and active men the University has had as President, was extraordinarily popular among the students, alumni, and the people of Georgia generally. He will go down in history as the Builder. He engineered the financing and construction of Sanford Stadium. He took full advantage of the liberal terms provided by the Public Works Administration, and during his term of office and that of President Caldwell (who carried out the program), nineteen buildings were erected at a cost of $2,155,000. Of this amount the state provided $1,332,000, the P.W.A. $823,000. Among the new structures were the Park Language Building, LeConte Hall, the Fine Arts Building, four men's dormitories, four women's dormitories, the Agricultural Extension Building, the Forestry Building, the

Dairy Products Building, the Home Economics Buildings, the Snelling Dining Hall, the dairy barn, as well as important additions to the Law School, the Commerce-Journalism Building, Moore College, Baldwin Hall, and New College. During President Sanford's time the scope and service of the School of Journalism was greatly expanded. In the year his term of office ended, the enrollment of the University was 2,948, and the faculty numbered 157.

Harmon W. Caldwell, '19, President (1935-1948), Chancellor (1949-   )

Mr. Caldwell, who succeeded President Sanford when the latter became Chancellor in 1935, had been Dean of the Law School and was quite a young man when elevated to the post of President. He participated in a large way in the building program already mentioned. When the Second World War came he succeeded in having the University designated as one of the five U. S. Navy Pre-Flight units, which brought, among other benefits, Stegeman Hall, the expansion of War Memorial Hall, the fine cinder athletic track, and the athletic field houses and new playing fields. In the matter of buildings, the crowning achievements of the Caldwell administration were the erection of Gilbert Memorial Hospital and the planning and financing of the Little Memorial Library, now in process of erection. Most of the paving of campus roads was done in Mr. Caldwell's term of office.

Mr. Caldwell, however, was more interested in improving the quality of the teaching and in encouraging graduate work and research than in the brick and mortar aspect of the growth of the University. He brought in large numbers of fine men and women, increased seven-fold the amount available for research, greatly increased the salaries of the professors, and established the Institute for the Study of Georgia Problems, an enterprise which has published numerous studies in the field of Georgia's financial, economic

and social problems.[6] Another contribution of President Caldwell to the intellectual life of the University and the state was
the establishment of *The Georgia Review*, a first-class quarterly that has published excellent articles in many fields
of interest. Another major achievement was the establishment of the Art Department.

I should not overlook another movement of great significance that occurred during Dr. Caldwell's tenure as President, namely the creation of the University of Georgia Foundation, incorporated in 1937. This Foundation was the joint
product of the devotion of a group of really outstanding
alumni, Cam D. Dorsey, Hughes Spalding, Dr. F. Phinizy
Calhoun, Dr. Frank Boland, and Hatton Lovejoy. Its purpose was to provide a channel through which alumni and
friends of the University might make gifts for the general
good of the University. The corpus of the fund is now
about half a million dollars. One of its first fruits was a gift
from the Bradley Foundation of Columbus towards the purchase of the palatial residence that is now the home of the
Presidents of the University of Georgia.

It was during the Caldwell administration that the University had to bear the strain of the Second World War.
The student body, or at any rate the male element, almost
disappeared. In 1939 the enrollment was 3,735, of whom
the men accounted for 2,343; in 1944 the enrollment had
shrunk to 1,836, the men numbering only 698. With the
coming of peace and the enactment by the Congress of the
liberal G.I. bills, veterans in vast numbers flooded the University and all other institutions of higher learning. The maximum enrollment occurred in 1948 when the figure reached
7,071, of whom 4,056 were veterans. The faculty that year
numbered 468, the largest in our history. Meanwhile the income of the University increased rapidly during Mr. Cald-

---

6 [Dean Brooks was Director of the Institute and the principal contributor
to its publications. *Ed.*].

well's time. In 1946, for the first time, the figures exceeded a million dollars; the next year it was $2,000,000, jumped to $4,000,000 in 1948, and was nearly $4,000,000 the following year.

JONATHAN C. ROGERS, PRESIDENT (1949-1950)

Upon the death of Chancellor Sanford in 1945, the Regents named as his successor Dr. Raymond R. Paty. He assumed office in January 1947, and resigned effective January 1, 1949. The Regents then promoted President Caldwell to Chancellor and Jonathan C. Rogers to the Presidency of the University. Mr. Rogers assumed office on January 12, 1949, and retired September 7, 1950.

In his brief tenure President Rogers made an excellent impression on the University community. He fought valiantly for the coordination of agricultural teaching, research and extension under the control of the University of Athens, a policy long advocated by President Caldwell. The successful culmination of the struggle was a tremendous achievement. President Rogers also succeeded in securing several much needed increases in the salary scale of professors. It was during his term of office that the new building for the School of Veterinary Medicine was pushed to completion.

OMER C. ADERHOLD, '23, PRESIDENT (1950-   )

On the retirement of President Rogers in 1950 the Regents named as his successor Omer C. Aderhold, a graduate of the class of 1923. Dr. Aderhold had been for some years the very successful Dean of the Peabody College of Education. In that capacity he became a real leader of the forces working for the better training of teachers and for better support of education at all levels. He was principally responsible for the Minimum Foundation Program for Education, and when that program was formally adopted by the General Assembly of Georgia, a new day dawned for the educational interests of the state. Since President Aderhold is

just at the beginning of his career, and since I claim no
prophetic powers, I shall have to leave to some future historian the job of evaluating his services. My guess is that
such a task will turn out to be a most pleasant one.

DISTINGUISHED GRADUATES, *1829-1901*

Having surveyed the administrations under which I served
from 1901 to 1951, I must speak of the University's main
product, its outstanding graduates. I shall confine myself,
however, to a survey of the classes which graduated before
my time. No one who keeps in mind the lack of public support during the first hundred years of the University, the
tiny enrollment, and the narrow scope of the curriculum,
can help wondering how the University turned out so many
men of eminence in so many fields of endeavor. Were space
available, an even more impressive list of great names could
be presented.

STATESMEN, LEGISLATORS, MILITARY LEADERS

Eminent in national affairs were Alexander H. Stephens,
'32, Member of Congress, Vice-President of the Confederacy; Robert Toombs, '28, United States Senator, Chairman of the Montgomery Convention that established the Confederate States of America, and Major General in the army
of the Confederacy; Howell Cobb, '34, Speaker of the national House of Representatives, Secretary of War in Buchanan's cabinet, Governor of Georgia, and Major General in the
Confederate Army; Thomas R. R. Cobb, '41, the first to
codify the laws of any state in the union, author of the constitution of the Confederacy, and Brigadier General in the
Confederate Army; Benjamin H. Hill, '44, United States
Senator. Other United States Senators were A. O. Bacon,
'59, William C. Dawson, '16, Herschel V. Johnson, '34,
Pope Barrow, '59, Thomas W. Hardwick, '93 (he was also
a Governor of Georgia); and William J. Harris, '90.

Graduates too numerous to name have been members of

Congress, Governors of Georgia, and leaders in the legislative halls of the state. A goodly number of the Governors are named in other connections. In addition there were James Johnson, '32, Nathaniel E. Harris, '70, William Y. Atkinson, '77, John M. Slaton, '86, Hugh M. Dorsey, '93, and Clifford M. Walker, '97. Especially eminent among the Members of the national House of Representatives were William M. Howard, '77, who was also a member of the United States Tariff Board and a Trustee of the Carnegie Endowment for International Peace; and Dudley M. Hughes, '71, co-author with Senator Hoke Smith of the famous Smith-Hughes Act, under the terms of which vocational education in the public schools of the nation was begun.

Our outstanding military leader was John B. Gordon, '53, who at the age of thirty-three became a corps commander under Lee. He was also twice Governor of Georgia and was elected United States Senator three times.

MINISTERS

To the ministry the University gave before 1900 George F. Pierce, '29, Methodist Bishop and founder of Wesleyan College, Macon; T. F. Scott, '59, Episcopal Bishop with a jurisdiction extending from British Columbia to the northern border of California; Charles M. Beckwith, '73, Episcopal Bishop of Alabama, and Edwin G. Weed, '65, Episcopal Bishop of Florida.

LAWYERS

Most of the graduates of the precentennial era who achieved fame were lawyers. In addition to those already named there were Joseph Henry Lumpkin, '16, who organized the Supreme Court of Georgia and was its first Chief Justice, and Eugenius A. Nisbet, '21, who was on the bench at the same time as Justice Lumpkin. Other members of the Georgia Supreme Court were Charles J. Jenkins, '23, James Jackson, '37, Linton H. Stephens, '43, Samuel Lumpkin, '66, Joseph Henry Lumpkin, '75, Joseph R. Lamar, '77, Richard

B. Russell, '79, and Marcus Weyland Beck, '81. At least two Georgia lawyers of the era were Presidents of the American Bar Association, Peter W. Meldrim, '68, and William A. Blount, '72. Two graduates, John A. Campbell, '26, and Joseph R. Lamar, '77, became members of the Supreme Court of the United States. Other Federal judges were Samuel H. Sibley, '92, now retired Judge of the Circuit Court of Appeals; Emory Speer, '69; and William H. Barrett, '85, District Court Judges.

Physicians and Surgeons

Crawford W. Long, '35, is, of course, the most famous physician the University has produced. As the discoverer of anesthesia he has an enduring place in the history of medicine. Three others, all still living, have achieved eminence in their profession. Dr. William L. Moss, '97, after completing his work at Johns Hopkins, taught at various times at Johns Hopkins, Yale, and Harvard, and then served for a number of years as Dean of the University of Georgia Medical College at Augusta. Dr. Frank K. Boland, '97, a surgeon, has been Professor of Surgery at Emory University, took an active part in the medical service in World War I, and is now a Colonel in the Medical Officers Reserve Corps. He is past president of the Southern Surgical Association and of the Southeastern Surgical Congress. Dr. F. Phinizy Calhoun, '00, is past President of the American Ophthalmic Society, and was a Major in the Medical Corps of the U. S. Army in World War I.

Scholars, Writers, Journalists

Scientists of note were John Le Conte, '38, Professor in the University of Georgia and founder of the University of California; and his brother, Joseph, '41, Professor in the University of California; and Charles H. Herty, '86, President of the American Chemical Society.

Among the important writers were Charles H. Smith, '47,

(Bill Arp); Francis R. Goulding, '30, author of *The Young Marooners* (he also invented the sewing machine); Cornelius DeWitt Wilcox, '80, Professor at the United States Military Academy and military historian; J. L. M. Curry, '43, author of *The Civil History of the Confederate Government;* U. B. Phillips, '97, Professor at the University of Michigan and at Yale, and leading Southern historical writer; and Henry Timrod, '47, the poet. Among the journalists of note were Henry W. Grady, '68, editor of the *Atlanta Constitution;* Clark Howell, '83, editor and owner of the *Atlanta Constitution;* John Temple Graves, orator and editor of the *Atlanta Georgian;* Pleasant A. Stovall, '75, editor of the *Savannah Press* (he was also ambassador to Switzerland).

EDUCATORS

The contribution of the University to education has been especially notable. The two Le Contes have already been mentioned. Walter B. Hill, '70, and David C. Barrow, '74, were both Chancellors of the University. Gustavus J. Orr, '44, was President of the National Educational Association. The University supplied to the nation in those days many college presidents and professors.

BUSINESS LEADERS

It is out of the question to list the University of Georgia graduates in the precentennial era who achieved prominence in the business world. Among the most notable graduates of this group were: Samuel Spencer, '67, organizer and first President of the Southern Railway Company; Preston S. Arkwright, '90, President of the Georgia Power Company; William D. Anderson, '91, President of the Bibb Manufacturing Company; A. R. Lawton, '77, Vice-President and General Counsel of the Central of Georgia Railroad Company; and Eugene R. Black, '92, Governor of the Federal Reserve Board.

WHAT OF THE FUTURE?

The changes in the past fifty years have been tremendous. There is every indication that the changes ahead of us will be no less remarkable. Some of them may be foreseen even now. For one thing, the future will see major emphasis laid upon off-campus activities. The far-reaching research and extension work in agriculture which emanates from Athens has already had profound effects throughout the state. In time it will revolutionize farm life and farm productivity. Our off-campus centers for adult education bring the benefits of college education to many thousands whom circumstances have prevented from studying at the University. In other words, the state is now our campus. The influence of the University, through research and through service, is reaching out into every community of Georgia. All colleges and departments share in this work.

On the other hand there is no doubt that, striking as the progress over the past fifty years has been, the University is quite literally at the crossroads. It would be unfair to say that its progress has been a mere matter of widening out instead of deepening; research has not been neglected, and many departments have risen to considerable scholarly stature. But with the influx of vast numbers of students seeking vocational specialization, the idea of general education has become endangered. It is one of the healthiest signs that both the faculty and the administration are profoundly aware of this problem and that the battle for higher standards and broader concepts never ends. The next decades will determine the issue. Shall we rest on our oars, glorying in past achievements, or move forward to ever greater service to the people of Georgia? Much will depend on the type of goal we set ourselves.

=11=

Quo Vadimus?

[1947]

The following article, reprinted with minor omissions and changes, appeared in the first issue of the Georgia Review, *Vol. 1, No. 1, (Spring, 1947), pp. 53-63.*

A QUARTER OF A CENTURY AGO THE CHANCELLOR OF THE University of Georgia invited the oldest member of the faculty to deliver the baccalaureate address. Although I was present on graduation day, I had long ago become adept in sinking into a comfortable state of near-Nirvana on such occasions, and I therefore remembered nothing except the title of the address, "The Memories of Age." In due course the University printed the address[1] and I have just been reading it, being curious to know just what memories the learned speaker recorded for the entertainment and instruction of his audience.

I

Dr. White was just completing his fiftieth year as Head of the Department of Chemistry. Few men manage to stretch out their days of travail as University teachers to a half century, and one might reasonably expect an educational leader of Dr. White's calibre to have had worthwhile experiences in a state university that for so many years had striven more or less valiantly and successfully to keep life in the embers

---

[1] H. C. White, *The Evolution of the University as Interpreted by the Memories of Age.* Baccalaureate Address, June 21, 1922. Bulletin of the University of Georgia. Vol. 22, No. 6.

of enlightenment amongst us. I found the paper most interesting.

Had Dr. White been a common or garden variety of annalist, I fancy he would have written something like this: "I joined the faculty of the University of Georgia in 1872, only two years after the close of the political phase of the Reconstruction Period and the final withdrawal of the Federal troops from the state. After some years of suspension because of the Civil War, the University had reopened its doors on January 3, 1866, with 78 students in attendance. By the time of my arrival in 1872 the student body had increased to 317, including 55 high school students, and the faculty numbered twelve members. The curriculum had been considerably broadened. In ante-bellum days only the A.B. degree had been offered with its set requirements of Latin, Greek, and mathematics for everybody. By 1872 the sciences had got a toe-hold and the University was offering the additional degrees of Bachelor of Science, Mechanical Engineer, and Civil Engineer, with appropriate requirements for each. The physical equipment consisted of a half dozen old buildings. The fifty years of my tenure have witnessed expansion in every respect. The student body now (1922) numbers more than 1,000 (not counting 1,274 summer school students); the faculty has grown to more than 100, not including numerous extension workers; the campus has spread from the original 30-odd acres to several thousand acres. Buildings too numerous to mention have been erected. The University has become a real university with a number of distinct schools and colleges, each with its own dean and special staff. The annual appropriation for maintenance has grown from nothing at all when I came to the present handsome sum of $165,000 per year."

Strangely enough Dr. White said none of these things. In a discourse which took considerably more than an hour to deliver, little mention was made of the material growth of the University; no talk about buildings or equipment; no statistics about the growth of the student body or faculty; no reference to the financial support except to comment upon its meagerness. Odd indeed that so intelligent a man as Dr. White did not realize that a University consists of a great campus, a multitude of magnificent structures, and an army of students! Well, what *did* he talk about?

First of all, he made clear his authority to speak about the University when he said: "I have been associated with and known intimately the University for a longer number of years than any man, living or dead."[2] He then devoted some time to a discussion of the charter of the institution, pointing out that for the first time in American history a political unit—the state—had accepted the higher education of its youth as a fundamental obligation of the whole people of the commonwealth. He also mentioned the fact that the Charter, while recognizing the maintenance of religion and morality as essential to the wellbeing of a well ordered state, dissociated the University from all forms of organized religious faith. But the chief distinction of the Charter, he went on to say, was its insistence that the function of the University was "to mold the youth of the state to a life of virtue and good order," "virtue" and "good order" being interpreted to mean "righteousness" and "justness." Higher education, he contended, should have as its purpose not specialization but general knowledge. "The experience of modern times has but confirmed the experience of the centuries that specialization of the intellectual faculties may not with advantage precede the development of the whole."

The object of all education was to cultivate the sound mind, which is marked by righteousness in thinking and justness in thought, by ability to think rightly and to reason justly. No justification, he thought, "could be found for

---

[2] He continued to teach until his death in 1928.

education at public charge of the craftsman rather than the man."

The speaker believed that on the whole the University had lived up to this high ideal. She had indeed produced a long line of notable leaders of men. In whatever aspect of public and private affairs, University men had provided that leadership without which a democracy cannot survive. Aside from government, war, religion, and business, University men have taken the lead in such diverse developments as the organization of our present system of high schools, in the creation of numerous other colleges in Georgia, including those for Negroes, in the establishing of the State Department of Agriculture, the planning of our wonderful system of highways, and the beginnings of the State Geological Survey, not to mention service upon numerous commissions such as those to reform the tax system. The University has fostered a truly remarkable type of loyalty to the institution and to the state. Dr. White ventured "to doubt if any similar institution in the world today can boast a larger measure" of such loyalty and spirit. "It is a spirit inherent to the institution, born with its birth and continuous through its life, a spirit which made bright and glorious those precious jewels of the University, the successive generations of Georgia youth who have filled its halls; a spirit of loyalty and love, loyalty founded upon respect and affection engendered of gratitude; a spirit which should appropriately mark the relation of alumni to alma mater; of alma mater to alumni; of foster-sons to foster-mother; of foster-mother to foster-sons."

II

This striking production of leaders, the intense loyalty of the alumni to their alma mater, their courage in defending her when attacked, had resulted, Dr. White believed, from three factors that had determined the character of the University. One of these is implicit in all he said, namely, the extraordinary ability of the faculty in the days when the position of University professor was a proud one, and of the general management of the institution; the other two are explicitly stated, the tradition of freedom, and the "instrument" that the University had used to develop men. These matters are certainly worthy of comment.

Many of the professors of fifty years ago I sat under and knew intimately—a few of them are still with us—and I can testify to their exceptional scholarship and devotion as teachers. As a rule they were not noted for research and writing, but they were learned and skillful in the arduous and exacting work of teaching. In those days of small student enrollment (the student body in the year of my graduation, 1904, totaled 359, the largest enrollment the University had had up to that year) the relation of student to teacher was on a far more personal basis than now when the huge size of classes ineluctably precludes personal contacts and makes it necessary to rely almost exclusively upon the lecture system.

It is my opinion that a university stands or falls on the character of its faculty. Great scholars, great scientific researchers, great teachers, men of culture and good breeding, make a university great. A collection of mediocre professors cannot give character and reputation to an institution, no matter how numerous they are nor how extensive the institution's physical equipment, nor however large its student body. There is no doubt whatever that fifty years ago, and even in later years, the University had on its faculty a really notable group of first class teachers. Irwin Edman in his delightful *Philosopher's Holiday*, reminiscing about his own undergraduate days at Columbia, remarked that "every college has five or six men who in essence are its educational system." He could recall only a half dozen teachers who had left any impress upon his mind and heart: Charles A. Beard, Carlton J. H. Hayes, E. A. Robinson, John Erskine, Frederick Woodbridge, John Dewey—*nomina clarissima*. I am sure that in times past the University of Georgia could measure up to that high standard, and I think the affection of the alumni is attributable in large measure to their memories of and associations with such men.

The tradition of academic freedom, Dr. White held to be a prime factor in the generation of the Georgia spirit. How many times have I boasted that the University, though poor in the goods of this world, was rich in the possession of a tradition of unhampered freedom of teaching and writing? Throughout her long history the professors have had little of the stifling and stultifying interference with academic concerns and with freedom of expression that other institutions in the land have suffered at the hands of politicians, the clergy, and business interests. In the one unhappy recent instance of political attack, everyone knows how our students and alumni rallied as one man to defend the institution. Without this freedom, Dr. White wrote, "there can be no conscientious discharge of professional duties; no genuine attachment of the student to the institution."

And, finally, Dr. White devoted much of his time to the pedagogical tools or "instruments," as he called them, that the University had employed in molding the youth of the state "to a love of virtue and good order," that is to say, in producing cultured men of good will qualified to serve the state as leaders. This instrument, Dr. White says, had always been the Humanities. In earlier days the term "Humanities" had meant the classical languages, mathematics, and philosophy. The catalogue of 1868-69 listed as the requirements for admission a correct knowledge of Caesar and Virgil, the Greek Reader, and of Algebra and one book of Geometry. Once in college, all students took the same courses; Latin, Greek, mathematics, and English were required in every term of every year. What would the twentieth century student think of that! Dr. White points out that in modern times it had become necessary to include the natural sciences in the concept of Humanities. Hence at the University "laboratories were added to libraries and the value of the methods of science given full recognition in the curricula." The new departments of science had flourished and had become "powerful additions to the energies of the inner urge toward intellectual righteousness," but—and this is of the essence of the matter—"the error was not committed that the sciences should replace or subordinate the classics and other agencies of culture; these too were strengthened and expanded and their efficiency increased the progress of the times." The classics, English literature, philosophy and the sciences—the aim and the method are the same: insistence upon a broad general type of education and avoidance of anything suggesting specialization or craftsmanship.

The success of the University seems completely explained at this point in Dr. White's memorable address—it was found in the calibre of the faculty, the maintenance of academic freedom, and the devotion to the Humanities.

III

I trust that this long analysis of Dr. White's address has not bored the reader to such a point that he will not be willing to bear with me in carrying on the story where Dr. White left off. Briefly stated, my purpose is to raise the question whether or not the ideals, conditions, and practices that presently dominate the University are such as to insure that she shall continue to function as the "mother of men."

The University recently has been going through a period of phenomenal growth. During the depression years of the thirties, largely through federal aid, many excellent buildings were erected; the greatly increased income of the state during the war years and the liberal attitude of the state government made possible appropriations for maintenance of a magnitude undreamed of a few years ago; the generous provisions of the federal government for the education of veterans has brought an overwhelming flood of ex-soldiers, with the result that the facilities of the institution are taxed to the utmost; many additions to the faculty have been made during the last two or three years. All these are indications of vitality and continued interest in higher education in Georgia and we are proud of them.

Despite these evidences of physical growth, uncomfortably disturbing doubts assail me when I try to rationalize these developments into indications of progress in the intellectual sense. John Woolman used to call these periods of doubt "stops" in his mind. Is the University drifting along, complacently confusing size with excellence; have we become an educational factory turning out a second-rate product; have not our classes become so large and unmanageable as to make impossible the sort of personal relation between teacher and student without which there can be no true university teaching? If we do not have that relationship we might as well depend entirely upon books for education and forget Cardinal Newman's warning: "If we wish to become exact and fully furnished in every branch of knowledge which is diversified and complicated, we must consult the living man and listen to his living voice."[3] Hence the need of institutions we call universities. Newman's idea of a University was penned in these immortal words:

> [The university] is a place where inquiry is pushed forward, and discoveries verified and perfected, and rashness rendered innocuous, and error exposed, by the collision of mind with mind, and knowledge with knowledge. It is the place where the professor becomes eloquent, and is a missionary and a preacher, displaying his science in its most complete and most winning form, pouring it forth with the zeal of enthusiasm, and lighting up his own love of it in the breasts of his hearers. It is the place where the catechist makes good his ground as he goes, treading in the truth day by day into the ready memory, and wedging and tightening it into the expanding reason. It is a place which wins the admiration of the young by its celebrity, kindles the affections of the middleaged by its beauty, and rivets the

---

[3] John Henry Newman, *The Idea of a University.*

fidelity of the old by its associations. It is a seat of wisdom, a light of the world, a minister of the faith, an Alma Mater of the rising generation.

Have we so diluted the requirements for graduation that even our best students get only a smattering of many subjects but no real mastery of any of them, with the result that our graduates are poorly prepared for life? I think I never saw the whole matter more neatly expressed than in an article by Sir Richard Livingston, Vice Chancellor of Oxford University. He said:

> Uneducated people are a danger to the world, but they are not so dangerous as a less recognized menace—the half-educated, who have learned enough to express an opinion on subjects which they do not really know, but have never learned to be aware of their ignorance. Such people are familiar pests in every department of life, and a main duty of education is to diminish their number. It cannot do this by giving the knowledge required—omniscience is not a practical aim—but it can show people what knowledge is, so that they are aware when they do not possess it, and this it achieves in a very simple way: by seeing that the pupil studies at least one subject in the curriculum so thoroughly and so far that he knows what knowledge is and how much industry, thoroughness, precision, and persistence it demands, if we are to have even a distant sight of it.[4]

We may as well be realistic in facing up to the question I have raised. No practical-minded man would now consider it at all possible to ignore the current of history and academic change and reconvert the University into a small classical college with the curriculum then prescribed. In its very nature a state university is forced, if it is to have any considerable measure of popular support, to offer work in a vast range of interests that touch the lives of its constituency. If thousands of parents and their progeny desire training in such utilitarian fields as Agriculture, Home Economics, Busi-

---

[4] Sir Richard Livingston, "Education for the Modern World," *Atlantic Monthly,* November, 1946.

ness, Forestry, and Pharmacy, a state university has no choice but to yield to such pressure, and many of our best students are content with the types of curricula that the force of circumstances has produced in these fields, all of which are, it goes without saying, important in our economy. Furthermore, it must be remembered that, since our system of admission is based primarily upon graduation from high school, there is practically no selective process in admitting students. We take all comers, in sharp contrast with the practice of private institutions with strictly limited enrollments.

IV

We shall continue to operate these professional and semi-professional schools and the numbers of students attracted to them will no doubt increase. My plea is that we strive not only to maintain but to enhance the prestige of the liberal arts college of the University and try to attract to it a larger proportion of students of first rate ability who are primarily interested in general education.

There appears to be a natural tendency for students of mediocre ability to gravitate toward the semi-professional divisions of a university. On this point I am not disposed to be too dogmatic or to speak with very great assurance, for unquestionably many students of superior ability register in schools and colleges other than the College of Arts and Sciences because of their genuine interest in the specialization available in these other lines; but how frequently have I heard students say, "I am taking a (blank) degree because I do not want the required language work in the A.B. degree" or, "I am avoiding the B.S. degree because of its emphasis on science!" Many students are wholly devoid of interest in philosophy, mathematics, language and literature, and pure sciences, and prefer more "practical" courses. I have had bitter arguments with students who wanted to be excused from some liberal arts requirement in order that they might take shorthand and typing, which they thought would be more "useful." With this sort of selection going on, it seems to me that there should be left in the College of Arts and Sciences a fairly excellent nucleus of students willing to hazard the arduous work in sciences, mathematics, languages, art, and literature.

Let us at any rate make the pleasant assumption that the College of Arts and Sciences enrolls large numbers of superior intellects, boys and girls qualified to endure the tough discipline that the A.B. and B.S. degrees have traditionally stood for, though heaven knows there are also plenty of indifferent students in the College. Let us also assume that this is the element of our students destined by tradition, native ability, and cultural background to become the leaders of tomorrow in the learned professions, in scientific achievement, and scholarly effort. Now, my complaint is that we do little to encourage such students to put forth their best efforts. Students of exceptional ability, those of the average sort, and those on the margin, so to speak, are all corralled indiscriminately into a given course, all must meet the same requirements, and the level must be within the reach of the average student so that the percentage of failures will not be too great. The superior students drift along with the rest, not having to put out any real intellectual effort, while the poor students may pass the course in the sweat of their brows, and, of course, some fail altogether. Our superior students cannot help holding the course in contempt, simply because it has not exacted of them any worthwhile effort. Eventually they are graduated and forever afterward are disgruntled and become members of the group, numerous in Georgia, who assert that standards are low in the University and that they obtained their degrees with a minimum of effort.

Oxford and Cambridge Universities long ago recognized this situation and provided for it in a very practical and efficient way. It was realized and frankly admitted by preparatory teachers, by the boys, and by their parents, that about half of the students (such at least was the proportion forty years ago) are of such low grade intellect and so lacking in ambition and energy as to be unfit for real university work. They are, nevertheless, permitted to enter Oxford, but they are classified as "Pass" students and the work required of them is pitched at a level within their reach—about like the work required in the average American college. The other fifty per cent of the students are called "Honors" men and they are expected to measure up to a very high standard. Most of their work is done through guidance given them individually by the teachers.

In this way there is a rough adjustment of requirements to ability. The general idea of the Oxford system has been introduced into the United States and I noticed in a recent study of higher educational practices the statement that three-fourths of the American colleges and universities on the approved list of American institutions now have Honors courses. The University of Georgia is not one of them.

An Honors program involves ignoring such matters as specific course requirements for the degree, attendance upon lectures, term examinations and reports—in fact practically all of the routine commonly associated with college work. To replace these requirements, several departments of closely allied interests (such as economics, government and history) organize seminars in which students meet in small groups and do first hand work in original sources and standard secondary works. Their reading follows a syllabus and their results are presented in the seminar where the papers are discussed by the members. The function of the professor is to lay out the plans of the seminar, prepare the syllabus, assist the student in finding the materials, teach him how to use the library, criticize his writing, guide the discussions, and check on the work of each student. The Honors program is a two-year one based upon two introductory years of general education. The student participates during his last two years in eight such seminars, all in related fields, and at the end of that period he is subjected to a comprehensive examination prepared and graded by outside examiners, that is to say, by experts from other colleges who have had no part in conducting the seminars.

This sort of program is clearly a radical break with American traditions for undergraduate work, although at the graduate level it has long been used. In the typical state university with its great mass of students, understaffed departments, large classes, and cramped physical conditions, the current method of teaching is to announce a text book, for the contents of which the student is held responsible. (There may also be in the library a reading shelf of reserved books to which the professor will make reference and either suggest or require additional reading, though few students take advantage of the opportunity). Then the teacher lectures for a quarter or a term, amplifying, explaining, amending and criticizing the text, having occasional tests, the papers being commonly read and graded by graduate assistants, and at the end of the course he prepares a final examination and he himself grades the papers. This process is repeated in institutions on a quarter system some 35 or 36 times, and in the course of three or four years the student accumulates enough "credits" in these homeopathic doses to qualify him for a degree. These courses are chosen more or less at random, under certain restrictions designed to provide continuity in a given department's work, and a certain degree of concentration is required in the student's field of major interest.

By contrast the student who pursues an Honors program consults scores or even hundreds of books on a given subject; he is not a mere receptacle into which the professor pours his knowledge in the often-times vain hope that some of it will not leak out; he does his own reading and thinking and comes to have a fair mastery of a few subjects rather than a smattering of many.

It goes without saying that such a change in the character of the University teaching cannot be forced upon students. At Swarthmore, the first American college to move in this direction, Honors work was introduced a quarter century ago on an experimental basis. The President, thoroughly sold on the idea, called together a group of the ablest teachers in the social sciences, explained the system he had in mind, won their enthusiastic approval, got committees to work in setting up the program, and then invited a group of the most promising students to meet for a discussion of the matter. Volunteers were called for and eleven students responded. From this small beginning in one segment of the college the principle has spread until now Honors courses prevail in all departments at Swarthmore. The intellectual life of the college has been revolutionized, the ablest students are engaged in work that taxes them to the utmost, and when they depart to take their places in the state and nation, they go forth with the feeling that they have got something worthwhile from their years in college.

Meanwhile the college goes on as usual, offering the old-fashioned programs for students with lesser ability. The superior minds are given a chance to flower in a way quite impossible under the traditional method, but this rigorous discipline is not imposed upon students of mediocre ability. Many of the best institutions in the land have introduced modifications of the Swarthmore idea. The first step has been taken at the University of Georgia in the appointment of a committee to study the whole matter.

The question which provides the caption of this paper cannot now be answered. I hope, however, that we may be on the threshold of a new day.[5]

---

[5][The Honors Program of the University of Georgia, initiated by this article, failed within two years. *Quo Vadimus?*—Ed.]

PART FIVE

TRIVIA

12

A Georgian in California

[1939]

On April 21, 1939, the University of California gave a dinner to the American Association of Collegiate Schools of Business. Dean R. P. Brooks, then President of the Association, delivered the after-dinner address.

SINCE THIS IS THE ONLY OPPORTUNITY THE PROGRAM GIVES me to speak officially, I avail myself of the chance to say that we from other parts of the union are enjoying in full measure our stay on the Coast. Your magnificent distances, your World's Fair, your many miles of toll bridges, your San Francisco fogs (the counterpart of which are to be found only in London) are all more or less unfamiliar to us Easterners. Your open-handed hospitality, while very enjoyable, is seriously interfering with the orderly conduct of the program.

The fact that I come here as a representative of the University of Georgia gives me the opportunity to remind you of the connection between the University of California and my own institution. Your first Acting President and third President was John Le Conte, a member of the class of 1838 of the University of Georgia, where he filled the chair of Physics and Chemistry from 1846 to 1855. Later he migrated to Berkeley and was one of the builders of this institution. His brother, Joseph, also a graduate of the University of Georgia (class of 1841), was for many years Professor of

Geology here. Another University of Georgia man who had a notable career with you is Hal Moreno, of the class of 1893.

Aside from the Le Contes, the Californian best known in Georgia is the great Burbank, a wizard with plants, equal in genius to Edison. Burbank's fame is somewhat marred with us by the prevalent belief that by crossing poison ivy on dog fennel he produced spinach, a vegetable hateful to all right-minded persons.

The speakers at the banquet last night had as their theme song the notion that crossing the state line into California somehow impairs one's moral fibre, transforming conservative truth-loving Americans into monumental liars. Indeed, whether native sons or emigres from the East, you seem all to admit that mendaciousness is a leading characteristic of coastal people. The epithet "liar" apparently means nothing, whereas in my part of the country the only other term more fight-producing is the one which reflects upon one's maternal ancestors.

My own observation in this matter would, I imagine, find general agreement among visitors. Your somewhat cavalier attitude toward the truth apparently emerges only when you are recounting the glories of the West. I for one feel bound to say that I do not think you exaggerate the wonders of this marvelous land. I notice, however, that in your panegyrics only Washington, Oregon, and California as far south as Santa Barbara are included. And you are wise, I am convinced, in keeping quiet about the states lying immediately eastward. The streamliner took the better part of the day coursing (sailing I believe is the correct nautical term now used by the Union Pacific) through Wyoming. From Cheyenne to Ogden stretches one vast desert of mesquite bushes—no cities or towns, no human habitations, no farms, no factories, no cattle, no outward signs of life of any sort. The dreariness of those hapless hours would have been insupportable but for the circumstance that among my fellow travelers were Dean Madden and Professor Elwell. It was Dean Madden, I recall, who discovered means aboard ship of refreshing ourselves at intervals. Somewhere in mid-Wyoming the alert New Yorker started a mild stampede toward his side of the car by claiming that he had seen a cow. Unfortunately a curve in the road obscured this vision and there were no other witnesses to the exciting event. The only animate creature I personally saw was a crow winging his solitary way eastward carrying his own vittles. I am bound to admit that there are several unaccountable lacunae in my mental picture of Wyoming and it is possible that in such moments I missed some of its more pleasing prospects.

I come from a state, Georgia, that is just about as far from California as one can get and still be in the United States. Her remoteness is perhaps no greater than your unfamiliarity with the economic and social conditions under which we Georgians live. From the multiplicity of things legendary and factual that might be related about the land of moonlight and magnolias (or, as Mencken named it, "the Sahara of the Bozart"), I have jotted down a few random items that may be of interest. At the outset I should say, however, that although I may modestly claim to know some pretty tall tales myself, I cannot possibly equal you accomplished Californians in the extent and variety of stories about your state and region. For one thing the material I have to work with is by no means so rich.

Like Gaul, Georgia is divided into three parts: the mountain counties of extreme North Georgia, a relatively small fraction of the whole area; the Piedmont Plateau, a country of hills, valleys and swift streams comprising one-third of our 59,000 square miles; and the Coastal Plain, a flat sandy land about three-fifths of the total area, being the portion of the state south of the fall line of the rivers, extending from

Augusta on the Savannah, through Macon on the Ocmulgee to Columbus on the Chattahoochee.

The mountains of North Georgia, some three or four thousand feet high, would, I presume, scarcely be recognized as mountains by persons who know the Rockies or the Sierras. Until recent times the mountain section of Georgia has been without adequate means of communication and transportation. Its inaccessible valleys and hillsides have for two centuries provided homes for an element of our people sometimes referred to as our contemporary ancestors. Although Negroes constitute more than one-third of the population of Georgia, there are practically none in this area. The population is almost wholly made up of Scotch-Irish people whose ancestors moved southward in the eighteenth century from the states to the north. The Appalachians constituted a formidable barrier to the westward movement. Many of the pioneers got stranded in the mountains and for some generations lived isolated lives, cut off from the social and economic movements which went on apace in the coastal area and the more fertile lands further south. The mountaineers are excellent people but are culturally retarded. Most of the present-day illiteracy and poverty among the Southern whites occurs among the mountain people.

The leading products of this area are corn and children. The fertile valleys, the heavy rainfalls, the long dreary winter days and nights, and the lack of transportation facilities are said to favor activities which result in a heavy production of these two commodities. The corn has traditionally found its way to market in the form of "moonshine" or "white mule," and the young people are providing part of the labor supply for the rapidly growing industries of the Piedmont region to the south. Of late years the power companies have acquired control over large areas of the region, converting many valley farms into storage lakes. Many dams and power houses are now to be seen on the streams. Furthermore, the federal and the state government have acquired hundreds of thousands of acres in these counties and are converting them into beautiful public parks. North Georgia is rapidly becoming an attractive play ground for those who love the wildwoods, the streams, and lakes.

Piedmont Georgia, as the name indicates, comprises the foothill regions formerly covered with oak and hickory forests. The cotton planters and their slaves began their invasion of this country on its eastern side early in the nineteenth century and in a relentless march swept over the land, Alabama-bound. A clean culture crop like cotton tends to exhaust the natural fertility of the land; the lure of quick profits and the absence of scientific conservation methods have resulted in widespread erosion. Many thousands of acres of Piedmont Georgia are now classed as sub-marginal and are permanently ruined for agriculture. The boll weevil completed the story, almost wiping out the cotton industry in North Georgia. The town of Athens, where the state university is located, is in the heart of the Piedmont country. It was once the sixth inland cotton market in the United States. Twenty-five or thirty years ago some 180,000 to 190,000 bales of cotton were annually marketed there; now no more than 25,000 bales are received. Since the climate and soil are apparently not well adapted to other types of large-scale farming, the Piedmont area has lost much of its former importance in agriculture. On the other hand it is admirably suited to manufacturing and most of the industrial development of Georgia has occurred there. Many people think that ultimately cattle raising and dairying will be the leading agricultural interests.

The University of Georgia, or rather the oldest unit of a state system of sixteen institutions now under the control of one Board of Regents, is located in Clarke County about 80 miles from the North Carolina line. The town of Athens, which the classically-minded, optimistic Georgians of the period expected to reproduce the atmosphere of a like-named city in ancient Greece of which you may have heard, was laid out in 1801 and was designated as the site of the University. In placing the University a hundred miles from the nearest considerable town, the purpose of the founders was to safeguard the students from the corrupting influences of the great Georgia cities of the time. (At the dawn of the nineteenth century the total population of the state was 160,000; Savannah, the largest of the metropolitan centers, reported a total of 2,300 persons. Savannah is 250 miles from Athens. The nearest town was Augusta, 100 miles away.) Much of the building material was hauled by wagon from Augusta. The particular spot selected was a hill overlooking the lovely Oconee River, and an important factor influencing the selection was the belief on the part of the Trustees that a plentiful supply of fresh fish would always be available.

Nothing of importance distinguishes the University of Georgia from any other state university, except perhaps its age. For many years we have been engaged in a verbal battle with the other oldest state university over the right to the designation. My practice is to claim that Georgia is the first state university unless North Carolinians are present; in that event I content myself with second place. After "doing" the University, the only interesting sight in the town of Athens is our double-barreled cannon, locally believed to be unique. This curious piece of ordnance now adorns the lawn of the city hall. It was the brain-child of an Athenian aroused to defend his native city from the ruthless heel of the conquering Northerners in civil war times. The idea had all the signs of genius. Each of the barrels was loaded with a cannon ball, the two being connected with a chain. Upon being discharged the balls were expected to separate to the limit of the chain's length and to proceed forward, mowing down the enemy in such a mass execution as was not thereafter dreamed of until the days of Charles McCarthy. According to the story told

by survivors of the first and only shot fired, it turned out
that the charges of powder in the barrels were not uniform,
or that they did not ignite simultaneously, or that the balls
were uneven in weight. For one or several of these reasons,
when the balls roared from the cannon's mouth, their normal
flight being hindered by the chain, they proceeded to do a
sort of horizontal Catherine wheel, panicking the bystanders.
After a moment of indecision this besom of destruction took
a due east course, hurtling off toward Charleston, some 200
miles distant. Athenians hopefully awaited reports from South
Carolina, whose citizens were none too popular in Georgia,
but nothing further was ever heard as to the final resting
place of this bizarre shot.

What with digressions and reminiscences of one sort or
another, I have already taken more than my share of the
time. As they pass along the road to the bourne from which
there is no returning, old men unfortunately accumulate a
vast amount of pointless anecdotes, useless facts, and untenable
beliefs and they never overlook the chance to inflict them
upon others, often in the vain hope of lightening the gloom
that is apt to descend upon dinners. I ought to stop now, but
I cannot leave Georgia without saying a few words about
the third geographical division of the state, the Coastal Plain.
I imagine many thousands of my fellow Georgians are crowded around their radios, listening sternly and getting ready their
Ku Klux regalia for a party in my honor, in the event I do not
treat their section fairly.

It is an odd paradox that the part of Georgia which was
formerly called the "pine barrens" and which the cotton
planters avoided because of the bad reputation of its soils
and the prevalence of malaria, has in the twentieth century
become the most prosperous section of the state. It is from
South Georgia that come the naval stores, tobacco, peanuts,
melons, early vegetables, pecans, and hog products which
are rapidly transforming Georgia from a one-crop state to a

commonwealth of diversified agricultural interests. Much of the cut-over pine lands has now been cleared, drainage and medical science are conquering malaria, marvelous concrete roads traverse the entire region, and thriving towns everywhere give evidence of new life since the devastation wrought by the boll weevil.

A couple of years ago, emerging from a New York theater where I had been seeing "Tobacco Road," I overheard a young woman say: "I never realized before what Georgia people are like." She had nothing on me there. Fifty years of life and travel in Georgia had never brought to my sight any such depravity. Social workers assure me, however, that there are plenty of such families as the Jeeter Lesters in the state. And it is not to be denied that in many of the studies of comparative social and economic conditions, Georgia comes perilously near the bottom. Some of our impatient young people think that the only thing to do about Georgia is to apply the well-known treatment accorded to nut grass, namely, move away and leave it. There is, however, another more sensible view. While Georgia is decades behind such progressive states as Ohio, California, or North Carolina, when one compares Georgia's conditions now with those that prevailed a generation ago, quite wonderful progress becomes evident. At any rate we have no earthquakes, no dust bowls, no floods, no long periods of drouth, and few tornadoes; and while we have no oil fields, Hollywoods, Sequoias, nor World Fairs, we do produce an abundant supply of beautiful and gracious women and of men who know how to enjoy themselves, taking advantage of our fine climate, which encourages life in the open perhaps to the disadvantage of scholarly activities; mint grows well throughout the state; and we are not too far from Broadway. All in all I am not minded to migrate to California. At least not as long as it is necessary to pass through Wyoming to get there.

=13=

Of This and That

[1947]

Read in 1947 at a meeting of Dr. Brooks' dinner club. Unpublished manuscript, revised for inclusion in this volume.

CONSIDERING THE SUPERABUNDANCE OF READING MATTER that confronts the reader of today, one ought to think twice before sitting down to write. Books, books, books, article after article, on every imaginable subject! What justification could I have for adding my mite to this immense flood! My only excuse is to plead a well-defined case of *cacoethes scribendi.* I have, I confess, the irresistible urge to write. Yet I am not sanguine enough to think that I have anything of importance to say. Like John Randolph of Roanoke, I am compelled to confess: "I am an ignorant man." It is fundamental, I think, that one should write only about matters of which one has more than common knowledge. An honest appraisal of my experience convinces me that the only subject I am really qualified to discuss is the business of being an academic dean. I therefore propose to take up this matter first. The rest of this paper will be given to a hodge-podge of observations on a variety of unrelated subjects. These the reader should peruse, if he can stand them, without hope of profit.

OF BEING A DEAN

One of the apocryphal anecdotes told of me is that once upon a time I was angered by a student who persisted in falling asleep in one of my classes, and that I finally dismissed him for the remainder of the hour. Shortly thereafter, the story goes, I returned from a meeting of the national association of deans and at the first class meeting apologized to the offending student for my harshness, remarking that I had not realized before attending the recent meeting how dull deans could be.

The general attitude toward deans was amusingly put some forty-odd years ago by an English don. He wrote a slender volume of parodies under the title "Misfits." Much of the volume purported to be recently discovered manuscripts of short essays by Sir Francis Bacon, written, of course, in the style and with the spelling of his day. Of "donnes" (as teachers are called at Oxford), he wrote:

> Certainely there bee that affect to find Usage in Donnes; And set them Downe as proper to the Body Politique; as needs they must; For they should else be at a Stond, to Thinke what should be in it, that such Things bee; which neither make for Pleasure, as is very Certaine; Nor yet for Advantage. . . . Of the Reason for Donnes, then, I give this Account; That it is by some Approved; But by others not. And of which the views be wiser, I say not; Though I know well.

And of Donnes that might be called deans he says:

> And other Donnes there bee, of an exceeding Difficilnesse. For these be mainly interested in the Reiglement of Colleges; and the Sustentation of Laws. Alle manner of Bruit they utterly Abhorre; and will not listen to any Excusation thereof; Though it be very cunning. With such I am distasted; For Zelants be alwais Absurd.

At the time of his elevation to the deanship the typical dean was probably neither duller nor less sparkling than the average teacher. The nature of his duties is what kills his spirit. His primary and really important function is to guide his faculty in building up a sound curriculum and to keep the degree requirements current with the best thought in his field; to add able members to the staff, and to keep constant pressure on the administration to increase his budget. The budget is always uppermost in his mind, no matter what the allocation may be. Once when the association of deans was meeting at Harvard, a group of us visitors paid a courtesy call on the Dean of the Harvard Graduate School of Business. We found the old gentleman in a towering rage with the President. His budget for the next year had been fixed at only $800,000. "How does he think it possible for me," he demanded, "to run this enterprise on such a grossly inadequate amount?" I recall that at the moment I was trying to get our Business School budget raised from $25,000 to $30,000.

If the dean's time and energies could be restricted to these primary activities, his life would perhaps be endurable. In actual administration, however, his waking hours are consumed by the endless chore of answering the daily correspondence, administering an infinity of university and college regulations upon all sorts of subjects; trying to keep peace among the warring factions of the staff; holding conferences with students, generally the delinquent ones; making up schedules of class meetings and of examinations; preparing material for the annual catalogue; attending faculty and committee meetings. These routine duties reduce the dean to a machine, leaving him little time or strength to prepare for his teaching work, if he elects to teach, as he usually does, and none for research and writing.

Unfortunately, it has come about that the leading man in a college or a department in the college of arts and sciences (many of which are of college size and have comparable problems) is promoted to the top position. This practice is partly a hangover from the days when the colleges and departments were very small, and the best man was naturally made the head; and, of course, prestige and especially salary are also involved. In order to reach the highest salary one had to become a dean or department head. Not infrequently the result has been to spoil the careers of promising scholars by the unavoidable substitution of routine drudgery for creative research and writing.

The way out of this bad situation would appear to be putting a premium upon scholarship and creative research rather than upon administrative work. The best men should be headed away from administration by reducing their teaching loads and by providing them with salaries that would make administrative posts unattractive. Another helpful device, perhaps not always applicable to colleges, but certainly to departments of the college of arts and sciences, would be to have no heads but rotating chairmanships, the incumbent holding office for only one or two years. If there were, say, a dozen eligible men in the college or department, no one of them would be obliged to sacrifice any considerable part of his professorial career to uninteresting and relatively minor routine activities.

I should not overlook one quite important consideration. Some men (and women) are born deans. Not greatly interested in the life of the scholar nor in writing or teaching, they love administrative detail and do the job well. Such men should be given their chance. This variety of dean not infrequently becomes President of the institution. They understand financial problems, are good administrators, shine in public relations work, and are good platform performers. There are, of course, exceptional cases in which deans combine these qualifications with a genuine love of learning and manage to turn out creditable creative research in the face of heavy odds.

OF GROWING OLD

Some years ago I taught in the months of June and July at the University of Colorado, in Boulder, an ideal spot for a summer sojourn. At the boarding house I met a Mr. and Mrs. Jones of Fort Worth, who had somehow discovered

Boulder and went there every summer to escape the Texas heat. Mr. Jones was a well-to-do retired businessman of some seventy-five years. He had no interest in fishing, which is excellent in those parts, did not play golf, knew nothing of bridge or other card games, did not collect stamps, read nothing but the daily newspapers. One day I asked him how he managed to kill the time. He arose early, he said, had a substantial breakfast (characteristic of old men), strolled down to the business section of the town, bought the morning newspaper, went back to the boarding house, read the paper, took a nap on the front porch, and was then ready for lunch. After lunch he had a brief nap and then he and Mrs. Jones went for a walk, after which he bought and read the afternoon paper. Dinner over, the boarders commonly sat around and chatted awhile, the Joneses in the group. By then it was bedtime. After thus reviewing his ordinary day's activities, Mr. Jones looked me squarely in the eyes and said solemnly, "I am just waiting around to die."

I shall never forget the incident. Here was a man of means, sound of body and mind, with ample leisure, but totally lacking in intellectual resources and having no interest in any form of stimulating recreation. To him the world of ideas was a closed book; he was completely unaware of the inexhaustible mine of delight to be had from the great books of the past or the vast output of the present. His life, now that he had reached the time of retirement from active business, was as dull and boring as Ulysses found his when he got back to barren Ithaca. Mr. Jones had surrendered, unlike the great Homeric hero who, tired of inaction, got his old comrades in arms together and fired them with desire to strike out afresh over the wine-dark sea in search of new adventure. Tennyson, in those immortal lines of the greatest old man's poem, has Ulysses say:

> for my purpose holds
> To sail beyond the sunset, and the baths

Of all the western stars, until I die.
It may be that the gulfs will wash us down;
It may be we shall touch the Happy Isles,
And see the great Achilles, whom we knew.
Tho' much is taken, much abides; and tho'
We are not now that strength which in old days
Moved earth and heaven; that which we are, we are;
One equal temper of heroic hearts,
Made weak by time and fate, but strong in will
To strive, to seek, to find, and not to yield.

A famous Princeton professor, George McLean Harper, was said to have been unable to read aloud Wordsworth's "Michael." His voice would choke with emotion and he would have to give it up. The concluding lines of Tennyson's Ulysses affect me the same way.

Schoolboys in my youth were made to read Cicero; why, I can't imagine, unless the schoolmasters regarded his Latin as easy. Cicero's speeches and letters meant nothing to boys ignorant of the background of his writing. We also read *De Senectute*, an even sillier requirement, since nothing is less interesting to youth than wise reflections about the problems that come with advancing years. After a half century I have just reread *De Senectute* in translation. It is humiliating to confess that reading the original would have been the task of a week. I had it in mind to suggest that all men of sixty-five or more ought to be required to read the essay, but such a suggestion would be footless, for Cicero elaborates upon the delights of old age when a man is prepared for it, intellectually, emotionally, and economically. He must have stored his mind with the wisdom of the ages; he must be philosophical about the loss of sensual pleasures; and he must have laid by a competence, for poverty-stricken old age is unendurable. If a man has not already made this preparation, it is of course too late to do anything about it once he is old. So I would change my prescription and recommend *De Senectute* to young men and women of thirty or so.

·De Senectute* was written in the form of a conversation between the aged Cato, in his eighty-fourth year, and two young noblemen who had asked why old age seemed no burden to him. Putting his ideas into the mouth of Cato enabled Cicero to do quite a bit of anticipating (he was only sixty-three when he was assassinated), and to express opinions that one would scarcely have expected of him. For example, I never heard of Cicero's taking any interest in farming, a circumstance in which he differed from many of the Senators and other important Romans of his day. Cato is made to say that farming is an ideal avocation for an old man, and he comments learnedly upon such agricultural operations as irrigation, thorough preparation and manuring of the soil, and most surprisingly, grafting, which he says is "surely the most ingenious invention ever made by husbandmen." He also remarked that in Homer, a classic for centuries before Cato was born, mention is made of manuring the soil. How modern these ancients often were!

My net conclusion on this subject of growing old is therefore that, while it is a calamity to continue in life after one's mental and physical powers are exhausted, a satisfying period may be enjoyed by those who read, love the outdoors, and have a substantial amount of E-Bonds.

OF BODILY AILMENTS

After finally shedding all administrative responsibility, I should have been in a more cheerful frame of mind, and perhaps would have been but for a protracted siege of sciatica. Was it not in *Three Men in a Boat* that one of the characters claimed that he had had symptoms of all known ailments except housemaid's knee? Lately I have checked through a medical encyclopedia to see whether or not I could truthfully make the same statement; and, while to my surprise I find that I have escaped a few of the more unusual oriental diseases, the number of my ailments is still impressive and makes a list that any hypochondriac might well be proud

of. Beginning with the feet and proceeding heavenward, ath-
lete's foot has been a hardy perennial, contracted no doubt
in club shower baths. In early youth osteomyelitis struck me
down, leaving me partially crippled in one leg. For a long
time I navigated on crutches. I suppose it was at that period
that I acquired my life-long love of reading. While in college I developed a "mouse" in my left knee-joint. The original mouse has produced numerous progeny, visible to the
X-ray. It was while I was still in college, moreover, that I
underwent an operation for varicose veins.

Moving upward, some twenty years ago I suffered a
serious attack of pleurisy and spent three months in an Ashe-
ville hospital. The younger members of my staff watched
the situation with bated breath, hoping that the matter of
succession would arise. Still earlier, during World War I,
a captain's commission was offered me in an organization to
keep track of the history of the War. At the conclusion of
the required physical examination in Washington the major
examiner said: "Well, I suppose you know about your
heart?" I was startled because my heart was about the only
major organ with which I had had no trouble. The doctor
sternly said that I was unfit for any except sedentary work,
and added that if he had my heart he would never take another drink, nor smoke, nor play tennis or golf, nor follow
dogs quail-hunting, nor do any mountain climbing, nor run
after a street car, nor bring up a scuttle of coal from the
basement. That verdict was pronounced thirty years ago and
I am still here. (I compromised by giving up tennis.)

At intervals, happily rare, I have been laid up with lum-
bago, an ailment that I cannot recommend as an agreeable
way of escaping work for a few days. Six or eight years ago
I was operated on for double hernia. From the neck up I
have had plenty of trouble, My eyes were congenitally weak
and I put on glasses at sixteen. Much of my annual income
has gone to dentists. For many years I was tortured by sinus

infection and had to make weekly visits to a specialist in Atlanta.

I close this touching account of my bodily infirmities with a fuller reference to sciatica, which with me has been *facile princeps* in agony. No language at my command can give an adequate idea of what sciatica entails in the way of torment. I have compared notes with other sufferers and they are unanimously agreed that sciatica surpasses all other ailments in searing and unremitting pain. It has now worked down to my toes, which at the time of this writing feel as if they were immersed in a cauldron of molten lead. In this connection I have made a discovery that I freely pass on to the world. It is of such major importance that if I were an Englishman I believe it would earn me a knighthood. Sufferers say, take off your shoes whenever possible—that will relieve the pressure. I say unto you, remove your sox also. They seem to restrict the feet even more than do the shoes.

Many writers have professed themselves puzzled by the physical frailties of mankind and have come up with bizarre notions on the subject, as did Henry Mencken in one of the early issues of *The American Mercury*. Many people flout the notion of evolution and cling to the old-fashioned idea of special creation of all the million varieties of creatures that presently encumber the earth. If we adhere to special creation and assume omnipotence and good-will on the part of the Creator, the problem is how to account for so poor a job of manufacturing as man is. Mencken's answer was that the designing of the human body must have been delegated by the supreme Authority to a committee of lesser gods, and, since differences of opinion arise in all committees, the final decisions represented a compromise. Compromises are usually bad. No records of the committee meetings have come down to us, but we know the subcommittee on the hand did a perfect job. The subcommittee on the teeth however failed miserably, to the eternal delight of dentists.

OF MURDERING THE LANGUAGE

Professional students of the English language look with tolerance upon most departures from current "good usage." While I approve this objective and broadminded attitude, I confess that I harbor certain pet prejudices against many popular yet dubious expressions. Here are some of them: *contact* as a verb; *enable* in such sentences as *the draining of the swamp enabled the use of the land for farming; until* instead of *that* (*I am so busy until I cannot come*); the wrong case of pronouns (no one was ever heard to say *they invited I to dinner*, but millions say *they invited Jack and I to dinner*); the universal confusion of *lie*, meaning recline, and *lay* (practically everybody says *I laid down* and *I am going to lay down*); *enormity* as the equivalent of *vastness;* the expression *some place else;* and that prime irritant, *different than.* Communications addressed to the editor in the "letters" section of *Time* magazine usually begin *Re your article.* My observation has been that nothing of interest or importance is ever said by a person who begins his letter with *Re*, or *Anent*.

Of all the current instances of bad grammar, the misuse of *like* is the commonest, and in the South we have invented a new word, *liketer* (or *like-tuh* or *like-ta*), as the equivalent of *almost*, as when we say *he liketer fell.* I see no reason why the grammarians should not accept *liketer* as a good word, and I was much interested to be told recently by a lexicographer that in a book he has just completed he so recommends.

In the South we are inaccurately charged with two oddities of language usage that I especially want to comment upon. One of these is the notion deeply ingrained in the minds of gagsters, funnymen, and writers of comic strips that we pronounce the first person pronoun *I* as if it were spelled *Ah.* I dare say that one could live a quarter-century in Georgia and never once hear that pronuciation. I have heard it only twice in my life. In one of the cases a girl student unmistakably said *Ah*. On inquiry it turned out that she was from Pennsylvania (the other case was a native South Georgian). In reading a recent book the scene of which was the north country of England, I was interested to find that the natives of the peasant variety invariably pronounce *I* with the *Ah* sound.

The other oddity is the mistaken notion that we use *you-all* in the singular. I am led to discuss the matter because several years ago, when inadvertently listening to some radio comedian (Senator Claghorn, I think), the expression came over the ether. For a half century I have traveled up and down and hither and thither in the South and never have I come upon an instance of *you-all* in the singular. Mencken (in *The American Language*) gives a complete bibliography of the subject and concludes that the expression, though occasionally used by the most ignorant element of Southerners, is to all intents and purposes unknown in the South.

Nevertheless there must be good ground for the view prevalent in other parts of the Union that we do use *you-all* in the singular, and I think the answer to the puzzle is that Southerners do in fact commonly say *you-all* when, speaking to one person, they intend to include more than one in the remark. For a dozen years a Kansan by birth was a member of the faculty of the University of Georgia. He stoutly maintained throughout his stay that *you-all* in the singular was generally used in Athens. Once on a Sunday I dropped in for a call and found my friend sitting alone on his front porch. He greeted me triumphantly with the statement: "Well, at last I have a perfect case to report." In those days automobiles were still rare. An automobile-owning neighbor had come over and, finding the Kansan sitting alone on the porch, had said to him: "How would *you-all* like a drive this afternoon?" "Did you accept?" I asked. "Yes, my wife and I enjoyed the outing," he replied. "And how did she get in on the party?" I asked. "Of course, Mr. Green included her in the invitation." "He certainly did," I came back, "and when he asked if *you-all* would like a ride, he had her distinctly in mind." (Knowing Mr. Green it was not hard to guess that the last thing on earth he would want to do was to take my Kansan friend out without his wife; in fact, the husband was excess luggage.)

OF THE TOTAL DEPRAVITY OF INANIMATE THINGS

It is a matter of common observation among paper-shuffling people that the document required at the moment is invariably at the bottom of the pile, if indeed it is in the pile at all; and that a letter or paper filed—however rational the filing system—is permanently lost. A similar situation exists in the home. With the passage of the years my wife and I have collected what must be the majority of the items listed in the American Pharmacopoeia. But look for an aspirin in the medicine cabinet, and never will it be found. On a fishing trip have the misfortune to pull up a catfish armed with powerful, murderous fins. The only way to extract the hook safely is to use a pair of pliers. Your tackle box will yield plugs, hooks, lines, sinkers, and corks by the dozen, but no pliers. The cussedness of inanimate things is also sometimes seen in the way machinery works. The windshield wiper of your car is likely to stall only when it is raining; the lights work perfectly in the daytime, only to flash out when you are in the country on a dark night. The electric clock in my house, after working perfectly for a half dozen years, took to gaining time at the rate of three hours in twenty-four. The man in the repair shop could find nothing wrong with it. I took it home and it worked perfectly.

My concern with the vagaries of inanimate things dates back to the first years of the century when, as a youngster,

I was secretary to the Chancellor of the University, Walter B. Hill, of blessed memory. It was he who coined the phrase *the total depravity of inanimate things*. The expression is a good one, for I am beginning to suspect that so-called inanimate objects are in reality sentient but by nature depraved. After all, they are ultimately made up of atoms and parts thereof, just as are human bodies. There are differences between things and human beings, though. In some unfathomable way the bunch of atoms that we call human beings acquired consciousness, a sense of sin, a fear of punishment for it, and a method of salvation. As time passes, the conduct of mortals appears to be improving to some slight extent. We tend to become less self-seeking, more socially-minded, more generous in our attitudes towards our fellows. I regret to report, however, that I can see no improvement in the conduct of so-called inanimate things, and this makes me disconsolate and unhappy.

OF NOSTALGIA

My wife spends a considerable fraction of her life responding to calls from our daughters who need help at critical times. During such periods of bachelordom my radio enjoys a well-earned rest. Only occasionally, when some important event such as the world series or a football game is being broadcast, do I turn on the current. I did this the other night and was rewarded by a wistful voice crooning "W'y, oh w'y did I leave Wyoming?"

Now I should have thought it most unlikely that anyone would grieve over having left Wyoming. I know little enough of the state, and I have never visited Yellowstone National Park, undoubtedly one of the wonders of this world. But I did once drive from Estes Park, Colorado, to Cheyenne, following Route 30 through eastern Wyoming to Ogden, Utah. The high point of that drive was a night spent at Rawlins where we enjoyed buckwheats of a quality that might well create profound nostalgia in a crooner who thinks of them. Buckwheat cakes of that kind give me the spiritual uplift that I get from playing a two-pound bass, gazing down in the Grand Canyon, or toying with a Bourbon highball.

Nevertheless, Wyoming was the home state of my radio crooner and he yearned for his boyhood surroundings. There are numerous such nostalgic songs and poems, ranging in poetic excellence from Browning's "Oh, to be in England Now That April's There" to the Wyoming song. Many of these songs originated in or were written about the romantic South, such as "Carry me Back to Old Virginny," "My Old Kentucky Home," "Carolina Moon," and "Swanee River." Such songs are likely to involve magnolias, mocking birds, and darkies singing and picking cotton. One that I remember, no doubt inaccurately, is about Tennessee, and ran:

> Back home in Tennessee
> Just try to picture me
> There on my mother's knee,
> She's all the world to me.
> All I can think of tonight
> Is a field of snowy white,
> Banjos ringing,
> Darkies singing,
> All the world seems bright
> Tonight in Tennessee.

The most beautiful of these songs about states, I have always thought, is "The Banks of the Wabash," the lyric written by one of the Dreisers, the music by the other. The refrain runs:

> Oh, the moonlight's fair tonight along the Wabash,
> From the fields there comes the breath of newmown hay;
> Through the sycamores the candle lights are gleaming
> On the banks of the Wabash far away.

The only nostalgic song I know about cities is "The

Sidewalks of New York." Perhaps the names of cities do not lend themselves to compositions of this character. Who was ever heard tearfully pleading to be carried back to dear old Cicero, Ill., or Wilkes-Barre, Penn., or Lickskillet, Georgia?

Yes, we all think sentimentally of the old country, the old state, the old home town, and long to get back there. It sometimes happens, however, that the returning native does not find himself as happy as he had expected when at last he gets home. Reading Carl Crow's fascinating *Foreign Devils in the Flowery Kingdom*, I was impressed by Crow's observation that tough old "China Hands" yearn to get back to the States and prepare years in advance for the great event, but when they finally manage it, they frequently return to China after a short visit home, never to try it again. Conditions have changed, old friends and relatives have died or scattered, things are not as they were in the good old days. Expatriated Chinese, on the contrary, never seem to lose their love of native land. A strong organization is maintained in this country through which Chinese finance the return of their bodies home for burial.

OF RECREATION

> I ain't gwinter wuk no mo'
> Labor am tiresome sho'
> Best occupation
> Is recreation
> I ain't gwinter wuk no mo'.

Since man finds that most of the goods and services he needs or desires are scarce, he has throughout history had to work, usually long and hard, to obtain them. For the masses of mankind life has been a ceaseless round of toil: the sentiment of the doggerel that heads this section has a strong appeal. In modern times the application of machinery to industrial processes and the coming of the factory system have so increased the productivity of labor that with a much shorter day it has been possible to raise the standard of living and at the same time leave the workers a measure of freedom for recreation. Unfortunately, this desirable development has not affected in any notable way agricultural labor or domestic service, but for factory and other workers who are on an eight-hour day, society is providing recreational facilities, the sound principle being that mere idleness is socially undesirable.

That segment of the population which lives by its wits, the professional classes, for example, has never been accustomed to fixed hours of employment. While many professional people and those citizens who are in the managerial class oftentimes work longer hours than manual laborers, they can usually so regulate their lives as to make reasonable allowance for sports and other forms of recreation.

Very ancient records of human life give evidence of indulgence in sports and games. In Rawlinson's history of Assyrian archeological excavations I noticed a contemporary drawing of men shooting birds on the wing with bows and arrows. Lovers of Homer will remember how Ulysses in his wanderings after the fall of Troy came upon Nausicaa and her maidens playing ball—probably not big league ball: nothing is said about any DiMaggio ending the game in the ninth with a home run.

Among the multifarious forms of recreation I rank sports and reading first. Sports today offer such a range of activities to lovers of the outdoors that anyone can find his opportunity, whatever his physical power may be. Between mountain climbing or football, at one extreme, and croquet at the other, all one needs for sport is fondness for games. I have gone in for quite a number of sports, though I have always been a mediocre performer and have never known the thrills that champions must enjoy. Though never a good shot, I have killed my share of birds; not a notably skillful fisherman, I have found more relaxation and pleasure in fishing than in any other sport—my biggest fish, barring sharks, has been an eight-pound bass; no great golfer, rarely under ninety; fairly good at tennis, as several European silver cups attest.

But one grows older and in the process finds (or rather I have found) indoor forms of recreation of major interest. I rank these in the inverse order of importance as card games, conversation, and reading. The only card game I presently play is bridge, that fearful time consumer. Of conversation, I cannot imagine anything more enjoyable than talk in a group of well informed, urbane, catholic-minded men and women. Membership in our dinner club is one of my chief joys.[1] But best of all is reading.

The last time I read Ecclesiastes I came across the familiar saying, the origin of which I had forgotten: "Of the making of many books there is no end." Indeed there is nothing new under the sun, as the Preacher himself states on high authority. Yet he would have suffered much severer headaches had he been confronted with the deluge of books now pouring from the presses of the world. What to read is indeed the problem, how to select from the many thousands of books at hand! Twenty years ago, during a period of enforced idleness, I resolved to read some books which I had never more than glanced through, and what an orgy of good reading it turned out to be: Frazer's *Golden Bough*, Boswell's *Johnson*, Wynwood Reade's *Martyrdom of Man*, *The Compleat Angler*, *Moby Dick*, and other classics.

Since reaching maturity I have never been an assiduous reader of novels. Dickens, Thackeray, Scott, Victor Hugo, Dumas I read in early youth and remember them to this day.

---

[1] Several writers have undertaken to reduce to book form the sort of conversation that occurs in such a group. Two of the best are Edna Vincent Millay's *Conversation at Midnight* and G. Lowes Dickinson's *Symposium*. In 1931 I had the pleasure of several days' association with Dickinson at the home of Mr. Albert Kahn in suburban Paris. He was really a great man, for many years a professor at Cambridge. His book is not so conversational in arrangement as is Miss Millay's; it is rather a series of short essays on specific subjects, contributed by the members of the club in one evening.

Of late years I have never been able to reread any of these massive novels, with the sole exception of *The Tale of Two Cities*. I invariably bog down and quit after a few chapters. Even *Pickwick Papers* bores me. I think it is because they are too long-drawn out and I am too impatient. Long modern novels I eschew—the last one I managed *in toto* was *The Forsyte Saga*.

Mystery stories seem to be getting poorer and poorer. I find none now published that compare with Sherlock Holmes or Maurice LeBlanc, or of a younger generation, Dorothy Sayers and E. C. Bentley. The English, it seems to me, write infinitely better detective stories than do Americans. Their writing is more pleasing, more leisurely, and contains more local color. A few Americans have concocted good mysteries, notably Rex Stout with his inimitable Nero Wolfe and Archie the audacious. I have grown weary of Perry Mason, and that imitation Englishman, Philo Vance, has never charmed me. Books of this sort I read only after retiring for the night, as a substitute for phenobarbital.

For steady reading, to keep current with what is going on in the world, I rely upon such periodicals as the *Atlantic*, *Harper's*, *Time Magazine*, and the magazine section of the Sunday *New York Times* (the best of them all for informed articles on domestic and foreign affairs). A category of books that I have always found absorbingly interesting are books that have to do with the life and customs of foreign people, whether they are written expressly with this end in view or are novels that reveal a clear and comprehensive knowledge of foreign parts. The number of such books is legion, beginning with Herodotus' account of his visit to Egypt in the fifth century before Christ and coming down to the present day. Of the more recent books of this character, one I have reread many times is James Norman Hall's *On the Stream of Travel*, especially the sketches of life in Tahiti. Another book about the same area is O'Brien's *White Shadows in the South Seas*. Many excellent books have to do with China—Pearl Buck's *Good Earth*, about peasant life; Nora Waln's *House of Exile*, dealing with upper-class Chinese; Carl Crow's delightful *Four Hundred Million Customers* and *Foreign Devils in the Flowery Kingdom*, about business and social life in contemporary Shanghai and thereabout; and, best of all, Smith's *Chinese Village Communities*, written seventy-five years ago, but accurate and engrossing. Upfield's mystery stories contain the best descriptions I know of life in Australia; E. M. Forster's *Passage to India* I rank as the best I know of India. John Buchan, a really great writer, produced some fine books about Scotland, among others *John McNab*. Anyone interested in stirring stories of adventure would enjoy his *Greenmantle*, *Three Hostages*, and *Thirty-Nine Steps*. Our own Logan Pearsall Smith and Irwin Edman, excellent writers both, have in *Unforgotten Years* and *A Philosopher's Holiday*, made penetrating observations on contemporary life in England and the continent.

Another category of writing of which I am inordinately fond is the all too rare humorous book. To me Mark Twain is the greatest of the humorists; for a time I kept up with P. G. Wodehouse, but I have tired of him. The funniest single piece of writing I know of is Stephen Leacock's "Spiritual Outlook of Mr. Doomer," in *Moonbeams From The Larger Lunacy*. Cabell's *Jurgen* is an unfailing source of laughter, as is Booth Tarkington's *Plutocrat*. The conversation between Tinker and his guide at the tomb of St. Augustine is sidesplitting. Tarkington, I feel, has not been fully appreciated.

Unhappily, just as we are becoming sufficiently civilized and educated to get maximum returns from meeting other minds through the printed word, we find the last curtain descending and the end of knowledge and pleasure at hand.

OF GENERAL EDUCATION

This has been a rambling piece. I should like to close it, five years after it was written, with a postscript on general education. My thoughts were once more turned to this vital matter recently as I listened to an address of Dr. Robert D. Calkins, Director of the General Education Board. His general point of view was much the same as the one I had expressed some years ago in *Quo Vadimus?*

Dr. Calkins did not deprecate scientific and technical training, which produces specialization of a kind that is essential to the modern world. But he was concerned over the inroads which specialization has made in the liberal arts departments. Teachers in these departments, he felt, are becoming more and more specialized; they like to devote themselves to some narrow portion of their field, and they encourage their students to do likewise.

In this process, the ideal of general education is apt to get lost. Dr. Calkins believes that we ought to get back to it. General education is education for living, not training for special and narrow tasks. General education should teach the student to think; it should develop his curiosity about the world and prepare him for leadership in his community. Students should leave college with sound views on nature and on man, his society and his government. Above all, general education should plant them firmly on the road to a healthy, vigorous life of the mind. Amen, I say.

Bibliography of the Writings of
Robert Preston Brooks

By Gregor Sebba

This bibliography contains the published writings of R. P. Brooks with the exceptions noted below, and a small but representative selection of his unpublished papers. It does not list book reviews, individual newspaper articles, and administrative reports. The following abbreviations are used:

BG   Bulletin of the University of Georgia
GAR *Georgia Alumni Record*
GB   *Georgia Business*, published by the Bureau of Business Research, College of Business Administration, University of Georgia
GBR *Georgia Business Review* (predecessor of *Georgia Business*)
GSt   *Georgia Studies* (refers to this volume)
Ms   Manuscript
SN   Serial Number
UGa University of Georgia

The notation "BG 23:10c (SN 351), Jun '23. 14pp." means: "Bulletin of the University of Georgia, Volume 23, Number 10c (Serial Number 351), June 1923. 14 pages."

1. 1902. "Agricultural Education in Georgia." *The Georgian*, published by the UGa Literary Club, 7:1, Oct '02, 6-12. [With portraits of R. C. Berckmans and Dudley M. Hughes.]

2. 1902. "The Forest of Arden." *Ibid.*, 7:3, Dec '02, 115-116.

3. 1903. "The Imagination." *Ibid.*, 7:5, Apr '03, 230-237. ["$50.00 (Horace Russell) Prize Essay in Psychology." Partial reprint.]

4. 1907. Ms. *Oxford University*. Paper read before the Athens University Club in 1907. 24pp. [Cf. No. 11.]

5. 1910. *A Preliminary Bibliography of Georgia History*. BG 10:10a (SN 127), Jun '10. 46pp. [300 titles.]

6. 1911. Ms. *Georgia Plantation Schedules, 1911.* 2 vols. Charts, tables, map. (UGa Library, Rare Book Collection.) Vol. 1: Special Census Schedules. Vol. 2: Summary Report.

7. 1911. "A Local Study of the Race Problem: Race Relations in the Eastern Piedmont Region of Georgia." *Political Science Quarterly,* 26:2. June '11, 193-211.—Abridged in *GSt,* Ch. 1.

8. 1912. Ms. *Inquiries I, 1912.* Replies Received to a Questionnaire Directed to Georgia Planters in Reference to the Reorganization of the Agricultural Labor System after 1865. (UGa Library, Rare Book Collection.)

9. 1913. *History of Georgia.* Chicago, New York, etc.: Atkinson, Mentzer & Company, 1913. xvii, 444pp.—Ch. 18 reprinted with minor omissions in *GSt,* Ch. 7.—Second revised edition (abridged) under the title *An Elementary History of Georgia.* 1918. xi, 341pp.

10. 1914. *The Agrarian Revolution in Georgia, 1865-1912.* Bulletin of the University of Wisconsin, No. 639 (History Series 3:3, '14, 393-524). Madison, Wisconsin, 1914. 129pp.—Abridged in *GSt,* Ch. 2 [Doctoral thesis.]

11. 1914-15. "The Rhodes Scholarships." *The Georgian,* published by the Demosthenian and Phi Kappa Literary Societies of the UGa, 19:1, Nov '14, 26-31 (admission requirements); 19:4, Feb '15, 67-76 (organization of Oxford University); 19:5, May '15, 115-124 (social life at Oxford.) [Partially taken from No. 4. An article on athletics at Oxford, though announced, was not published.]

12. 1915. Ms. *The Influence of the Plantation System on Southern Life.* Read before the University Club of Atlanta, Ga. 1915. 34pp.

13. 1916. "A Program for the Study of Local History." *The High School Quarterly,* UGa, 4:2, Jan '16, 133-136.

14. 1916. "History Teaching in Georgia High Schools." *Ibid.,* 4:3, Apr '16, 217-221.

15. 1916. "A Southern Professor on Lynching." *The Nation,* 103:2675, Oct 5, '16, 321-322.—Reprinted without first paragraph in *GSt,* Ch. 8.

16. 1916. "Conscription in the Confederate States of America, 1862-1865." *The Military Historian and Economist,* Harvard University Press, 1:4, Oct '16, 419-442.—Reprinted in *GSt,* Ch. 4.

17. 1917. "The Need for a New Historical Organization in

Georgia." *Proceedings of the First Annual Session of the Georgia Historical Association*, Atlanta, Ga., Apr 10, '17, 12-20. [With brief survey of historical associations in the South.]

18. 1917. "Howell Cobb and the Crisis of 1850." *The Mississippi Valley Historical Review*, 4:3, Dec. '17, 279-298.—Reprinted BG 18:1 (SN 285), Jan '18, and again in *GSt*, Ch. 4.

19. 1918. "Fall Term Examinations in History in the University of Georgia." *The High School Quarterly*, UGa, 6:3, Apr '18, 182-185.

20. 1918. "Georgia in the Great War." *Proceedings of the Second Annual Session of the Georgia Historical Association.* Atlanta, Ga., Apr 6, '18, 29-32. [On the preservation of fugitive sources.]

21. 1918. (With William K. Boyd). *A Selected Bibliography and Syllabus of the History of the South, 1584-1876.* BG 18:6 (SN 292), Jun '18, 133pp.

22. 1919. "Report on the Effect of the Great War on Agriculture in Georgia." *Proceedings of the Third Annual Session of the Georgia Historical Association.* Atlanta, Ga., Apr 12, '19, 15-25.

23. 1920. "The American Cotton Association." *The South Atlantic Quarterly*, 19:2, Apr '20, 97-108. [Origin of the A.C.A.; critique of its initial program.]

24. 1920. "Preliminary Work of the General Campaign Committee." GAR 1:1, Aug '20, 5. [UGa War Memorial Fund.]

25. 1920. "The Legislative Deadlock." GAR 1:2, Sep '20, 30-31. [University System Appropriations.]

26. 1920. "The University System and How it is Supported." GAR 1:4, Nov '20, 73-75.

27. 192? *What is Worth Fighting For in American Life?* Paper read before the Athens Dinner Club. Uncertain date. 11pp.

28. 1921-22. (Ed.) "Howell Cobb Papers." *Georgia Historical Quarterly*, UGa, 5:1, Mar '21, 50-61; 5:2, Jun '21, 29-52; 5:3, Sep '21, 35-55; 5:4, Dec '21, 43-64; 6:1, Mar '22, 35-84; 6:2, Jun '22, 147-173; 6:3, Sep '22, 233-264; 6:4, Dec. '22, 355-394. [A selection of unpublished letters and papers, supplementing U. B. Phillips' *Correspondence of Robert Toombs, Alexander H. Stephens, and Howell Cobb* (1913).]

29. 1921. (Unsigned.) *Sons of "Old Georgia."* For Church or Court / Commerce or Camp / For Factory or Farm / Men!

GEORGIA, Maker of Men! / The University of Georgia, 1785-
1921. Pamphlet, 12pp. [Honor roll of UGa alumni of the 19th
century.]

30. 1922ff. Art. "Georgia." *Encyclopaedia Britannica,* 12th edition. Revised in the subsequent editions. Supplement in *Britannica
Yearbook* 1940ff.

31. 1923. *Taxation and the Support of Higher Education in
Georgia. A Symposium of the Georgia State Press.* BG 23:10b
(SN 350), Jun '23. 54pp.

32. 1923. *Support of Higher Education in Georgia and Other
States: Some Startling Facts.* BG 23:10c (SN 351), Jun '23. 14pp.

33. 1923. "Is the University [of Georgia] a Rich Man's College?" GAR 4:1, Oct '23, 3-4.

34. 1924. *History of the First Methodist Church of Athens,
Ga.* (Ms. 9pp.) [Reprinted as a pamphlet on the occasion of the
Church's Centenary in 1924.]

35. 1924. "The Alumni Office." GAR 4:6, Apr '24, 123-126.

36. 1925. Ms. *Legislative Representation in Georgia.* Address
before the annual convention of the Georgia League of Women
Voters, Atlanta, Ga., 1925.—Abridged in *GSt,* Ch. 5.

37. 1925. Ms. [*On University Administration and Administrators.*] Paper read before the Georgia Chapter, American Association of University Professors, 1925. 5pp.

38. 1925. "The University Budget, 1925-6." GAR 5:6, Apr
'27, 127, 142-144; 5:7, May '25, 152-154, 167.

39. 1925. "What the War Memorial Fund has Meant to the
University." GAR 5:8, Jun '25, 179-180, 184.

40. 1925. "Larger Support Denied" [to the Georgia University System]. GAR 6:2, Nov '25, 31. [Failure of voters to support educational bonds.]

41. 1926 ff. (Contributor) *Dictionary of American Biography.*
Centenary edition. New York: Scribner's. 1946 ff. [48 articles on
outstanding Georgians in vols. 1-20. Article on Eugene R. Black
in Supplement One.]

42. 1926. *The University and the State. A Comparative Study
of the Support of American State Universities.* BG 26:2a (SN
397), Feb '26. 24pp.

43. 1926. "Bonds for Education Defeated." GAR 6:7, May
'26, 121-122. [With map showing the result of vote on the bond
issue by counties. Cf. No. 41.]

44. 1926. "Georgia Goes Marching On." *Forum*, 76:5, Nov. '26, 748-755.—Condensed in *GSt*, Ch. 9.

45. 1926(?). Ms. *The Rise of Manufacturing in Ante-Bellum Georgia.* Uncertain date. 20pp. 3 tables, chart.

46. 1928. Ms. *The Need of a Bureau of Business Research in the School of Commerce of the University of Georgia.* Read before a meeting of business men in Atlanta, May 8, '28. Mimeographed. 11pp. [This memorandum was instrumental in winning support for the establishment of the Bureau in 1929.]

47. 1929. "School of Commerce." GAR 9:5, Feb '29, 102, 112.

48. 1929. *The Industrialization of the South.* UGa, School of Commerce, Bureau of Business Research, Study No. 1, Apr '29. 20pp. ["Southern agriculture as well as manufacturing is passing through revolutionary changes, manufacturing at a faster pace." Agricultural diversification would be aided by an accelerated movement of farmers to the cities, combined with still greater industrial development.]

49. 1929. "The Collapse of the Stock Market." GBR 1:2, Nov 21, '29, 8-9.

50. 1929. (Ed., with Chauncey S. Boucher) *Correspondence Addressed to John C. Calhoun, 1837-1849.* Report of the Historical Manuscript Commission. *Annual Report of the American Historical Association for the Year 1929.* Washington, U. S. Government Printing Office, 1931, 125-569.—Also printed separately, same pagination.

51. 1929-37. (Ed.) *Proceedings of the Institute of Public Affairs*, UGa, Third to Eleventh Annual Session. 9 volumes in 15 parts. [For the history of the Institute see *Proceedings, Sixth Annual Session (1932)*, Part I, BG 23:3 (SN 527), Sep '32, v-xi, Introduction by R. P. Brooks.]

52. 1930. "The Business Cycle." GBR 1:5, Feb 26, '30, 7-8.

53. 1930-31. "Globetrotting with a Georgian." [A series of weekly articles in the *Atlanta Constitution* and the *Constitution Magazine*, published between June 7, 1930 and September 20, 1931.]

54. 1931. "The Causes and Course of the Depression." GBR 3:3, Nov 30, '31, 7-8.

55. 1931. *The Independence Movement in India.* Albert Kahn Foundation for the Foreign Travel of American Teachers. Reports, Vol. 10. Printed by the Trustees. New York, 1931. 66pp.

["The British Raj in India," *Proceedings of the Institute of Public Affairs*, Fifth Annual Session, 1931, pp. 119-126, is a condensed reprint of a chapter.]

56. 1933. "What of the South?" *The American Oxonian*, 20:1, Jan '33, 39-46. [The members of Dr. Brooks' dinner club wrangle with the question "whether there is anything distinctive in Southern thought and ways of life."]

57. 1933. Ms. (With J. H. T. McPherson and Malcolm Bryan). *Memorandum on Taxation.* Department of Public Relations, UGa, Jan '33. Mimeographed. 25pp.

58. 1933. Ms. *The World Economic Conference.* Address before the Underwriters' Association in Atlanta, Jun 30, '33. 8pp. ["Should the Conference fail, it would mean the recrudescence of Nationalism in even more violent manner than during the past decade."]

59. 1934. *The Sales Tax. Facts and Opinions.* Revised reprint of articles in the Atlanta *Georgian-American*, n.d. [See No. 60.]

60. 1934. *Georgia's Financial Problems. Reprinted from the Atlanta Georgian-American, with Revisions Made by the Author* . . . n.d. 20pp. ["On March 11, 1934, The Atlanta Georgian-American began publishing a series of Sunday articles on economic and social conditions in Georgia, written by Professor R. P. Brooks. The last article appeared in the issue of December 30, 1934." (Preface to No. 60). "Public interest has been marked from the outset, but when the live tax question was opened up, interest quickened and the demand for the articles grew . . .; and when the series on the Sales Tax started, on June 17 (1934), the Georgian-American began to be swamped with requests for extra copies." (Preface to No. 59). The articles in No. 59, slightly revised, are included in No. 60. File of the original articles and of some reactions to them in the Rare Book Collection, UGa Library. This series of articles played a great part in rousing sentiment for tax reform in Georgia.]

61. 1935. Ms. *The Monetary Policies of the Roosevelt Administration.* Paper read before the Lawyers Club of Atlanta, Mar 8, '35. 10pp. [Holds the dollar devaluation ineffective and stresses the danger of Treasury ascendancy over the Federal Reserve System.]

62. 1935. Ms. *Some Reflections on the Relation of Taxes to Economic Security.* Address before the Business Womens Club, Atlanta, Mar 18, '35. 9 pp.—Excerpt in *GSt*, Ch. 6.

63. 1935. Ms. (With O. A. Park and Malcolm H. Bryan). *Suggested Alterations in the Revenue System of Georgia.* 30pp. [Report for a group of Atlanta business leaders, favoring a three per cent general sales tax, though R. P. Brooks at that time still opposed it.]

64. 1935. Ms. *Sources of Additional Revenue.* Memorandum Prepared for Governor [E. D.] Rivers. 59pp.

65. 1936. "School of Commerce." GAR 15:4, Jan '36, 108-109.

66. 1936. "Over Forty Years: John Morris." [Biographical sketch.] GAR 15:6, Mar '36, 167-168, 185.

67. 1936. Ms. *The Property Tax Limitation Amendment.* Speech before the Albany, Ga., Rotary Club. April 9, 1936. 7pp. —Excerpts in *GSt*, Ch. 6.

68. 1936. Ms. *The Tax Limitation Amendment.* Paper read before the City Officials of Atlanta, Ga. June 19, '36. 14pp.—Excerpts in *GSt*, Ch. 6.

69. 1937. Ms. *Georgia's Revenue System.* A Report Made to Mr. Hughes Spalding [for the use of the E. D. Rivers administration.] Jan '37. 80pp.

70. 1937. "Trend of Georgia Finances." *University Items,* UGa, Dec '37, 16-17.

71. 1938. *Georgia State Taxes.* Citizens' Fact Finding Movement of Georgia, Jun '38. 21pp.

72. 1938. "Poverty and the Support of Public Welfare Services in Georgia." GAR 17:9, Jun '38, 256-257, 272.

73. 1938. "Points West." GAR 17:9, Jun '38, 261, 283. [A travel report.]

74. 1939. *Georgia Faces a Financial Crisis.* Institute for the Study of Georgia Problems, Pamphlet No. 1. BG 39:2b (SN 723), Jan '39. 16pp.—Revised excerpts in *GSt*, Ch. 6.

75. 1939. *A Georgian in California.* Address before the American Association of Collegiate Schools of Business. Berkeley, California, April 21, 1939.—Reprinted in *GSt*, Ch. 12.

76. 1939-40. Art. "Georgia" in *Collier's Yearbook.*

77. 1940. *Tax System: Georgia State Finances.* Citizens' Fact Finding Movement of Georgia, Series III, No. 9. Jun '40. 33pp.

78. 1940. (Ed.) *Contemporary Georgia. Readings.* Revised. UGa Press, 1940. 314pp.

79. 1941. Ms. [*The Financial History of the Rivers Adminis-*

tration.] Speech before the Georgia Association of Colleges. Atlanta, Ga., Feb '41. 13pp.

80. 1942. Ms. *The Problem of Price Control.* Address before the Atlanta Cotton Association, Apr 10, '42. 10pp. [Dr. Brooks served at the time as Regional Price Executive, Office of Price Administration, Atlanta, Ga.]

81. 1942. Ms. *The University of Georgia in the War Emergency.* Speech before the Kiwanis Club, Atlanta, Jul 7, '42. 9pp.

82. 1942. Ms. *Taxation of Banks in Georgia.* 34pp. A Study Undertaken for the Bankers Association and the Clearing House Banks of Atlanta. Sep '42. 34pp. [History of Georgia bank taxation since 1805; present system in Georgia and neighboring states. Cf. No. 96, 97, 99, 100.]

83. 1946. *Financing Government in Georgia, 1850-1944.* Institute for the Study of Georgia Problems, Monograph No. 5. BG 46:9 (SN 907), May '46. x, 76pp.

84. 1947. Ms. *John Porter Fort.* Paper read on Apr 13, '47, at the unveiling of a portrait of J. P. Fort. 7pp. [On the history of the Fort family.]

85. 1947. "Quo Vadimus?" *Georgia Review* (UGa Press), 1:1, Spring '47, 53-63.—Reprinted with slight changes in *GSt*, Ch. 11.

86. 1947. "Tax Reform in Georgia." GB 7:1, Oct '47, 6-8. [Brief survey of the Georgia tax reform movement, 1918-1947, and the groups and individuals behind it.]

87. 1947. *Of This and That.* Read before Dr. Brooks' dinner club in 1947. 24pp. Revised in *GSt*, Ch. 13.

88. 1948. (With R. L. McWhorter, Jr.). "Faculty Memorial to Dr. W. H. Bocock." GAR 27:7, Apr '48, 124.

89. 1948. "Honors Work in Special Subjects." BG 48:10 (SN 943), Jun '48, 6-18. [A discussion of honors programs at Oxford and in American universities, introducing the UGa honors program. Cf. No. 85.]

90. 1948. "Potential Sources of Tax Revenue in Georgia." GB 7:9, Jun '48, 4-7.

91. 1948. *State Supervision of Local Fiscal Affairs in Georgia.* Institute for the Study of Georgia Problems, Monograph No. 6. BG 49:5 (SN 955), Nov '48. 35pp.

92. 1949. "Dr. R. P. Brooks Lauds Caldwell at Dinner Hon-

oring Chancellor." GAR 28:4, Jan '49, 71, 74. [On UGa administrations since 1901.]—Incorporated in *GSt*, Ch. 10.

93. 1949. "Where Is the Money Coming From?" GB 8:5, '49, 4-7. [On the financing of the Minimum Education Program and other essential services.]

94. 1949. "Comments on a General Sales Tax." GB 8:6, Mar '49, Supplement. 4pp. [Open reply to letters about No. 93.]

95. 1949. Ms. *Georgia Should Have a General Sales Tax.* Aug. 27, '49. 15pp. [Memorandum prepared for the use of the (Herman) Talmadge administration.]—Excerpts in *GSt*, Ch. 6.

96. 1949. Ms. *Bank Taxation in Georgia, 1949.* Aug 29, '49. 13pp. [Continuation and extension of No. 82.]

97. 1949. Ms. *Georgia Banks Should Seek to Have the Share Tax Voided.* Oct. 3, '49. 14pp. [See note to 96.]

98. 1950. *The Georgia Property Tax: History and Administrative Problems.* Institute for the Study of Georgia Problems, Monograph No. 7. BG 50:5 (SN 981), Jan '50. 27pp. [Study undertaken for the Georgia Tax Revision Committee. Partly incorporated in the final Commission report of Jan 1, '50.]

99. 1950. Ms. *The Taxation of Banks in Georgia.* Feb '50. 57pp. [Final report, with statistical appendix listing the ratio of assessed to true value of Georgia banks, state and local. Cf. No. 82, 96, 97.]

100. 1950. Ms. *State Taxation of Banks After the Richmond Decision.* Paper read at the first meeting of the School of Banking of the South, Louisiana State University, Jun 12, '50. Mimeographed. 19pp.

101. 1950. Ms. *The Struggle for Sound Banking in the United States.* Paper read at the first meeting of the School of Banking of the South, Louisiana State University, Jun 10, '50. Mimeographed. 11pp.

102. 1950. Ms. *Robert Ligon McWhorter.* Memorial read at the General Faculty Meeting, UGa, Jul 25, '50. 4pp.

103. 1950. *Georgia in 1950.* Institute for the Study of Georgia Problems, Monograph No. 8. BG 51:7a (SN 1000), Sep '50. vii, 33pp. [Study made at the request of Mr. W. M. Lester, Director, Tax Revision Committee, for the use of the General Assembly.]

104. 1951. "Georgia's Economy in Transition." GB 11:2, Nov '51, 1-9. [An edited portion of the last chapter of No. 108.]

105. 1951. Ms. *The Development of the Georgia Revenue System*. A Sesquicentennial Address (UGa), Feb 14, '51. 12pp.

106. 1951. Ms. *The University of Georgia: One Hundred and Fifty Years of Service*. A Sesquicentennial Address (UGa). Feb '51.—Revised and incorporated in *GSt*, Ch. 10.

107. 1951. "Thirty Years of It." *The American Oxonian*, 38:2, Apr 51, 71-74. [Experiences as Georgia secretary of the Rhodes Scholarship Committee.]

108. 1952. *The Financial History of Georgia, 1732-1950*. Institute for the Study of Georgia Problems. Monograph No. 9. BG 52:8 (SN 1048), Apr '52. viii, 85pp.

109. 1952. *Georgia Studies: Selected Writings of Robert Preston Brooks*. Edited and with an Introduction by Gregor Sebba. UGa Press, 1952.

Index